Praise for *The Eld*

"Rooted in the deep soil of Reformed faith and practice, *The Elder* is also a treasure at a time when much gets lost in translation from theory to practice. I heartily recommend this book for current elders, elders-in-training, aspiring elders, and those who seek to be blessed by their labors."
—**Michael Horton**, Westminster Seminary California

"Cornelis Van Dam provides a full and intelligent discussion of the biblical texts that inform our understanding of the office of the elder in the church today. This book is a must for those who are elders or who think they might be called to that office."
—**Tremper Longman III**, Westmont College

"Displaying the carefulness of a biblical scholar and the wisdom of a pastor, Cornelis Van Dam examines key passages related to elders in the church. Readers will find themselves challenged, stretched, and edified as they encounter seasoned insights on matters such as shepherding, church discipline, and personal character. The work shows particular promise as a tool in training elders in Reformed churches."
—**Christopher W. Morgan**, California Baptist University

"In my judgment the monograph *The Elder: Today's Ministry Rooted in All of Scripture* by Cornelis Van Dam is an excellent treatment of a neglected topic. Written from a self-consciously Reformed perspective, Van Dam looks at the office of elder in a broad redemptive-historical context, rooting the New Testament givens in their Old Testament background, and carefully noting both the continuity and discontinuity between the testaments with respect to this office. By thus situating the eldership in the broad metanarrative of Scripture, Van Dam (himself an Old Testament scholar) gives a perspective which is sorely lacking in most contemporary treatments of the topic. Although written for a broad audience, the book is based on solid scholarly research and interacts with a broad range of biblical and theological scholarship. A specific strength of the book is the way it draws on the rich Dutch sources that are available on this subject, which are generally inaccessible to a North American audience. A further unusual strength is its treatment of the flexibility of Old Testament law as a guide for the contemporary elder's pastoral care. It thus takes seriously the Reformed confession that the "truth and substance" of the Old Testament Torah is still relevant to the lives of Christians today, and refutes the widespread misconception of that Torah as rigid and inflexible."

—**Albert M. Wolters**, Redeemer University College

"Dr. Van Dam's book enlarges a growing body of material designed to assist churches and church leaders in applying Scriptural teaching to the organization and government of God's people. Because it is rich in biblical teaching and careful reflection, this book will be useful for group study and church leadership training. It belongs in every church library and in the hands of every elder and church member as a manifesto of mutual expectations. May it be serviceable to the greater glory of Christ and the well-being of his church."

—**Nelson Kloosterman**, Mid-America Reformed Seminary

"*The Elder: Today's Ministry Rooted in All of Scripture* is not just another book on church leadership, but a refreshing biblical and theological look at local church leadership by elders, in which cultural considerations receive their proper place. Besides arguing for this office as fundamental to local church leadership, Van Dam counters the contemporary tendency to locate church leadership roots and practice mostly, or only, in the NT with an extensive and lucid discussion of relevant OT material. By showing OT wisdom literature's peculiar contribution to successful church leadership, Van Dam also corrects an often neglected aspect of leadership. As a unique contribution to church leadership literature, *The Elder* is a must read for churches wishing to reinvigorate their own

traditions of local leadership or to train those elders or presbyters elected to exercise Christian pastoral care."
—**Arie C. Leder**, Calvin Theological Seminary

"I know no other book that explains the continuity (and discontinuity) between the OT and the NT offices as clearly as Dr. Van Dam does in this book. The book gives guidance to ministers and elders who struggle with practical questions such as: How can we equip (candidate) elders for the office? Should the eldership be permanent or should it have an indefinite tenure? In my estimation, this book will have a long life span. It is a book that will be read and reread for many years to come."
—**Arjan De Visser**, Theological College of the Canadian Reformed Churches

"Dr. Van Dam's contribution to the churches is for many years to come. He is a professor of Old Testament but also a churchman with a deep love for the local church. Out of this commitment, he has studied what the Bible says about elder rule in order to encourage elders and churches to reconnect with the biblical teaching on wise governance that is distinctive from contemporary models of leadership. Because elder governance is not unique to the Presbyterian form of government, I expect leaders in many different churches to benefit from reading and applying this book to their lives and to contribute to the kingdom of the Lord Jesus Christ."
—**Willem A. VanGemeren**, Trinity Evangelical Divinity School

Praise for the Explorations in Biblical Theology series

"Under the trusty captaincy of Professor Robert Peterson, a crew of seasoned Reformed sailors has set out to encompass a new Treasure Island—an up-to-the-minute, mid-range, pastorally focused collection of Explorations in Biblical Theology, covering the main themes of the Reformed faith and the main biblical books that set them forth. These are books to look out for, and to collect as they see the light of day. It is already clear that they will demonstrate afresh the truth, life, light, and power that the old Reformed faith can still bring to a befuddled and benighted world."

—**J. I. Packer**, Regent College

"Explorations in Biblical Theology is a valuable new series of books on doctrinal themes that run through Scripture. The contributors are competent scholars who love to serve the church and have special expertise in the Bible and its theology. Following a thematic approach, each volume explores a distinctive doctrine as it is taught in Scripture, or else introduces the various doctrines taught in a particular book of the Bible. The result is a fresh and unique contribution to our understanding of the Bible's own theology."

—**Philip Ryken**, Tenth Presbyterian Church, Philadelphia

"Explorations in Biblical Theology is a gift to God's people. Biblical theology was never meant to be reserved for academics. When the verities of the Reformed faith are taken from the 'ivy halls' of academia and placed in the hearts and minds of the covenant people of God, reformation and revival are the inevitable result. I believe God will use this series as a mighty tool for the Kingdom."

—**Steve Brown**, Reformed Theological Seminary

"This new series of volumes on important Christian doctrines is projected to teach Reformed theology as it is most helpfully taught, with clear grounding in Scripture, mature understanding of theology, gracious interaction with others who disagree, and useful application to life. I expect that these volumes will strengthen the faith and biblical maturity of all who read them."

—**Wayne Grudem**, Phoenix Seminary

"Only a worldview that is informed by both biblical and systematic theology can withstand the intellectual challenges that face us today. The series Explorations in Biblical Theology is designed to meet this very need. I commend these volumes enthusiastically, for they explain what the Scriptures teach from the standpoint of biblical theology. What we desperately need to hear and learn today is the whole counsel of God. This series advances that very agenda for the edification of the church and to the glory of God."

—**Thomas R. Schreiner**, The Southern Baptist
Theological Seminary

"This is a series that the church needs more than ever, as we forge fresh links between the world of biblical studies and our Reformed theology. The contributors remind us again that the Bible is a book about God and his purposes and encourage us to preach and teach the message of salvation which it contains. It will be an inspiration to many and will give us new insight into the faith once delivered to the saints."

—**Gerald Bray**, Beeson Divinity School

"The aim of these volumes is clear: as regards God's Word, rigor; as regards other scholars, respect; as regards current issues, relevance; as regards the Lord himself, reverence. Effective witness and ministry currently require more than extra effort and better methods: the call is heard from churches across the board for renewal in our grasp of Christian truth. Each author in this series contributes admirably to that urgent need."

—**Robert W. Yarbrough**, Trinity Evangelical Divinity School

"The authors are first-rate, and they write to build up our faith by pointing us to Christ. That's what biblical and systematic theology at their best have always done, and the best application of Scripture has always shown us in practical ways how to draw on the rich blessings of Jesus' salvation. I hope that many will read these books and take them to heart."

—**John Frame**, Reformed Theological Seminary

"Able and godly scholars trace the golden thread of grace that unites all Scripture to make the wonders of our God's redeeming love shine and win hearts anew. The writing is warm, winsome, and respectful of those who differ. The motives are clearly to reveal truth and expose error by glorifying the message and manner of the Savior."

—**Bryan Chapell**, Covenant Theological Seminary

The Elder

Explorations in Biblical Theology

Robert A. Peterson, series editor

The Elder

Today's Ministry Rooted in All of Scripture

Cornelis Van Dam

P&R PUBLISHING

P.O. BOX 817 • PHILLIPSBURG • NEW JERSEY 08865-0817

Unless otherwise indicated, all Scripture quotations are from the Holy Bible, New International Version®. NIV®. Copyright © 1973, 1978, 1984 by International Bible Society. Used by permission of Zondervan Publishing House. All rights reserved.

Scripture quotations marked ESV are from The Holy Bible, English Standard Version, copyright © 2001 by Crossway Bibles, a division of Good News Publishers. Used by permission. All rights reserved.

Scripture quotations marked NASB are from the New American Standard Bible®. Copyright © 1960, 1962, 1963, 1968, 1971, 1972, 1973, 1975, 1977, 1995 by The Lockman Foundation. Used by permission.

Scripture quotations marked RSV are from The Holy Bible, Revised Standard Version, ©1946, 1952, 1971 by the Division of Christian Education of the National Council of the Churches of Christ in the United States of America.

Other versions mentioned include KJV (King James Version), NKJV (New King James Version), NEB (New English Version), and TEV (Today's English Version).

Italics within Scripture quotations indicate emphasis added.

Printed in the United States of America

Library of Congress Cataloging-in-Publication Data

Van Dam, Cornelis, 1946–
  The elder : today's ministry rooted in all of Scripture / Cornelis Van Dam.
    p. cm. — (Explorations in biblical theology)
  Includes bibliographical references and indexes.
  ISBN 978-1-59638-141-4 (pbk.)
  1. Elders (Church officers)—Reformed Church. 2. Elders (Church officers)—
Biblical teaching. I. Title.
  BX9425.v36 2009
  262'.042—dc22
                                2009026097

For Jenny Van Dam–van Rijswijk
and
in memory of Schalk Van Dam
(1922–2000)

My parents were the first
to teach me the meaning of
the office of elder.

Contents

CONTENTS

Part 5: Maintaining and Building on the Heritage

Series Introduction

BELIEVERS TODAY need quality literature that attracts them to good theology and builds them up in their faith. Currently, readers may find several sets of lengthy—and rather technical—books on Reformed theology, as well as some that are helpful and semipopular. Explorations in Biblical Theology takes a more midrange approach, seeking to offer readers the substantial content of the more lengthy books, on the one hand, while striving for the readability of the semipopular books, on the other.

The series includes two types of books: (1) some treating biblical themes and (2) others treating the theology of specific biblical books. The volumes dealing with biblical themes seek to cover the whole range of Christian theology, from the doctrine of God to last things. Representative early offerings in the series focus on the empowering of the Holy Spirit, justification, the presence of God, preservation and apostasy, and substitutionary atonement. Examples of works dealing with the theology of specific biblical books include volumes on the theology of 1 and 2 Samuel, the Psalms, and Isaiah in the Old Testament, and books on the theology of Mark, Romans, and James in the New Testament.

Explorations in Biblical Theology is written for college seniors, seminarians, pastors, and thoughtful lay readers. These volumes are intended to be accessible and not obscured by excessive references to Hebrew, Greek, or theological jargon.

Each book seeks to be solidly Reformed in orientation, because the writers love the Reformed faith. The various theological themes and biblical books are treated from the perspective of biblical theology. Writers either trace doctrines through the Bible or open up the theology of the specific book they treat. Writers desire not merely to dispense the Bible's good information, but also to apply that information to real needs today.

Explorations in Biblical Theology is committed to being warm and winsome, with a focus on applying God's truth to life. Authors aim to treat those with whom they disagree as they themselves would want to be treated. The motives for the rejection of error are not to fight, hurt, or wound, but to protect, help, and heal. The authors of this series will be godly, capable scholars with a commitment to Reformed theology and a burden to minister that theology clearly to God's people.

ROBERT A. PETERSON
Series Editor

Preface

CERTAIN GIFTS OF GOD need to be constantly rediscovered, lest they be taken for granted and neglected. The eldership is one of those gifts. Although this office is from the distant past, it is still very much relevant and vital for the well-being of the church today.

One of the current challenges in properly appreciating the eldership is that it has more often than not been detached from its historic roots. This study seeks to redress this deficiency by going beyond the New Testament to the very beginnings of this office in ancient Israel. God's revelation in the Old Testament helps us to see something of the grandeur of this glorious office. Although there are discontinuities between the Old and New Testament, the enduring principles that guided the elder in antiquity remain normative, relevant, and a blessing for the church today.

All of this has real-life implications. Indeed, my practical experiences as a pastor for ten years made me realize that a study of the eldership based on the entire Scripture was needed to create a more clear understanding of what the identity and duties of this office actually entail. Understanding the background and history of this office helps us to appreciate what the ruling and teaching elders have in common, where their responsibilities differ, and how their tasks are to be handled in justice and righteousness.

The reader will notice that everyday concerns and lessons constantly surface as we trace the eldership through biblical times. This practical benefit came out repeatedly when I conducted workshops on material that forms the bulk of this book. It is, therefore, my hope that this publication can serve as a resource and an encouragement for the elders and their work.

Understanding the key biblical principles impacting this office will empower them to do their task much more confidently and effectively. This book is, however, not intended solely for the elder. I cherish the hope that theological students, church leaders, and church members will also be able to benefit from it and gain a greater appreciation for the elder office.

Questions for study and reflection are included at the end of the book. They are meant to be used by ruling and teaching elders, seminary and college students, as well as by church Bible study groups. Those with a more scholarly inclination who wish to delve deeper into any particular aspect can consult the footnotes and the selection of additional specialized resources found at the end of this volume.

May this publication serve to enhance a biblical understanding and functioning of the office of elder and in this way be a blessing for God's people to his praise and glory.

Acknowledgments

I WISH TO EXPRESS my gratitude to Robert Peterson for accepting this publication into his series. It has been a great privilege to work with such a perceptive, prompt, and encouraging editor. Furthermore, I thankfully acknowledge the parts that Allan Fisher, Marvin Padgett, and Eric Anest played in the publication process.

It is also my pleasure to thank the following who read all or parts of the manuscript prior to publication and commented on it. I have benefited from their contributions: Adriaan J. de Visser, Nicolaas H. Gootjes, Gerhard H. Visscher, James Visscher, G. I. Williamson, and Albert M. Wolters. Needless to say, the views expressed as well as any remaining inaccuracies are my responsibility.

For the questions for further study I have been much helped with the assistance of Douwe Agema, Nelson Kloosterman, Gijsbertus Nederveen, Gerard Nordeman, and Rodney Vermeulen.

I am also very grateful for the editorial assistance of Chris Morgan and Beth Ann Brown. Their efforts greatly improved the work.

My thanks also to Margaret Vandervelde, librarian at the Theological College of the Canadian Reformed Churches where I teach. She was always ready to be of assistance.

Last but not least, throughout this enterprise I have been able to count on the unfailing support of my wife, Joanne. She has also helped with proofreading and preparing the indices.

Part 1

Introduction

An Overview of the Office

WHAT DOES IT MEAN to be an elder in the church today? Do elders still have a real function, or is their office just an antiquarian curiosity from the past? One sometimes gets the impression that elders are not always honored in the measure that their office would warrant. Indeed, experience teaches that it is not unusual for this office to be undervalued, even by those who stand to gain the most from it, namely the members of a local congregation. Faithful elders are typically the unsung heroes in many Presbyterian and Reformed churches, and their toil is often neither fully understood nor appreciated.

And yet this office is needed more than ever in the church today. The eldership is a great blessing from God. Elders can be encouraged by the reality that they stand in a long line of elder office bearers whom the Lord our God has been pleased to equip and use for the benefit of his people. After all, the office goes all the way back, not just to the New Testament church, but to the Old Testament people of God! This tremendous heritage is usually not fully appreciated. However, if we can uncover and understand the key normative principles underlying the faithful execution of this office in Old and New Testament times, we will rediscover what a precious gift this office is. We will also be better equipped to meet the challenges facing the church today.

History has shown that the office of the elder cannot be taken for granted. It needs to be constantly rediscovered and its

3

great value reappraised again and again. This book therefore wishes to serve teaching and ruling elders, theological students, church leaders, and interested church members by encouraging a renewed appreciation for this office. We hope to reach this goal by determining and considering the crucial normative features of the eldership as found in the Old Testament and developed further in the New, and by seeing how these principles impact the well-being of the church.

By way of orientation we begin by reflecting on:

- What is an ecclesiastical office?
- The continuity of the office in the Old and New Testament
- The discontinuity of the office between the Old and New Testament
- The plan of this book

This initial survey will help us to understand the need to go all the way back to the Old Testament in order to do justice to the office of elder and realize its significance for today.

What Is an Ecclesiastical Office?

An elder is called an office bearer—that is, he has a certain office. What precisely is an office? An ecclesiastical office can be defined as a task given by God for a specific continuous and institutional service to his congregation with a view to its edification. Such a special office is to be distinguished from the general office given to all believers. As the Heidelberg Catechism reminds us in Lord's Day 12, all Christians share in Christ's anointing so that as prophets they confess Christ's name, as priests they present themselves as living sacrifices of thankfulness, and as kings they fight against and triumph over sin and Satan. This book concerns itself with the special office of elder.

Now when God gives a task, he also provides the necessary gifts. However, the right to ecclesiastical office does not reside in the gifts that one may have, but in the Lord who calls one to the office. As John Murray noted, "For office there must be a corresponding gift, but not all gifts bestowed by the Spirit and necessarily exercised within the unity of the body of Christ and for its edification, invest the participants with office in the sense in which this applies to apostles, prophets, pastors, rulers in the church, and diaconate."[1]

Our egalitarian and democratizing age is unsympathetic to the idea of authority, including the special office, that is, of someone being given a specific task by God with all the connotations of authority and divine legitimacy this concept brings with it. Yet, if we are to fully grasp the biblical notion of office and more specifically the office of elder, we need to be clear about this point. The exercise of authority by one person over another is justified and can be justified only by the fact that God gives the office. God is the source of this authority, not the congregation. God also sets the limits of this authority. God alone is sovereign.[2]

A Task Given by God

God in his good pleasure calls certain persons to serve him in a special office. What a daunting truth! He is the living God of heaven and earth whose appearance on Sinai brought fear and trembling to the people (Ex. 20:18–21). And he, the Holy One, not only covenants with humankind but also gives certain individuals a specific task among his people so that these office bearers can be his instruments and even his voice.

Needless to say, the Lord has supreme authority and therefore he can set someone over others for a specific service in different ways. For instance, we are informed in quite some detail how the priests were ordained to office and started their work amidst an awesome display of the glory of the Lord (Lev. 8–10). The process of being recognized as an elder with authority in

---

1. John Murray, "Office in the Church," in *Collected Writings of John Murray*, 4 vols. (Edinburgh: Banner of Truth Trust, 1976–82), 2:358.
2. See K. Sietsma, *The Idea of Office* (Jordan Station, ON: Paideia, 1985), 37–40.

Israel was considerably less dramatic, but this did not in any way diminish the authority of this office and the respect that was to be shown to it.

There were apparently two basic ways of coming to the office of elder in ancient Israel. The first we could characterize as being directed by the providence of God. In this scenario, no specific moment of being ordained to office is noted, but because of the structure of Israelite society at a certain point in history, some individuals acquired a position of leadership and became elders, be it elders of the people (Ex. 3:16) or of a tribe (Judg. 11:5) or of a city (Judg. 8:14). That such elders indeed held office is evident from the term "elder" being used with or in place of official titles (Josh. 24:1; Judg. 8:14; 1 Kings 8:1; Ezra 10:8).

The second way of coming to the office was by being appointed after having been chosen by the people (Deut. 1:13–16). The involvement of the people in the Old Testament dispensation in the receiving of office bearers with authority over them is noteworthy.

With respect to the New Testament church, Paul and Barnabas appointed (*cheirotoneō*) elders in every church during their first missionary journey (Acts 14:23). It is quite likely that what occurred is relayed here in a compressed manner so that only the last act, the appointment, is mentioned and the intermediary steps, such as the participation of the congregation, are left out. The NIV text note thus suggests that they "had elders elected." Similarly, when Paul charged Titus to appoint (*kathistēmi*) elders in Crete (Titus 1:5), this duty did not mean that the congregation had no part to play.[3] Such participation would not be unexpected given the involvement of the congregation in the Old Testament in the receiving of office bearers. Indeed, the congregation had chosen the seven in Acts 6. The apostles had then laid their hands on them and set them aside for the distribution of food among the needy. The churches also chose (*cheirotoneō*) a brother to accom-

3. See George W. Knight, *The Pastoral Epistles*, New International Greek Testament Commentary (Grand Rapids: Eerdmans, 1992), 288. The basic meaning of *cheirotoneō* is "stretch out the hand, for the purpose of giving one's vote in the assembly." See G. H. Liddell, R. Scott, H. S. Jones, *A Greek-English Dictionary*, 9th ed. with revised supplement (Oxford: Clarendon, 1996), 1986a.

pany Paul and Titus (2 Cor. 8:19). Furthermore, that the apostolic letters are directed to the congregation, and not just to the leadership, underlines that the congregations were responsible for their own affairs and could therefore be expected to participate in the selection of their leaders. This office belonged to the local church (see, e.g., Acts 20:17; 1 Peter 5:1). Indeed, the Didache, or Doctrine of the Twelve Apostles, probably a first- or early-second-century document, instructs the churches: "And so, elect [*cheirotoneō*] for yourselves bishops and deacons who are worthy of the Lord."[4]

Today one usually becomes an elder through a process that includes a recognition of one's gifts and election by the congregation, followed by the appointment to office by the session or consistory. At his ordination the elder acknowledges this to be God's way of calling him to the office. In the Reformed tradition, this acknowledgment takes place when he affirmatively answers the question: "Do you feel in your heart that God himself, through his congregation, has called you to this office?"

Because the elder receives his office from God, he represents God himself in the execution of his task. This gives great weight and solemnity to the office. Since the origin of the elder's office is from God, his authority does not, for example, derive from a church hierarchy, nor from the congregation but from the head of the church, Jesus Christ. It is through Christ that God gives the office today.[5]

The divine commission of the eldership places great demands on the office bearer, which he of himself is unable to fulfill. He therefore needs to do his task prayerfully in consecrated dependence on the Word and Spirit (Acts 14:23).

A Specific Service for Edification

The service of the elder in Israel differed from that of the priest, prophet, or king. We will see in more detail later that the

---

4. Didache 15:1. For the text and translation see Bart D. Ehrman, *The Apostolic Fathers*, 2 vols., Loeb Classical Library (Cambridge, MA / London: Harvard University Press, 2003), 1:440–41.

5. See chapter 6, under the heading "The Congregation of Christ."

eldership had two key tasks. Elders were to give sound leadership and guidance to the people and their affairs in a manner pleasing to God. Elders were also to act as judges. In this way they participated in the discipline of God's people and watched out for their welfare.

As will become evident in the course of this book, one could sum up the task of the office of elder as preserving and nurturing life in covenant with God. The task was to be a very positive one. As God's representatives in their areas of jurisdiction, the elders had to bring their wishes and desire to bear on the people. Through their office, something of the glory of God who set his people free and who wanted them to enjoy life with him was to be seen and experienced.

Finally, it should be noted that the service of the elder for edification is indeed to be characterized by serving. This is in keeping with what the Lord of the church said: "I am among you as one who serves" (Luke 22:27; Mark 10:43–45). There is, therefore, to be no lording over the flock, but rather a seeking of its well-being (1 Peter 5:3). The admonition of the apostle Peter also counts for office bearers: "Each one should use whatever gift he has received to serve others, faithfully administering God's grace in its various forms. . . . If anyone serves, he should do it with the strength God provides, so that in all things God may be praised through Jesus Christ" (1 Peter 4:10–11).

The Continuity of the Office of Elder in the Old and New Testament

Is it legitimate to compare an ancient Israelite institution with what we find in the New Testament and then relate all that to today? Although we will be returning to this issue in more detail in chapter 6, it is important to consider this question in a preliminary way at this point. Sometimes Old Testament Israel is simply seen as a nation from the distant past with no direct relevance for the church today. Yet the church of the Lord today has a direct continuity with the people of God in the Old Testament. This fact impacts how we view the office of elder.

We first need to note that the Old Testament nation of Israel was God's chosen people (Ex. 19:6; Deut. 7:6) who had received the promises of the coming messianic king and suffering servant (Gen. 49:10; Isa. 53). When the promised Messiah, the Lord Jesus Christ, came (Luke 24:25–27), those who believed in him continued to be God's special people. Thus, Peter, for instance, could call the recipients of his first letter "a chosen people, a royal priesthood, a holy nation, a people belonging to God" (1 Peter 2:9). Such a manner of referring to Christians was obviously an allusion to similar words spoken by God from Mount Sinai when he promised that Israel would be for him "a kingdom of priests and a holy nation" (Ex. 19:6). Indeed, the church is even specifically called "the Israel of God" (Gal. 6:16). The New Testament church is therefore the new Israel of God, and those who believe in the Christ are children of Abraham (Gal. 3:7).[6]

As the new Israel, the church has retained the use of the old office of elder. That the Christian eldership is rooted in the Israelite and Jewish office need not be doubted. When Luke mentioned this office for the first time (Acts 11:30), he did so without any explanation because none was needed. For the same reason, he also first introduced the appointment to this Christian office (Acts 14:23) without explanation. To the first Christians who were Jewish and had grown up with the synagogue and its elders, it would have seemed a matter of course that the eldership would be instituted in each congregation as it was established. Continuity with the past was maintained.

That the old office of elder became a Christian office indicates its abiding significance. At the same time, this continuity also shows that the eldership as it now functions in the church cannot be properly understood without the Old Testament background. After all, there is a long history behind this office.

6. See further O. Palmer Robertson, *The Israel of God: Yesterday, Today, and Tomorrow* (Phillipsburg, NJ: P&R, 2000); and Paul S. Minear, *Images of the Church in the New Testament* (Philadelphia: Westminster, 1960), 71–84.

This history did, however, involve much change and upheaval. Profound political transformations took place, especially from the time of the exile and through the intertestamental period. Yet the essentials of the office of elder in giving godly leadership for the nurturing and preserving of life in covenant with God basically stayed intact. The elders continued their work both in exile (Jer. 29:1; Ezek. 8:1) and in postexilic Judah (Ezra 5:3–11). The manner in which they exercised their responsibilities, particularly on the national scene, was influenced by historical developments. When the tribal units were in effect dissolved, individual families gradually became more important and certain families achieved national prominence. Elders from this nobility had the leadership. By the second century B.C. there was evidence for the existence of "a council of elders," which consisted of seventy or seventy-one members and was the forerunner of the Sanhedrin (1 Macc. 12:6; 14:20). At first the members were generally spoken of as elders (*presbyteroi*). As time went on, this term became used more and more to distinguish the "lay" members, who probably came from the nobility in Jerusalem, from those with a priestly lineage, as well as from those who were scribes. This situation is reflected in the New Testament where the triad of chief priests, scribes, and elders is often referred to as the Sanhedrin (e.g., Mark 14:43, 53, 55; 15:1). This body is, however, also referred to as "the council of the elders" (Luke 22:66; Acts 22:5).

During the upheavals of exile and return, the system of local elders continued (Ezra 10:7–17). It is this local eldership that is especially important for our topic since it retained the fundamental features of its ancient Israelite counterpart. Each Jewish community had its council of elders (Judith 6:16). When the synagogue became an established institution, the elders directed its activities and, as could be expected, were responsible for godly leadership in what they perceived were God's expectations for his people. They were also responsible for the discipline in the congregation. Although the Gospels show that the zeal of the synagogue and the elders associated with it was often misguided, their desire to safeguard their understanding of the Scripture is evident. Two examples come to mind. First, the elders had decided to discipline anyone who confessed Christ by excluding him from their synagogue (John 9:22; Luke 6:22). Second, the ruler of the synagogue, who was probably chosen from the elders, was indignant that Christ healed on the Sabbath (Luke 13:14). Such instances show that the elders, though mistaken, took their task seriously.

When the first Christian congregations were established by Jewish believers, these were considered, not surprisingly, to be new synagogues. Thus in what appears to be the oldest Christian document, the letter of James,[7] the Christian assembly or meeting is referred to as a "synagogue" (*synagōgē*; James 2:2). Although James also refers to the church (*ekklēsia*; James 5:14), the fact that he uses the word "synagogue" is notable, given the Jewish connotations it carried. Elsewhere in early Christian writings the term "synagogue" is also used to describe the Christian assembly or place of assembly.[8] This usage underlines the continuity of the Christian congregation and the synagogue assembly which the Jewish Christians left behind. Indeed, it could even be construed as an implicit challenge to the synagogue in the sense that the Christian church is its legitimate successor. Now as the synagogue could not be imagined without the office of elder, neither could the Christian church. Without implying that the Christian church adopted the entire organizational framework of the Jewish synagogue, which it definitely did not do, the New Testament office of elder can nevertheless be seen as coming out of the Jewish synagogue heritage, which in turn has deep Old Testament roots.

It is this office, with which the first Jewish Christians were only too familiar, that continued in the Christian church under the direction of the apostles. There is therefore continuity with

7. James was probably written in the middle 40s A.D. See the discussion in Douglas J. Moo, *The Letter of James*, Pillar New Testament Commentary (Grand Rapids/Leicester, England: Eerdmans/Apollos, 2000), 9–27.

8. See G. W. H. Lampe, *A Patristic Greek Lexicon* (Oxford: Clarendon, 1961), 1296.

the past. However, while this is so, there are also areas of discontinuity that need to be noted by way of orientation.

The Discontinuity of the Office between the Old and New Testament

A major difference between the Old and New Testament periods with respect to our topic is that in the Old Testament there was a very close relationship between what we today call the church and state. The societal and civic tasks of the elder, as described in the Pentateuch, were at the same time done within the religious congregation of the Lord. Israel was a theocracy. Now to be sure, the covenant assembly and the nation were not identical. Only the circumcised who lived within the borders of Israel were part of God's holy congregation (Ex. 12:38; Josh. 8:35). Yet, in the functioning of the elder, it would have been very difficult to categorize or differentiate his tasks as strictly belonging to either the civic or religious realm. The elder's giving leadership and judging took form according to the governing civil structures in place. At the same time they were done within and for the benefit of the people of God.

This Old Testament situation no longer holds true for the New Testament church. This changed context means that we have to be careful in distilling principles regarding the work of the Old Testament elders which are to have abiding significance in our day and age. To take an obvious example, neither the elder nor the church today has any civil authority to mete out the death penalty. This, however, does not mean that this Old Testament legal material is of no relevance now for the task of the elder in today's church. One could argue that as the death penalty removed unrepentant members of the Old Testament church from the body of God's people, so the application of church discipline by excommunication does essentially the same today. But the point is clear. In deriving the relevant principles for the task of the Old Testament elder for today, we need to be sensitive both to the abiding truths and to the changing outward circumstances. An assessment of the relevant New Testament data will be indispensable for achieving such a balanced understanding.

The Plan of This Book

Our chief concern is to obtain a renewed understanding of and appreciation for the office and task of the elder by taking into full account the relevant Old Testament material. To that end we will first consider the general image of the shepherd and his flock since this metaphor is fundamental for a good understanding of the leadership offices in Scripture, including that of elder.

After looking at the basic meanings and implications of the Old and New Testament terms for "elder," we will focus on the Old Testament elder and his leadership and judicial duties. Since the Old Testament does not contain a "handbook" on the office of elder, we will need to go through the evidence and sort out the relevant information so that we can form as coherent a picture as possible about this office in ancient Israel. Only after we have a clear understanding of the place and practice of the eldership in ancient Israel will we be able to derive the principles that carry through into the New Testament church and are still relevant for today's elder.

When describing how the Christian church inherited this office, we will also consider the Old Testament background of the apparent distinctions of ruling and teaching elder made in the New Testament. Furthermore, the elder's leadership and judicial roles in preserving and nurturing life in the covenant community today will be examined in the light of the Old Testament principles discussed earlier.

In the concluding section of this book, we will briefly consider two current issues: whether Scripture opens the office of elder to women, and definite or indefinite tenure of the eldership.

Finally, we will reflect on the privilege of this office both for the elder and for the congregation.

In summary, by integrating the Old Testament principles of the office into an examination of the New Testament elder we hope to rediscover the abiding relevance of these principles. In the process, we also wish to give the elders today, as well as all those interested in the eldership, a clearer sense of what this office entails. We cherish the hope that all of this may be of some assistance for the actual work of the elders.

The Shepherd and His Flock

"THE LORD is my shepherd, I shall not be in want." These well-known words from Psalm 23 have comforted untold numbers through the ages. The shepherd image brings to mind pictures of tender care and faithful perseverance which see to all the needs of those in the shepherd's care. And now the wonder is that God uses this compassionate and positive shepherd image to describe his basic expectations for various leadership offices, including that of the elder. The message is clear. The elder, along with other leadership offices such as the king, the prophet, and the priest, had to reflect something of the Great Shepherd who is the Lord. It is obvious then that if we are to understand anything of the specific office of elder, we must have a good grasp of what the general job description of the shepherd entails.

We will therefore consider:

- The Shepherd and his sheep
- The Lord as Shepherd
- The human undershepherds

The Shepherd and His Sheep

The task of the shepherd was, in short, to take care of the flock. This care involved several overlapping responsibilities which are

15

probably not as obvious to a typical twenty-first-century urbanite as they were to the average Israelite or Jew living in biblical times.

To care for the flock meant that the shepherd saw to it that the animals had enough food and water. This responsibility may seem obvious but it was absolutely critical. One simply could not assume that the sheep would take care of themselves. A sheep rancher once told me that sheep require constant guidance and care. Especially in periods of drought it would have been exceedingly difficult for sheep to find appropriate pasture along with sufficient water on their own. It was up to the shepherd to lead the sheep to the green pastures (Pss. 23:2; 77:20). Note, the shepherd led the sheep and did not drive them ahead of him. Sheep followed the lead of the shepherd and were dependent on him (Pss. 77:20; 78:52; 80:1). Sheep are followers.

> They must have a human conductor. They cannot go to predetermined places by themselves. They cannot start out in the morning in search of pasture and then come home at evening time. They have, apparently, no sense of direction. The greenest pasture may be only a few miles away, but the sheep left to themselves cannot find it. What animal is more incapable than a sheep? He realizes his impotence for no animal is more docile. Where the shepherd leads, the sheep will go. He knows that the shepherd is a guide and that it is safe to go with him.[1]

This leadership responsibility of the shepherds was helped by the incredible ability of sheep to remember the voice of their shepherd and to listen to him and to him alone. As the Lord Jesus put it, the shepherd "calls his own sheep by name and leads them out. When he has brought out all his own, he goes on ahead of them, and his sheep follow him because they know his voice. But they will never follow a stranger; in fact, they will run away from him because they do not recognize a stranger's voice" (John 10:3–5). This truth is confirmed by those who have witnessed

---

1. Charles Edward Jefferson, *The Minister as Shepherd* (1912), 47, as quoted by Alexander Strauch, *Biblical Eldership: An Urgent Call to Restore Biblical Church Leadership*, rev. ed. (Littleton, CO: Lewis and Roth, 1995), 25–26.

flocks congregated at a water well. Each flock would be given an opportunity to drink water in turn. They would do so when they heard the voice of their own shepherd. Never was a voice of another shepherd mistaken for that of theirs.[2]

The shepherd required much wisdom and patience to guide the flock. Not only did he have to ensure an adequate supply of food and water, but he also had to be careful not to lead the sheep at a pace that was too fast for the weak and the young (Gen. 33:13–14). A good shepherd "gathers the lambs in his arms and carries them close to his heart; he gently leads those that have young" (Isa. 40:11). By so doing, the shepherd kept the flock together, as was his duty. Indeed, if but one was lost, it would need to be found (Ezek. 34:12; Luke 15:4). To make sure none was missing, shepherds normally counted their animals when they returned to the sheepfold for the evening by letting them pass under their hand (Jer. 33:13; Ezek. 20:37; Lev. 27:32).

The care for the flock included protecting the sheep from danger. Perils could come in the form of disease or a broken limb. The shepherd would have to keep a very careful eye on the flock to make sure no one was in distress and suffering. He would need to know his flock from firsthand knowledge of them. Danger could also come from outside the flock, and the sheep would have to be sheltered in pens or sheepfolds (Mic. 2:12; Hab. 3:17; John 10:3). The shepherd needed to defend his sheep against thieves (John 10:1, 8, 10) as well as predators like lions, bears, or wolves (1 Sam. 17:34–35; Acts 20:29). Without a caring shepherd, the sheep would be scattered and vulnerable (Ezek. 34:5–8). A shepherd therefore had to be able to recognize danger for what it was and take appropriate countermeasures.

In short, the life of a shepherd was to be characterized by a genuine love and concern for the sheep in all respects. Office bearers, as those set over the flock, are to emulate such shepherd love. Actually, they need to do better than that. They need to pattern their love after God's love, and their concern for the

---

2. See, e.g., E. Post, "Sheep," in J. Hastings, ed., *A Dictionary of the Bible*, 5 vols. (New York: Charles Scribner's Sons, 1898–1904), 4:487.

flock after God's concern for his people. After all, the Lord God is *the* Shepherd of the sheep, *the* standard for the work of the office bearers. He is the one who gives the different offices of his undershepherds their content and meaning. They are to represent and reflect God's wishes, criteria, and interests. It is his agenda that they are to promote.

We will therefore consider the picture of the divine Shepherd that Scripture gives us and then reflect on the human shepherds in that light. This will help us to get a general sense of what the office of elder in its most basic essentials is all about.

The Lord as Shepherd

From a very early date God's people knew the Lord, their covenant God, as their Shepherd. This is evident in both a personal and collective sense.

Two examples of the personal relationship of God, the Shepherd, to his people come to mind. When Jacob at the end of his life blessed Joseph's sons Ephraim and Manasseh, he referred to "the God who has been my shepherd" (Gen. 48:15; cf. 49:24). What a confession for Jacob to make! His life had been difficult, as he had confided to Pharaoh (Gen. 47:9). He had been a fugitive before murderous Esau, lasting marital bliss had eluded him as his two wives bickered, and the disappearance of Joseph had caused tremendous grief. But he knew that God was his Shepherd without whom he could not have survived. As the Hebrew text suggests, the shepherding action was ongoing right into the present. Jacob therefore characterized his entire life as one that was under the Lord's care for him. He even described this shepherding care as deliverance by an angel from all harm (Gen. 48:16).

A similar but more detailed personal confession is evident in a second example, the well-known Psalm 23. This song begins with the confession: "The LORD is my shepherd, I shall not be in want." David continued by showing how the Lord had provided for him in so many different ways. In his tumultuous life the

Lord had always been there and sustained him so that he lacked nothing. Even in the most difficult moments, the Lord's shepherd's rod and staff both corrected and disciplined him, as well as protected and comforted him. As a friend, the Lord had made him a guest at his table. In short, David's divine Shepherd had not only provided for all his needs, but also assured him of his unending care and presence.

The many connotations that the shepherd metaphor calls to mind when used in a general way are very suggestive of the tremendous extent of God's provision as protector and guide. The Lord cared for, sustained, and watched over people like Jacob and David as a shepherd. He provided comfort when that was needed, as well as correction and redirection. He saw to it that when nurture was required, it was there. He also provided hope for the future. All these and many other aspects can come to the fore when the shepherd image is used by individuals who benefited from and experienced the divine shepherding. No single aspect of shepherding dominates the picture it conveys.

Such a general usage of the shepherd image is employed in the collective sense as well. The call to worship in Psalm 95 is justified with the words: "for he is our God and we are the people of his pasture, the flock under his care" (v. 7). The clear intimation is that the Lord is their Shepherd who provides for all the needs of his people. Nothing specific is in view. It is a general all-around provision such as a shepherd provides, including the protection, feeding, and leading of the flock. A similar general usage is evident in other passages such as the prophecy in Isaiah 40:11 that the Lord who comes with power "tends his flock like a shepherd: He gathers the lambs in his arms and carries them close to his heart; he gently leads those that have young." All the positive connotations that the divine Shepherd conveyed to the individual were also there for the flock as a whole.

Besides this general use of the shepherd image there are those instances that bring out specific aspects of the shepherding task. The Lord's leadership can be the issue. This is the case when Psalm 77 speaks of the Lord as the Shepherd who brought the entire nation out of Egypt during the exodus. "You led your people like a flock by the hand of Moses and Aaron" (Ps. 77:20).

In other contexts, the focus can be especially on the shepherd's ability to save his flock from distress and foes. As Psalm 28:9 articulates it: "Save your people and bless your inheritance; be their shepherd and carry them forever." Or think of the cry of distress in Psalm 80:1–2:

> Hear us, O Shepherd of Israel,
>   you who lead Joseph like a flock; . . .
> Awaken your might;
>   come and save us.

Through Jeremiah, the Lord promised that "He who scattered Israel will gather them and will watch over his flock like a shepherd" (Jer. 31:10; cf. Ps. 121:4–5, 7–8) and "I will bring Israel back to his own pasture and he will graze on Carmel and Bashan; his appetite will be satisfied on the hills of Ephraim and Gilead" (Jer. 50:19).

In a similar vein, Ezekiel delivered a moving prophecy which was directed at a scattered and disheartened people. The Lord as the Shepherd of his people promised:

> I myself will search for my sheep and look after them. As a shepherd looks after his scattered flock when he is with them, so will I look after my sheep. I will rescue them from all the places where they were scattered on a day of clouds and darkness. I will bring them out from the nations and gather them from the countries, and I will bring them into their own land. I will pasture them on the mountains of Israel, in the ravines and in all the settlements in the land. I will tend them in a good pasture, and the mountain heights of Israel will be their grazing land. There they will lie down in good grazing land, and there they will feed in a rich pasture on the mountains of Israel. I myself will tend my sheep and have them lie down, declares the Sovereign LORD. I will search for the lost and bring back the strays. I will bind up the injured and strengthen the weak, but the sleek and

the strong I will destroy. I will shepherd the flock with justice. (Ezek. 34:11–16)

The promised shepherd of Ezekiel 34 is ultimately the Messiah (Ezek. 34:23; 37:24). He came to deliver and rule God's people (Mic. 5:2–5a), although this salvation would only come about by the shepherd first being struck and the sheep being scattered (Zech. 13:7; cf. Matt. 26:31).

And so the image of the divine Shepherd found its New Testament expression in the Lord Jesus Christ. All the positive attributes of the shepherd find their realization in him who is the Shepherd of Israel (Matt. 2:6). In a general sense, he is "the Shepherd and Guardian" of our souls (1 Peter 2:25 NASB), "that great Shepherd of the sheep" (Heb. 13:20) who provides for all our different needs. More specifically, he is the Good Shepherd who laid down his life for his sheep (John 10:11; cf. Zech. 13:7; Matt. 26:31). As the Lamb of God he will be the Shepherd of his people who "will lead them to springs of living water. And God will wipe away every tear from their eyes" (Rev. 7:17). As the Good Shepherd, he knows his sheep and they know him. He will gather together all his sheep "so there will be one flock, one shepherd" (John 10:14–16).

It is the image of the divine Shepherd that serves to provide the undershepherds, the office bearers whom God appoints and sets over his people, with the criteria they need to follow in order to exercise their office in a manner pleasing to the Shepherd above. It will be helpful to briefly consider the undershepherds whom God appointed and so place the office of elder within a broader framework.

The Human Undershepherds

Old Testament Shepherds

Interestingly, the God-appointed office most often referred to as shepherd was the office of king.[3] As king under the King of

3. As sovereign Lord, God could even designate foreign kings like Cyrus to do his bidding as his shepherd (Isa. 44:28). Our interest is of course in the leaders of God's people.

kings, he especially had the responsibility to shepherd the flock of God's people, with all the positive connotations that the image of a shepherd evoked. For example, the Lord had said to David: "You will shepherd my people Israel, and you will become their ruler" (2 Sam. 5:2). As Psalm 78 puts it, the Lord

> chose David his servant
>   and took him from the sheep pens;
> from tending the sheep he brought him
>   to be the shepherd of his people Jacob,
>   of Israel his inheritance.
> And David shepherded them with integrity of heart;
>   with skillful hands he led them. (Ps. 78:70–72)

Many positive elements of shepherding were included in the task of a king by virtue of the shepherd image that was used for this office.

However, in the Old Testament the image of shepherd was also used for other offices. It could, for instance, depict the task of an elder, an office predating the monarchy. Indeed, the image of the shepherd could picture any ruler or leader in Israel. Thus, when Moses was concerned about who would succeed him, he asked God who would provide leadership so that "the LORD's people will not be like sheep without a shepherd" (Num. 27:17). Other examples likewise illustrate the wide scope of this image in picturing the leadership of the people in general. The prophets often lamented the dearth of godly leadership, and such leadership could include leaders at all levels of Israelite society. When the Lord through Jeremiah bemoaned the fact that "the shepherds of the people rebelled against me" (Jer. 2:8 NEB), he distinguished these shepherds[4] from the priests and the prophets and their sins. Thus "shepherds" here include those in leadership positions at all levels, and modern translations reflect that. The metaphor of shepherd is flexible. When Jeremiah complained that "the shepherds are senseless and do not inquire of the LORD; so they do not

4. NIV translates more freely "leaders."

prosper and all their flock is scattered" (Jer. 10:21; cf. 23:1–5), he undoubtedly had the kings in mind, but probably the prophets and other religious leaders as well. Similarly when Jeremiah noted that the shepherds had led Israel astray and caused them to roam and wander (Jer. 50:6), the shepherds included all their leaders, kings, prophets, and priests. Indeed, the context of Israel's repentance and seeking the Lord in tears (Jer. 50:4–5) suggests that religious leaders were especially prominent here. They may very well have included the elders since they too had responsibilities in passing on the knowledge of the law, as we shall see in chapter 4. In like manner, elders could be referred to (along with priests) when the Lord promised his people shepherds who would lead them "with knowledge and understanding" (Jer. 3:15).

Such a diversity of those represented by the image of shepherd is also likely in Ezekiel 34 where the Lord enjoined Ezekiel to prophesy against the shepherds of Israel who had been taking care of themselves and neglecting the sheep. The result was that the sheep were scattered because they had no shepherd (Ezek. 34:1–6). Therefore the Lord was against those shepherds and would require the sheep from their hand. These shepherds would have included all leaders in Israel and thus the elders as well. They too would have been expected to seek the well-being of the people and shepherd with justice.

The image of shepherding is all-encompassing, dealing as it does with protecting, feeding, and leading the flock. It is well suited to describe in a general sense the awesome privilege and responsibility of holding an office, a specific task given by God himself, within the covenant people, including the office of elder. The responsibility of the human shepherds was to emulate the high standards of the heavenly Shepherd whose sheep they were entrusted with. In a word, that standard is the great love and covenant faithfulness that the heavenly Shepherd has for his sheep— traits which include both encouraging obedience and punishing disobedience. If the human shepherds did not live up to the expectations of the heavenly

Shepherd, he would demand the sheep from their hand. He held them responsible (Ezek. 3:17–21; 33:2–9).

Shepherds of the Good Shepherd

The demands are no less stringent for the New Testament church. Christ is the Good Shepherd (John 10), and those who are in his service must exemplify his love, faithfulness, and diligence for the flock. As Christ put it in a parable regarding the love of a shepherd: "Suppose one of you has a hundred sheep and loses one of them. Does he not leave the ninety-nine in the open country and go after the lost sheep until he finds it? And when he finds it, he joyfully puts it on his shoulders and goes home" (Luke 15:4–6). A shepherd knows his sheep and guides them step by step. "He calls his own sheep by name and leads them out. When he has brought out all his own, he goes on ahead of them" (John 10:3–4). Such is the love and care of Christ who is the Good Shepherd (John 10:11) and whose example his undershepherds must emulate. It is therefore noteworthy that when Christ commissioned the twelve disciples for a mission tour, he sent them out as shepherds "to the lost sheep of the house of Israel" (Matt. 10:6 ESV).

As risen Christ, the Lord Jesus is still the Good Shepherd who gathers his flock (John 10:14–16, 27–29; 1 Peter 2:25), although it is through the ministry of undershepherds. When Peter was reinstated within the circle of disciples after his triple denial of the Lord Jesus, Jesus charged him three times: "Feed my lambs. . . . Take care of my sheep. . . . Feed my sheep" (John 21:15–17). In this way, Peter was restored as a shepherd of the sheep. The apostle Paul wrote to the Ephesians that Christ "gave some to be apostles, some to be prophets, some to be evangelists, and some to be shepherds and teachers" (Eph. 4:11 in a literal translation). The words "shepherds and teachers" are best considered as belonging together and probably referring to the same office, namely that of a teaching elder (1 Tim. 5:17).[5] This combination

---

5. See chapter 6 note for a discussion on the identity of the eldership and specifically on Eph. 4:16.

of terms underlines that the teaching task can never be divorced from the overall concern of shepherding, with everything this implies. Teaching is guiding the sheep and lambs along the ways of the Lord's choosing and away from error and falsehood. Teaching is also sustaining and feeding the flock with the Word of God. A teaching elder or pastor can never divorce the aspect of shepherding from that of instructing.

Elsewhere the shepherd image is used of ruling elders. When the apostle Paul bade farewell to the Ephesian elders, he used the shepherd image and in so doing he eloquently detailed the guarding and watching aspect of their task. He said in part: "Be shepherds of the church of God, which he bought with his own blood. I know that after I leave, savage wolves will come in among you and will not spare the flock. Even from your own number men will arise and distort the truth in order to draw away disciples after them. So be on your guard!" (Acts 20:28b–31a). Elders are to be on the alert for the flock that is their charge. The apostle had prefaced these words with the reminder that he was "innocent of the blood of all men" because he had not hesitated to proclaim to them the whole will of God (Acts 20:26–27). This calls to mind the Lord's words to Ezekiel that he would hold the watchman set over his people responsible for the blood of those who had not been warned of the dangers they faced (Ezek. 3:17–21; 33:2–9).

Peter wrote to the elders serving congregations scattered throughout Asia Minor:

> Be shepherds of God's flock that is under your care, serving as overseers—not because you must, but because you are willing, as God wants you to be; not greedy for money, but eager to serve; not lording it over those entrusted to you, but being examples to the flock. And when the Chief Shepherd appears, you will receive the crown of glory that will never fade away. (1 Peter 5:2–4)

With these words, the love that must motivate their performing the duties of the office is emphasized. Such love and unselfish serving will be rewarded by the Chief Shepherd himself on the day of his appearing. Ultimately, it is indeed love for the Lord and his sheep and faithfulness to the call that is absolutely critical to living up to the high demands of being undershepherds in the service of the Great Shepherd above. Peter knew from experience what he wrote. Had the Lord not reinstated him into his office only after he reaffirmed three times his love for the Chief Shepherd (John 21:15–17)?

Conclusion

The image of the shepherd for the leadership office, including that of elder, is rich and evocative. Being in the service of the Good Shepherd means that the task of shepherding can only be done with the love, devotion, and caring of Christ. There are no easy shortcuts. Shepherding is hard work that involves the responsibility for the total well-being of the flock. There is no aspect of the life of the flock that the shepherd can ignore. The flock needs shepherds. It is vulnerable and defenseless without them.

Shepherds therefore need to lead and feed the flock. We will return in greater detail to these points, but in the present context it is good to underline how comprehensive and vast this task is. As a shepherd must become familiar with the lay of the land and where the good pastures and watering places are, so the modern elder must know how he is to lead and feed with the Word of God through which the Chief Shepherd guides and nourishes his flock. Like his pastoral counterpart, he who shepherds human beings must know where the danger is, so that the sheep can be protected and equipped for life's trials. He needs to be constantly on the lookout for perils that could harm the flock so he can warn and, if necessary, discipline and correct the sheep.

This heavy burden can be successfully borne only by those who are motivated by a true love for the Lord and his sheep and who know that their strength must be in the Lord, whose Word they know and heed and whose favor they beseech in prayer and supplication.

A Bearded Head

HAVING SEEN some of the implications of the shepherd image for the office of elder, we now need to consider three other introductory topics.

- The names used for this office
- The origin and place of this office within kinship
- The requirements for the eldership

What's in a Name?

The Hebrew term used for the office of elder in the Old Testament (*zaqen*) is derived from the word meaning "beard" (*zaqan*). An elder is therefore a male old enough to have a full beard. He is no longer a young man. Indeed, the Hebrew word used for elder can also simply mean "old man." The Aramaic term for elder (*sib*) means "one with grey hair." The Greek word for the office, used both in the ancient Greek translation of the Old Testament (Septuagint) and in the New Testament (*presbyteros*), means "old(er) man." It is clear that the terms used for the elder suggest that reaching a certain age was a basic criterion for this office. With age come experience and wisdom. Job rightly asked, be it sarcastically: "Is not wisdom found among the aged?" (Job 12:12). This truth is illustrated by the older counselors' giving

Rehoboam good advice, although the king accepted the foolish counsel of the young men (1 Kings 12:6–8).

Even though reaching a certain age was important, all old men did not automatically qualify for the office. As noted, the Hebrew term used to designate an elder can refer simply to an old man who is "full of years" (Gen. 25:8), without any regard for the office. Old age and office must as such be kept distinguished. They are not the same. Furthermore, the gift of wisdom was not necessarily found with those oldest in years. God reprimanded the friends of Job who were elderly because they had not spoken rightly of God as had Job (Job 42:7; cf. 32:6–9). Indeed, wisdom could be with the young rather than the old (Eccl. 4:13). Ultimately, wisdom and the qualifications for the office came not from acquiring a certain age, but from God (Job 32:7–9).

How young could one be and still be eligible for the office of elder? The Bible is silent on this specific and somewhat theoretical point. Although the matter of how one became an elder will have to be considered in answering this question, there are some factors that can be noted at this point. Scripture divides life into three clearly defined phases: first, children (including sucklings, Deut. 32:25, and young boys and girls, Ps. 148:12); second, young, but fully grown and sexually mature, men and women who can also be referred to as youth (Deut. 32:25; Ezek. 9:6); and third, the mature, who in the case of males have full beards (Ezek. 9:6; Ps. 148:12). This division indicates that a distinction was made between being physically grown-up, such as young adults are, and maturity that comes with a ripening into full adulthood. In the case of the male, the latter includes a full beard. It is possible that until such a beard could be attained the chin was shaved. In general this would probably mean that one would be past the age of full legal maturity, which in Israel was twenty (Ex. 30:14; 38:26; Num. 1:3, 18). Since the office of elder in ancient Israel required maturity, wisdom, and insight, men who attained this office would normally have been considerably over the age of twenty. Similarly, the New Testament listing of qualifications for the office, such as being temperate, managing his own household well, and having a good reputation with outsiders (1 Tim. 3:1–7; Titus 1:5–9), underline the need for a certain maturity and age.

There are indications that the age of thirty was the minimum required for positions involving authority and leadership in the Old Testament and Judaism. It is striking that the census of the Levites who had to take care of and tend the tabernacle was limited to those from thirty to fifty years of age (Num. 4:3, 23, 30), even though the age of service for a Levite was from age twenty-five (Num. 8:24–25). There is something attractive about the ancient Jewish interpretation that one was first an apprentice for five years, and only at age thirty did one assume all the responsibility for the weighty Levitical office. It is noteworthy that David, who had waited for God's time to become king, was proclaimed such at the age of thirty (2 Sam. 5:4). This was, incidentally, the same age at which Joseph was elevated to second-in-command of Egypt, under Pharaoh (Gen. 41:46). In the Jewish Essene community at Qumran (late second century B.C.–A.D. 68) the minimum age of thirty was required for having a position of leadership.[1] It is also striking that the Lord Jesus had years of preparation and maturation (Luke 2:51–52) before embarking on his public ministry at the age of about thirty years (Luke 3:23). In light of the above, one therefore gets the impression that the age of thirty was the minimum age. However, Scripture gives no specifically prescribed age for this office.

In the culture of the Hellenistic and New Testament world, those aged under forty years were still considered young. Depending on which sources are followed, the boundary of old age was considered to be either forty or fifty years. However, one gets the impression that holding office in the New Testament church followed Old Testament tradition. Paul, for example, is said to be "a young man" (Acts 7:58), and Timothy is exhorted not to let "anyone look down on you because you

1. Rule of the Congregation (1QS vi.8); see Florentino García Martínez and Eibert J. C. Tigchelaar, eds., *The Dead Sea Scrolls Study Edition*, 2 vols. (Leiden/Grand Rapids: Brill/Eerdmans, 1997–98), 1:82–83.

are young" (1 Tim. 4:12). The terms used suggest ages ranging from about twenty-five and thirty to about forty.[2]

Besides the normal Hebrew and Aramaic terms for elder, the office could also be referred to by the broader designation "head." This general term, which is attested in languages older than biblical Hebrew, could also have the specific meaning of elder. Based on a study of the relevant passages, the conclusion can be drawn that the "heads" were the leaders or elders at the subtribal and settlement levels, or parallel to the "chiefs" at the tribal level. When both the "head" and the "elder" are mentioned, the elder is in second rank. The "heads" or "chiefs" were taken from the ranks of the elders. On occasion, the term "head" can have the meaning of "elder" (e.g., 2 Chron. 28:12).[3]

In addition to *presbyteros*, another Greek word sometimes used for elder is *episkopos*, "bishop" or "overseer." It appears to be synonymous with *presbyteros*, judging from its usage in passages such as the following: first, from Miletus Paul summoned the elders of the Ephesian church to himself (Acts 20:17), yet he calls them overseers (Acts 20:28). Second, Peter appealed to the elders of the churches but urged them to fulfill the office of bishop (1 Peter 5:1–2). Third, Titus is enjoined to ordain elders and then is told what the qualifications are for a bishop (Titus 1:5–7).[4]

As noted earlier, the common New Testament word for elder (*presbyteros*) indicates an older man and thus one who does not belong with the younger men. *Presbyteros* is the regular translation of the Hebrew expression for elder used in the ancient Greek

2. The term *neanias* in Acts 7:58 indicates a young man of about twenty-five to forty. W. F. Bauer, F. W. Danker, W. F. Arndt, and F. W. Gingrich, eds., *A Greek-English Lexicon of the New Testament and Other Early Christian Literature*, 3d ed. (Chicago/London: University of Chicago Press, 2000), 667. In 1 Tim. 4:12 the term *neotēs* derives from a term suggesting an age of thirty to forty. H. G. Liddell, R. Scott, H. S. Jones, *A Greek-English Lexicon*, 9th ed. with revised supplement (Oxford: Clarendon, 1996), 1169. See also I. Howard Marshall, *A Critical and Exegetical Commentary on the Pastoral Epistles*, in collaboration with Philip H. Towner, International Critical Commentary (Edinburgh: T&T Clark, 1999), 239, 560.

3. Hanoch Reviv, *The Elders in Ancient Israel* (Jerusalem: Magnes, 1989), 1–21.

4. See for these and other passages Benjamin L. Merkle, *The Elder and Overseer: One Office in the Early Church*, Studies in Biblical Literature 57 (New York: Peter Lang, 2003).

translation of the Old Testament. When used in the New Testament, this term therefore provides a clear continuity with the Old Testament office. The term *episkopos*, on the other hand, comes from the Greek world where it denoted someone who watches over, an inspector or overseer (who is responsible to a superior power), and is so used in the ancient Greek translation of the Old Testament. Considering its origin, it is not surprising that this term is used as a synonym for elder only in the churches originating from the Gentiles.[5] On the other hand, the term *episkopos* is well suited as it highlights some of the responsibilities of an elder, as we shall see in chapter 9.

The Origin and Place of the Elder in Kinship

Nowhere does Scripture specifically tell us when and how the office of elder originated. It likely developed from the tribal structure of Israel. An elder was probably a head of a family or tribe. Presumably after his death, his oldest son would take his place. However, if the oldest son was incompetent, then the position could conceivably go to a younger son who would then be "the elder." The point is that to be an elder involved recognition by others, not only because of one's age and legal position, but also in view of one's gifts, authority, and ability to lead and to represent the interests and wishes of the people. As the tribes grew and the number of clans and families increased, so did the number of elders. The tribal chiefs would come from the ranks of the elders.[6] This origin of the office of elder in the tribe or family is reflected in much of the history of the office and leadership functions of elder in Old Testament times.

It may be helpful at this juncture to remind ourselves that under the overarching designation of being a nation, Israel had three clear levels of kinship: the tribe, the clan, and the

5. J. B. Lightfoot, *The Christian Ministry*, ed. with intro. by Philip Edgcumbe Hughes (Wilton, CT: Morehouse-Barlow, 1983), 37, 43.
6. John L. McKenzie, "The Elders in the Old Testament," *Biblica* 40 (1959): 532–34.

family. Thus when the covenant violator was sought whose sin caused Israel's defeat at Ai, Israel appeared before Joshua, first by tribe, second, by clan, then by family, and finally the guilty individual was chosen. His name was Achan, son of Carmi (his father's name), son of Zabdi (or Zimri [NIV; cf. 1 Chron. 2:6], the grandfather and head of the family), son of Zerah (name of the clan) of the tribe of Judah (Josh. 7:14–18). Although Achan was head of his family (in our western sense), he was nevertheless part of the larger family headed by his grandfather Zabdi. This larger family is also called the "father's house" and would have included the grandfather and his wife or wives, his sons with their wives, his grandsons with their wives, and any unmarried sons or daughters in the following generations, along with all unrelated dependents. Such a family could have comprised from fifty to one hundred persons, residing in a number of dwelling units.

These different levels of kinship are reflected in the terminology designating elders. On a national level, elders functioned as "elders of Israel" (e.g., Lev. 9:1; Josh. 7:6; 1 Sam. 4:3), on a tribal level as elders of the tribes (Deut. 31:28) or of a particular tribe, such as "elders of Judah" (2 Sam. 19:11; 2 Kings 23:1), and more locally as elders of a clan, such as "elders of Gilead" (Judg. 11:5), or of a city, like "the elders of Jabesh" (1 Sam. 11:3), of Succoth (Judg. 8:14, 16), or Bethlehem (1 Sam. 16:4). Although change was inevitable over the long history of Israel, yet it is difficult to overestimate the fundamental importance of the tribal, clan, and family organizations that were closely associated with the office of elder. In this connection, one must remember that Israel had traditionally lived in family groups. In the wilderness, the camp was divided along genealogical lines (Num. 2), and in the Promised Land, the land was allotted along these same tribal and family lines (Josh. 13–21). Over time there would be movement and change, yet throughout the history of Israel most people would continue to live close to their family's traditional inheritance. Thus the local elders would have been immediate relatives of those in their care, and the clan leaders would be direct relatives as well. Even the tribal elders would be family of everyone through the tribal genealogy.

In the ancient Near East, Israel was not unique with regard to these different levels of eldership. We read of elders of Pharaoh, of the land of Egypt (Gen. 50:7; Ps. 105:22), of Moab, Midian (Num. 22:4, 7), and Gibeon (Josh. 9:11). We may assume that their origin in these societies was similar to that in Israel. In Israel, however, the elders were directly associated with God's rule and their leadership function could never be divorced from the nation's covenant with the Lord. This will become more clear in the next two chapters.

When we come to the New Testament church, it is striking that the composition of the congregations often centered on the family unit, rather than simply individuals. Salvation was promised to Cornelius and his household (Acts 11:14). It was Lydia and her household, as well as the Philippian jailer and his household, who were baptized (Acts 16:15, 33–34). The same was true of Crispus and his house (Acts 18:8) and probably Onesiphorus as well (2 Tim. 1:16). The household of Stephanas were the first converts in Achaia (1 Cor. 16:15). Such households would typically include not only the immediate family but would also embrace the slaves and laborers associated with it. As the synagogues became closed to Christians, house churches developed and believers met in each other's homes (Rom. 16:5; 1 Cor. 16:19; Col. 4:15; Philem. 2; cf. Acts 20:20). The elders who would function in such congregations would be well known to everyone and quite probably related to a number of them. As in Old Testament times, the elders would have arisen from the community they served as their gifts were recognized by the congregation. So the New Testament church and the eldership developed within the context of the family and household.

The relationship of the home and family to the church, however, goes deeper. The very concept of a family is used as a descriptive image of the church. Those who believe in Christ are considered "the family of believers" (Gal. 6:10). More than that, the concept of family and kinship is basic to the very identity of the people of God. The church is the family or household of God (1 Tim. 3:15; Heb. 3:6; 1 Peter 4:17) in which the children of God find their home (John 1:12–13; Eph. 2:19; 1 John 3:1–2). Believers in the Lord Jesus are brothers and sisters of each other and children of their Father in heaven. The church family reaches as far as the unity in Christ extends (Rom. 8:29; 1 Cor. 15:58; 2 Cor. 6:16–18; Gal. 3:26; Phil. 4:1).

As the nation of Israel was of one seed and flesh of Abraham, so the New Testament church is one family, the family of God, the spiritual children of Abraham (Gal. 3:7, 29). The church may have been spread far and wide, but it was one body of brothers and sisters in the Lord. When difficulties and problems arose, they sent representatives to gather together and go through the problems. This happened when the church at Antioch sent delegates to the apostles and elders at Jerusalem to deal with the controversy that had arisen in Antioch between Christians of Jewish and Gentile background regarding the place of circumcision and the law of Moses (Acts 15).

The closest one comes to "national elders" in the New Testament is arguably those elders who served in Jerusalem. These were the elders who along with the apostles adjudicated the difficulties Antioch brought to their attention (Acts 15:23). The fact that these elders are mentioned along with the apostles in Acts 15 (vv. 2, 4, 6, 22–23), as well as with James, a brother of the Lord Jesus and leader of the Jerusalem church, seems to indicate that they had special qualifications that set them apart from all other elders. It would appear most likely that they had been eye and ear witnesses of Christ's public ministry. This would explain both their association with the apostles and their considerable influence and authority outside their own congregation. At the same time, these elders primarily functioned as local elders in the church at Jerusalem (James 5:14). They apparently rose to that rank by virtue of their authority and leadership as eyewitnesses of Christ's work, although we are not informed precisely how they became elders.[7]

7. For more on these elders, see chapter 6, under the heading "The Jerusalem Elders."

In any case, the New Testament church's continuity with Old Testament Israel made the familiar office of elder a "natural" fit for the new Pentecost age. Indeed, God ordained it in this way (see e.g., Acts 14:23; Titus 1:5), and the office so familiar to the Jewish believers could continue unbroken in the new Israel of God (Gal. 6:16). It endured to function within the context of the family of God.

Requirements for the Office

Although the nature of the requirements for being an elder will become more and more clear as we deal with their duties, it will be profitable at this point to give a general overview of the biblical criteria for being an elder.

Wisdom and life experience that come with growing older are obviously important and, as we have seen, are implied in the very name given to this office. Of great significance is exhibiting a heart and love for God's people and their needs, as a shepherd does for his sheep. Wise individuals with such love were often providentially placed within ancient Israelite society so that they assumed the leadership role of an elder almost as a matter of course. On the other hand, it was also possible that those endowed with insight and understanding would be recognized by others and by conscious decision of those involved would be given a place of authority in their community. As we have seen, such a process was witnessed in the time of Moses, and it was the normal course of events in the New Testament church. Moses mentioned the qualifications of those whom he invited the congregation to put forward so that he could appoint them to have authority over the people as heads of the tribes (or elders) to judge. They were to be wise, understanding, and respected (Deut. 1:13, 15).[8] Other qualifications included their being capable, fearers of God, trustworthy, and hating bribes

8. For the identity of those appointed in Ex. 18:21–25 and Deut. 1:13–15 as probable elders, see chapter 5, under "Elders and Courts."

(Ex. 18:21, 24). Note how moral qualities stand in the forefront, rather than, for example, intellectual abilities or social standing. Finally, no elder could function in his own strength. As we shall see in more detail in chapter 4, he needed to be enabled by the Spirit of God (Num. 11:16–17).

The New Testament's guidelines and criteria for the eldership are similar, but go into more detail. We find them in the apostle Paul's instructions to Timothy and Titus. In both cases he refers to the elders as overseers. He wrote to Timothy:

> Here is a trustworthy saying: If anyone sets his heart on being an overseer, he desires a noble task. Now the overseer must be above reproach, the husband of but one wife, temperate, self-controlled, respectable, hospitable, able to teach, not given to drunkenness, not violent but gentle, not quarrelsome, not a lover of money. He must manage his own family well and see that his children obey him with proper respect. (If anyone does not know how to manage his own family, how can he take care of God's church?) He must not be a recent convert, or he may become conceited and fall under the same judgment as the devil. He must also have a good reputation with outsiders, so that he will not fall into disgrace and into the devil's trap. (1 Tim. 3:1–7)

From this "trustworthy saying" we can note the following. In the years immediately following Pentecost when there was much resistance to the gospel, especially from the Jews, considerable sacrifice could be expected from an elder or overseer. Paul reminded Timothy that it is a noble task to which one may aspire, and in this way he subtly encouraged such aspirations. When the apostle listed the qualifications for the office, it is remarkable that one's relationship to his family is very important. This reminds us again of how the family was the matrix of the early Christian church. Understandably, an elder's relationship to his family will be indicative of how he will function in the congregation, the household of God. The apostle assumed the elder is married but he did not make the married state a necessary qualification for being an elder. In other words, single men also can qualify for the eldership (cf. 1 Cor. 7:27–35). The rest of the qualifications speak for themselves. He must be known both from within the church and by those outside as one of impeccable reputation with the qualities that one would expect from a Christian leader. But he must not be a recent convert, lest he become proud and fall into sin (cf. Prov. 16:18). This rule was followed by Paul, who did not appoint elders until he revisited the churches (Acts 14:23). Delaying appointments allowed for a period of evaluation. Similarly, deacons were to be tested first (1 Tim. 3:10).

In like manner, the apostle wrote Titus:

> An elder must be blameless, the husband of but one wife, a man whose children believe and are not open to the charge of being wild and disobedient. Since an overseer is entrusted with God's work, he must be blameless—not overbearing, not quick-tempered, not given to drunkenness, not violent, not pursuing dishonest gain. Rather he must be hospitable, one who loves what is good, who is self-controlled, upright, holy and disciplined. He must hold firmly to the trustworthy message as it has been taught, so that he can encourage others by sound doctrine and refute those who oppose it. (Titus 1:6–9)

As in his letter to Timothy, Paul also here says that the elder must be one who is apt to teach the true doctrine and defend it against the wiles of Satan. Furthermore, his reputation as a husband and father is very important. His family must be an example for others; that is, his children must not still be in the darkness of paganism or behave as unbelievers, but embrace the same Christian faith.[9]

As the occasion warrants in successive chapters, we will return to some of the qualifications of the elder mentioned above and elaborate further. But it is obvious from the above that elders must be chosen very carefully. Much is at stake in their office.

9. See, further, chapter 8, under "Loving Leadership."

Part 2

Old Testament Origins

Elders as Leaders in the Old Testament

IN ORDER TO APPRECIATE the present leadership function of the elder, we will survey how this responsibility was exercised in ancient Israel. This approach will enable us to learn from the past and to appreciate more fully what is involved.

We will consider:

- The leadership of the elders prior to the monarchy
- The elders during the monarchy
- The elders during and after the exile
- Summary and conclusions

The Leadership of the Elders prior to the Monarchy

Leaders as Representatives and Rulers

When Israel consisted of a household ruled by the patriarch Jacob, there was no mention of elders in Scripture. Elders arose as the tribes developed. We first hear of the elders of Israel in the days of Moses. It is to the elders that the Lord commanded Moses to go with the news that he would deliver his people from Egypt. It was with the elders that Moses had to go to Pharaoh with the divine demand that he let the Israelites go to sacrifice in the desert (Ex. 3:16–18). These elders were clearly Israel's leaders.

41

They recognized Moses as leader only after he had presented his credentials to them with the message that God was going to deliver them (Ex. 3:13–18). The elders also represented the people. When Moses spoke to them, he spoke to the people (Ex. 3:15–16).

The leadership position and representative role of the elders are seen in other instances as well when elders and the people are mentioned together. For example, when Moses and Aaron gathered the elders of the people of Israel, Aaron spoke and "did the signs in the sight of the people" (Ex. 4:30). Even though only the elders were present, Aaron's action was done "in the sight of the people" (cf. Ex. 17:5–6). We see a similar close relationship of the elders to the people as a whole when Moses "summoned the elders of the people" at Mount Sinai. He told them all the words which the Lord had commanded, and then "the people all responded together, 'We will do everything the LORD has said'" (Ex. 19:7–8). When Israel approached Moses because they feared God's speaking from Mount Sinai, they came in the persons of the heads of the tribes and the elders (cf. Ex. 20:18–20 with Deut. 5:23).

The representative function of the elders was also apparent when the covenant was being confirmed at Mount Sinai. The Lord asked Moses and Aaron, along with Aaron's two oldest sons, Nadab and Abihu, to come up the mountain. But God asked seventy elders to come as well (Ex. 24:1). They represented the people. This same function is obvious in the provision that if the whole community sinned, then the elders had to lay their hands on the bull of the sin offering before it was slaughtered (Lev. 4:15). Furthermore, the elders were summoned as representatives of the people for the inaugural sacrificial service of Aaron and the priests (Lev. 9:1).

The special place of the elders is evident in the days of Joshua as well. As leaders, the elders of Israel accompanied Joshua and mourned with him at the defeat at the hands of Ai (Josh. 7:6). With Joshua they led the campaign to do battle with Ai for a second and successful time (Josh. 8:10). When at the end of his life Joshua bade farewell and exhorted the people to obey the Lord, he summoned the people, with the elders being specifically mentioned first (Josh. 23:2). This action was repeated at the more official covenant renewal at Shechem (Josh. 24:1). As long as these elders lived, the people served the Lord (Josh. 24:31).

The elders could provide energetic leadership in times of crisis. When there was a need for a strong military leader to protect Gilead and meet the threat of the Ammonites, the elders saw to it that Jephthah became their leader. In the negotiations and agreement made, the elders represented the interests of their people (Judg. 11:4–11). Similarly, the elders of Jabesh-Gilead dealt with the military emergency facing them by negotiating with the Ammonites and sending out messengers to seek help (1 Sam. 11:3). The elders were clearly in charge. It was also the elders who thought it necessary to ask for a king. Although Samuel warned them that this request was a rejection of God's kingship, they spurned the admonition (1 Sam. 8). This incident shows that the elders did not always heed God's will, as was their duty.

In summary, one could say that the elders both represented the people and ruled them, but they were not autocratic. When matters were as they should be, the elders were conscious of their obligations to God whose people they led and represented before him. This realization meant that their leadership and rule were to have a serving character. This was evident from their mediating role in the covenant renewal at Sinai. It was also apparent from their decisive leadership in the days of the judges in securing Jephthah as military leader of Israel during a time of crisis. Faithful elders kept paramount the interests of the nation, which was in covenant with God.

Leaders Enabled

At a certain moment, not long after leaving Sinai (Num. 10:33), the awesome burden of an ungrateful people that clamored for meat caused Moses to complain to God that the load was too heavy. In venting his frustrations, Moses asked whether he had conceived and given birth to this entire people: "Why do you tell me to carry them in my arms, as a nurse carries an infant, to the land you promised on oath to their forefathers? . . . I cannot carry all these people by myself; the burden is too heavy for me" (Num. 11:12, 14).

To bear the burden of the people was, then, a very onerous and comprehensive duty. It encompassed everything needed to get the people to the Promised Land. This duty would therefore have included spiritual oversight and guidance. Indeed, the Lord's leading Israel to the Promised Land is later described with a similar image. Before entering Canaan, Moses reminded the people how the Lord had carried Israel in the desert "as a father carries his son" all the way to the Promised Land (Deut. 1:31). Isaiah used the same word to describe the Lord as a shepherd carrying the lambs in his bosom from Babylon back to Judah (Isa. 40:11). With the comprehensive task of carrying the people, Moses felt the weight of responsibility very acutely. The Lord responded to Moses's trouble:

> Bring me seventy of Israel's elders who are known to you as leaders and officials among the people. Have them come to the Tent of Meeting, that they may stand there with you. I will come down and speak with you there, and I will take of the Spirit that is on you and put the Spirit on them. They will help you carry the burden of the people so that you will not have to carry it alone. (Num. 11:16–17)

These men subsequently came and received some of the Spirit that was on Moses. "When the Spirit rested on them, they prophesied, but they did not do so again" (Num. 11:25).[1] Two men, Eldad and Medad, had not come to the tent of meeting, but they too received the Spirit and prophesied (Num. 11:26–27).

This incident makes clear that the Spirit was needed for the demanding work of leadership. Moses was endowed with the Spirit, and these elders who were to assist him were likewise equipped. The Spirit's presence was authenticated by the ability of these elders to prophesy for a short time. How this prophecy took place is not as important as the fact that it established the

1. The Hebrew text of Num. 11:25 suggests the abiding presence of the Spirit.

legitimacy of these elders as leaders who assisted Moses. Moved by the Spirit they could speak in agreement with the Word of God and show people the way (cf. Ex. 4:15–16; 7:1–2). This gave them the necessary leadership credentials of being empowered by the Spirit who had come to them to enable them for their task.

What happened to Eldad and Medad was remarkable. Although they were not at the tent of meeting, they too received the Spirit's credentials. According to Jewish tradition, Eldad and Medad had not come out to the tent of meeting because they felt inadequate. If this is so, the Spirit's being given to them nevertheless underlines the Spirit's sovereignty and the efficacy of God's call to the office. However that may be, the Spirit clearly worked in his own way and equipped for office those whom he desired.

In giving Moses this help in leadership, God showed his great mercy to those whom he appointed to lead. After all, the fact that these elders shared in the Spirit that was on Moses made it clear that Moses had received enough to enable him in his task. God however did not deny the request of Moses implicit in his complaint that the load was too heavy for him. God gave assistance by taking some of the Spirit on Moses and distributing to these elders.

On the other hand, Moses understood very well what the ultimate issue underlying the leadership crisis was. When Joshua urged Moses to stop the prophesying of Eldad and Medad because this seemed to threaten the eminent position of Moses, Moses retorted: "Are you jealous for my sake? I wish that all the LORD's people were prophets and that the LORD would put his Spirit on them!" (Num. 11:29). The ultimate issue was the leadership of the Lord. Moses would have liked to see God's Spirit in all the people so that all the people would be taught and guided by God himself. This wish of Moses points to the miracle of Pentecost (John 14:26; 16:13; Acts 2:33; 1 John 2:20). Now that the Holy Spirit has been poured out (Acts 2:1–36), God's people, the congregation, have all the more responsibility to heed the good leadership of the office bearers.

When Moses needed help, the Lord gave seventy elders. The Lord dispensed assistance generously. This number connotes completeness. By this number, the people were adequately shepherded. It is noteworthy that God specified not only the number seventy, but also that these people be from among those who already had places of leadership over all the tribes, being their elders and "officers" (Num. 11:16 ESV). Whatever the specific nuance of this term might be, it suggests that these men had important places of authority, which possibly included the military.[2] Those who were already recognized by the people as having sound leadership capabilities were entrusted with assisting Moses in "bearing the burden" of the people. This comprehensive task description suggests that spiritual oversight would have been part of their task as well. Whether these seventy were the same as those who went with Moses up Mount Sinai (Ex. 24:9) is not stated.

This enabling by the Spirit for leadership is later mentioned for the office of Joshua (Num. 27:18; Deut. 34:9; cf. Isa. 11:2), judges (Judg. 3:10; 6:34; 11:29; 13:25), Saul (1 Sam. 10:6, 10; 11:6), and David (1 Sam. 16:13–14; 2 Sam. 23:2).[3] Subsequent to Numbers 11, no elders are specifically mentioned as being enabled by the Spirit. However, this silence cannot be used to suggest that in later times the Lord no longer enabled godly elders with his Spirit to give leadership to God's people (cf. Isa. 63:10–14).

To summarize, no leader can do the work of leading God's people in his own strength. Even Moses could not do so. As the Lord needed to equip elders for the task then, he still needs to do so now. Since we live after the time of the outpouring of the Holy Spirit at Pentecost, our responsibilities are the greater, both as elders and as those who are to heed their godly leadership and rule.

Leaders in Ensuring Knowledge of the Law

Israel as God's covenant nation was to live by God's law. The elders as leaders had to ensure that those under their care lived according to the stipulations of the covenant. We see this responsibility in a number of passages. Although Moses alone

2. For the possible military overtones in being an "officer," see Deut. 20:5–9; Josh. 1:10–11; 3:2–4.

3. Exegetes disagree as to whether or not the Holy Spirit is meant with respect to Joshua in Num. 27:18 and Deut. 34:9. Cf. NASB and NIV (including text notes).

normally addressed the people, this did not happen at the covenant renewal at Mount Ebal prior to entering the Promised Land. Then "Moses *and the elders of Israel* commanded the people: 'Keep all these commands that I give you today'" (Deut. 27:1). This joint exhortation is significant for it impressed on the elders that they had a special responsibility to ensure that the covenant demands were indeed carried out, especially in the absence of Moses who would not enter the Promised Land.

It is furthermore noteworthy that after Moses had written the law, he gave it not only to the priests (who took care of the ark where the law had to be deposited) but also "to all the elders of Israel" (Deut. 31:9). Together with the priests, the elders too received the command from Moses that every seven years, at the Feast of Tabernacles, they read this law in the hearing of the people "so they can listen and learn to fear the LORD your God and follow carefully all the words of this law" (Deut. 31:12).

Furthermore, Moses summoned the elders first when he recited the words of his final song. The elders had the specific obligation to make sure that Israel would know the contents of this important covenant witness. It testified of the greatness of God, of his dealings with his people, of the rebelliousness of his people, and of the curses and blessings of the covenant (Deut. 31:28–32:47). Significantly, right in this song, Moses enjoined God's people to

> Remember the days of old;
>   consider the generations long past.
> Ask your father and he will tell you,
>   your elders, and they will explain to you. (Deut. 32:7)

The duty to teach one's children the precepts of the Lord was well known (Deut. 4:9; 6:7; 11:19; 32:46). The fact that the elders were placed in a parallel position with the fathers suggests similar responsibilities on the part of the elder to make known the great deeds of God. It also reminds us of the familial and tribal context of this office of leadership. When reference is

47

made to the elder, the family and tribal relationships are never far away.

Finally, the duty of the elders as leaders to instruct can be seen indirectly in Nehemiah's penitential prayer in which he alludes to the gift of the Spirit to the elders. In this prayer Nehemiah recalled, among other things, God's leading and guiding Israel through the wilderness. He then mentioned that God gave the Spirit to instruct Israel (Neh. 9:20). Given the context of leadership and manna, Nehemiah was probably referring to the gift of the Spirit to the elders in Numbers 11. This reference thus underlines the elders' teaching task.

The great importance of the leadership of the elders in guiding Israel in God's ways and ensuring familiarity with the law of God is also evident in the period after Moses. Israel served the Lord as long as the elders who outlived Joshua and who had seen God's mighty works for Israel were with the people (Judg. 2:7; Josh. 24:31). The implication seems to be that they taught God's ways. When the elders were unfaithful, the entire nation suffered the consequences, as seen in the chaos of the days of the judges when Israel did not obey the Lord and each man did what was right in his own eyes.

A vivid example of this unfaithfulness is the last recorded incident in the book of Judges. After the slaughter of the Benjaminites at the hands of the other tribes, Israel worried that Benjamin might not survive as a tribe. To get around the oath that the other tribes had taken not to give one's daughter in marriage to a Benjaminite, the elders of the assembly commanded the Benjaminites to seize for themselves a wife from the girls of Shiloh when they joined in the dancing at the annual festival there. The elders promised to help resolve any complaints (Judg. 21:16–23). This action of the elders went against the express commandment of God, which punished kidnapping with death (Ex. 21:16), and thus fed the moral chaos of the times.

Another example of the harm inflicted by unfaithful elders comes from the time of Eli. The battle against the Philistines was not going well, and so the elders urged that the ark be taken into battle. Such a demand was based on the pagan belief that they could force God to come and fight for them. The elders' ungodly leadership brought God's judgment on the people. They lost the ark and Shiloh was destroyed (1 Sam. 4; Jer. 7:12–14).

In summary, the rule and leadership of the elders over Israel included the crucial obligation of placing the demands of the great King of Israel, the Lord God, before the people. In this way they were to be a blessing and guide Israel in the ways of the covenant and nurture God's people in their life with God.

The Elders during the Monarchy—Leadership under Pressure

The elders probably retained their place of importance in the family and clan structure of Israelite society and provided a measure of continuity and stability from one era to the next. With the monarchy, however, certain changes in the status of the elder did occur and their position of leadership was often threatened.

The United Monarchy

Apart from a special judge whom God would raise up from time to time to deliver his people from dire distress, the elders were the constant, undisputed leaders of the nation before there was a king. It was "all the elders of Israel" who came to Samuel on behalf of the people and demanded that he appoint a king over Israel (1 Sam. 8:4, 19–20). It was also with the elders of Israel that Abner conferred after a falling-out with Ishbosheth, son of the slain King Saul, and suggested that they make David king over all the tribes (2 Sam. 3:17). It was all the elders who came to Hebron and anointed David king over Israel. Significantly, their going to Hebron is described as all the tribes of Israel going there (2 Sam. 5:1–3; 1 Chron. 11:1–3). The elders were the legitimate representatives of the people. These initiatives of the elders for the monarchy did, however, lead to an undermining of their traditional leadership authority.

49

Initially it did not appear to work out that way. The elders enjoyed the prestige reserved for those in important leadership positions. King Saul was eager for their support. On acknowledging his sin of not punishing the Amalekites as God had commanded, Saul had asked Samuel to honor him before the elders of the people anyway (1 Sam. 15:30). When David was a hunted man, he remembered the elders of Judah and sent them some of the spoils of Ziklag (1 Sam. 30:26). This action was not only indicative of David's gratitude to these elders and cities that had apparently assisted him (1 Sam. 30:31), but it also showed his respect for the elders and the leadership authority they possessed.

After David became king, the importance of the elders as leaders and representatives of the people was clear from their accompanying David, along with the captains of thousands and the Levites, in bringing up the ark from the house of Obed-edom to Jerusalem (1 Chron. 15:25). In a similar capacity, the elders were also present with David, clothed in sackcloth, when the Lord executed judgment for David's sin of ordering a census of his fighting men (1 Chron. 21:16; cf. Josh. 7:6).[4]

In spite of the importance of the elder, there is no record that as a monarch, David (or for that matter Saul) ever had the benefit of regular consultation with the elders as part of a normal decision-making process in establishing policy. Indeed, David appears to have alienated the elders of Israel. It is striking that the elders of Israel supported Absalom in his rebellion, as apparently did a good part of the regular (tribal based) army, referred to as "the men of Israel" or "Israel" (2 Sam. 15:13; 17:1–15; 18:6). The loss of significant support from the tribal army meant that David had to flee immediately with only his private mercenary force, known as "his servants" (2 Sam. 15:14–18). Without the backing of the elders and the army, the rebellion would not have come so close to succeeding.

4. It is striking that in the parallel passage (2 Sam. 24:15–25), servants are present with David (v. 21), indicating that the "elders" of 1 Chron. 21:16 may have been servants as well, just as the "elders" in 2 Sam. 12:17 are (senior) servants. These servants may have been royal counselors (cf. 1 Kings 12:6).

Whatever the grievances of the elders were, we are not specifically told, but they seem to have been related to the loss of influence for the elder and tribe in the kingdom. The growing centralization of political power and justice in Jerusalem at the cost of the relative tribal autonomy in these matters was probably part of the problem (2 Sam. 15:2–6). In any case it is significant that after the revolt was put down, David immediately sought to be reconciled to the elders of his own tribe, Judah. He asked them to take the initiative in restoring him to the throne (2 Sam. 19:11–14). David recognized again the great importance of having the backing of the elders.

Although tribal and clan structures survived throughout the period of the monarchy as socioeconomic and, to a lesser extent, as political units, especially locally, there is no denying that the ancient tribal structures came under increasing pressure from the demands of royalty. Years earlier Samuel had warned precisely about such developments. He had cautioned that the king would claim the resources of the families of Israel for himself (1 Sam. 8:10–18).

When Solomon came to the throne, he divided his realm into twelve districts that did not always coincide with the tribal possessions, each with an appointed governor (1 Kings 4:7–19). This action, whether intentional or not, did not enhance tribal identities (and hence the position of the elders) but fostered centralization in a Jerusalem bureaucracy. Perhaps for that reason we rarely read of elders in the days of Solomon and Rehoboam and the divided kingdoms that followed. To be sure, the elders were summoned by Solomon to be present as representatives of the people when the ark was brought into the temple (1 Kings 8:1–5; 2 Chron. 2:2–4), just as David his father had involved them when bringing the ark up into Jerusalem (1 Chron. 15:25). But we hear nothing further of them during Solomon's lifetime.

When Rehoboam became king, "he consulted the elders who had served his father Solomon during his lifetime" whether he should lighten the load Solomon had placed on the people (1 Kings 12:6; 2 Chron. 10:6). If these elders refer to the traditional tribal leadership, it would indicate that they had a place in the royal court, perhaps in recognition of their traditional importance in Israel. The reference, however, could also be to those who had counseled Solomon as his appointees and officials and who by this time would have been "old men" (ESV). This view too is plausible because the age of these men is contrasted with that of the young men in 1 Kings 12:8 (and 2 Chron. 10:8). Whatever the case may have been, one does not hear of traditional elders in the royal government during the time of Solomon.

The Kingdom of Israel

In light of earlier coronations, we can assume that with the breakup of the kingdom of Rehoboam, the elders as the acknowledged traditional leaders of the people were involved in contacting Jeroboam in Egypt and crowning him king over Israel (1 Kings 12:2–3, 20).

With respect to the northern kingdom we can briefly take note of the elders in Samaria. Samaria was a new city, the possession of the king (see 1 Kings 16:24). As a result, the elders who actually lived there were probably from elsewhere. They may have been specially designated to be in this royal city as representatives of the people before the king when needed. In any case, their presence indicates how important or necessary the house of Omri considered the availability of the traditional elders in their city.

The elders in Samaria are mentioned on three occasions. First, when King Ahab faced a severe political crisis because Ben-Hadad II, king of Aram, was besieging Samaria, he summoned "all the elders of the land" for advice (1 Kings 20:7–8). These elders were probably those available in the city who were to represent all the people (v. 8), although it is possible that elders from elsewhere who had taken refuge in Samaria were included in this instance. It would have been important for Ahab to have the support of the elders for whatever decision he would make in the face of Ben-Hadad's demands. Second, when Ben-Hadad III besieged Samaria in the days of Jehoram (or Joram), elders visited Elisha at his home (2 Kings 6:32). Perhaps they were there to get insight from the prophet so that they would be equipped to give proper advice to Ahab should that be asked. Third, when Jehu set about to destroy the house of Ahab, he recognized the authority of the elders in Samaria by addressing them, along with the officials and guardians who were there. When the elders pledged their loyalty to Jehu, he asked them to take the heads of Ahab's sons and come to him in Jezreel (2 Kings 10:1–6). From the above it is evident that the elders in Samaria had a place in the political processes of the day.

A telling example of the leadership authority that the elders still retained occurred when Israel and the Arameans attacked Judah (2 Chron. 28). Israel under King Pekah took many Judeans captive, but the prophet Oded told the Israelites to release them so that they would not incur God's wrath. Some elders, here designated as "heads of the men of Ephraim,"[5] responded positively and demanded that the prisoners be released. "So the soldiers gave up the prisoners and plunder" (2 Chron. 28:14). This was undoubtedly not a popular action to take and may even have contravened the king's command, but the incident shows the authority of the elders.

The Kingdom of Judah

The elders in Judah appear to have retained their place of importance in the crowning of new Davidic kings. When Joash was crowned king, the "heads of the fathers' houses," that is, the elders, participated along with the Levites in making a covenant with the king (2 Chron. 23:2–3).[6] We meet the elders in Judah again in a covenant renewal context in the days of Josiah. After the book of the law had been found, King Josiah was determined to work reformation and renew the covenant with God. "Then the king called together all the elders of Judah and Jerusalem"

5. Hanoch Reviv, *The Elders in Ancient Israel*, (Jerusalem: Magnes, 1989), 15–21, 132–34.
6. Ibid., 117.

(2 Kings 23:1; 2 Chron. 34:29). They came as representatives of the people for the covenant renewal. "Then all the people pledged themselves to the covenant" (2 Kings 23:3).

From other passages it is evident that the elder retained a position of leadership in Judah (Lam. 4:16; 5:12). The elder is called the "head" of the nation (Isa. 9:14–15). God told Jeremiah to take some elders and priests as witnesses of his prophecy (Jer. 19:1). Unfortunately, the elders also contributed to the downfall of the kingdom by their sin (Ezek. 8:9–12; 9:6).

Summing Up

In summary, one gets the impression that when worldly ideas of royal power prevailed, the leadership and prestige of the elders were under duress and suffered. When a king needed them, they were part of the political or decision-making process, but otherwise generally not, unless the king was godly like Josiah. The unfaithfulness of the elders themselves was sometimes part of the problem. The developments during the monarchy illustrate the fragile position of the office of elder. When there was unfaithfulness to the covenant demands of God, the office quickly lost its honored place and clout. However, obedience by the elders to God's demands in spite of pressure to the contrary was blessed, as seen in the case of the elders insisting that the prophet Obed's instructions be carried out (2 Chron. 28:12–14).

The Elders during and after the Exile

With the collapse of Judah and the exile of God's people in Babylon, the elders came more to the foreground. They were, in effect, the sole authoritative leaders among the people since the centralized bureaucracy of the monarchy completely disintegrated. When Jeremiah wrote to the Israelite community in Babylon, "the elders of the exile" headed the list of recipients, which included the priests and prophets (Jer. 29:1; cf. Ezek. 7:26). The continuity that these elders had with the past is indicated by their being called "elders of Judah" and "elders of Israel" (Ezek. 8:1; 14:1; 20:1, 3). These elders provided counsel (Ezek. 7:26; Jer. 18:18) and would therefore come to Ezekiel for guidance (Ezek. 8:1; 14:1; 20:1). In a sense, the situation of the elders in exile was very similar to that of the Israelite elders during the Egyptian bondage recounted in Exodus. They were respected by their own people, but without any real power beyond that circle.

It is noteworthy that when the elders came to Ezekiel for guidance, the Lord refused to answer them, but rather confronted them with their sins. Their sin of idolatry was especially singled out as bringing God's judgment on Judah and Jerusalem (Ezek. 8, 14, 20). In this way, the tremendous responsibility of the elders for the well-being of God's people was underlined. Unfaithful elders were a curse for God's people; God held these leaders accountable (Ezek. 34).

The prominence of the elders after the return from captivity is evident from the fact that they were the acknowledged leaders. They were the ones questioned by the governor and officials of Trans-Euphrates about the rebuilding of the temple (Ezra 5:9). In the decree of Darius, the elders are mentioned as being in command, and the enemies of the Jews were told not to interfere in their work but to help them (Ezra 6:7–8, 14). Also, the elders, together with the officials (probably local leaders whose areas of jurisdiction would touch and overlap those of the elders), issued the proclamation calling for all the exiles to come to Jerusalem to deal with their sins of intermarriage. Failure to come would result in severe penalties of losing both property and membership in the community of the exiles (Ezra 10:8).

A noteworthy feature of postexilic life that needs to be factored in is that the significance of the tribes yielded to the importance of individual families. A certain nobility based on family standing emerged in the postexilic community. The authority of the elders, therefore, became based on the special position of their families within the people rather than on their own position within a clan or tribe. As mentioned in chapter 1, this eventually led to the establishment of the Sanhedrin consisting of seventy elders, although the local elder continued his important function of local leadership.

Summary and Conclusions

We will now pull together and integrate our main findings about the elders as leaders. We will concentrate on those areas that have the most impact for discerning abiding principles that are still operative today.

The Family Context

The Lord God chose a form of leadership that fitted the situation of Israel to a tee. The office of elder was tied to and very much integrated into the basic family structure of Israelite society. This had important implications and consequences.

First, it meant that their authority was limited and concentrated in the first place on the family and those people most closely related to them. The elders had wider tribe and clan responsibilities as well, which we will discuss later. But here it needs to be stressed that since the family was the matrix of this office, the authority of the elders was intrinsically limited.

Second, because of the close bond that the eldership had with the family, their authority was to be unselfish, caring, and loving, and not self-serving. The elder would above all have to exhibit the firm direction and loving-kindness of the Father of all Israel (see Deut. 1:31; 32:6; Isa. 63:16; 64:8).

Third, also with such authority, the authority of the elder in a family, clan, or tribe was to be representative of God's good authority (Deut. 1:17). At the same time, the nature of the family, clan, and tribe meant that the elder as one of their own, even their own flesh and blood, represented their interests and concerns in his duty as their leader. Thus an elder was to be a representative both of God and of the people to whom he was giving leadership.

These basic points have further repercussions with respect to the qualifications and role of the elders.

56

Qualifications

An elder needed to be respected; otherwise he could not function with credible authority and leadership. This respect could come with age, but reaching a certain number of years was of itself not enough. Critical was a consistent demonstration of wisdom and insight, which inspired confidence. At the most basic level, the fear of the Lord as the beginning of wisdom was needed. Submission to the Word and guidance by the Spirit of God was a must.

Let us pause at these requirements for a moment. Although the word used for the office of elder can also mean old man, there was no set number of years at which one could become an elder. Much more important than a certain age as a qualification for this office was the recognition of the necessary gifts in a particular person. An elder was someone who was normally honored and respected in the community (cf. Lam. 4:16; 5:12). One would become leader of an extended family or clan only if those gifts were obvious. Such gifts would of course need time to become obvious, and so a certain maturity was necessary for such recognition.

One of the most crucial gifts was wisdom. After all, an elder must be able to give counsel. That was to characterize him (Jer. 18:18; Ezek. 7:26). Jewish tradition says that an elder is "only he who has acquired wisdom."[7] The biblical concept of wisdom is rich in nuance and meaning. For our purpose it is enough to note that wisdom was a very practical concept which included prudence and good sense but also deep insight. The woman who saved Abel Beth Maacah by convincing her fellow citizens to give the head of the rebel Sheba to Joab was described as going to the people "in her wisdom" (2 Sam. 20:22 ESV). Solomon asked God for wisdom. This included all the discernment, insight, and understanding needed to govern the nation (1 Kings 3:7–9). God granted Solomon his wish (1 Kings 3:12).

Indeed, God alone is the source of true wisdom. "The fear of the LORD is the beginning of wisdom, and knowledge of the

---

7. *Babylonian Talmud*, Kiddushin 32b.

Holy One is understanding" (Prov. 9:10; 1:7). It is striking that the reading and teaching of the Word of God was a key responsibility of the elders (Deut. 31:12; 32:7). It is difficult to escape the impression that herewith the Lord was also equipping the elders for their task of leadership. It was only in the wisdom of God as revealed in the Word that the necessary insight for the execution of their office, as well as the norms for the people's obedience, would be found. When the elders did not understand God's will and made a bad decision, such as having the ark of God taken into battle, the results were disastrous (1 Sam. 4:3–11).

Coupled with the need for the Word was the necessity of the empowering Spirit. When the Lord gave Moses the assistance of seventy elders, he enabled them with his Spirit (Num. 11:16–17).

A well-qualified elder was honorable, and the presence and glory of the Lord himself would be associated with him. His walk of life and wise counsel would reflect God's will and holiness (see Ps. 119:100).

The Role of the Elders as Leaders

The leadership of the elders had two aspects: the political and the spiritual. The latter is most relevant for our purposes, but the former has something to teach us as well.

Politically, the elders represented the people and served them. We have seen some examples of how the elders exercised their political power. For our purposes, it is now important to note that by representing the people, the elders tended to counter efforts to centralize political power. In other words, the institution of the elders, arising from the family and tribe, tended to diffuse political authority and to be antihierarchical. Ideally, the king was not to be an absolute monarch, but needed to respect the place and authority of the elders (1 Sam. 15:30). When the power of the elders waned during David's rule, the elders were involved in the revolt (2 Sam. 17:4, 14). Solomon's political reforms concentrated power in the monarchy to the detriment of the place of the elders.

Although the monarchy weakened the tribal unit and hence the national position of the elder, the tribe nevertheless remained a very important political and social factor, undoubtedly due in no small part to the prestige and important role that the elders continued to play locally. The role of the elder was crucial in the trauma of the exile as well as in the difficult rebuilding that took place afterwards. Then more justice was done to their office again and their leadership was acknowledged.

As spiritual leaders, the elders represented the people before God as necessary. They did so when seventy elders ascended Mount Sinai and saw God (Ex. 24:9–11), when they laid their hands on the bull of the sin offering (Lev. 9:1–2), and when the ark was brought into Jerusalem both in the time of David (1 Chron. 15:25) and Solomon (1 Kings 8:1–5).

Most importantly, the elders represented God before the people. This status was evident from their responsibility (together with the priests) to read the law every seven years at the Feast of Tabernacles (Deut. 31:9–12). The fact that the elders had to teach and explain "the days of old" (Deut. 32:7) reinforced this duty.

Although the duty of teaching rested primarily with the priests (Lev. 10:11; Deut. 33:10; Mal. 2:6–9), those who were not priests also had obligations. The fact that Jehoshaphat sent five officials to accompany nine Levites and two priests in teaching the people the law of God in Judah (2 Chron. 17:7–9) indicates a teaching role for these officials whose position was not always clearly distinguishable from that of the elders.[8] In a more general way, it is striking that the elders are often associated with the priests (Deut. 17:8–13; 2 Chron. 19:8–11; Lam. 1:19; 4:16), a feature accentuating their place as representatives of God, along with the priests.

In so far as the elders assisted Moses, Joshua, and the people in the time of the judges (Num. 11:17; Judg. 2:7), and later the kings (2 Chron. 28:12–14; 1 Kings 20:7–8) with their counsel according to the Word of God, they also represented God's wishes. Elders

---

8. These officials (*sarim*) were probably chosen from the elders. Elders and *sarim* are sometimes mentioned together with no clear distinction, as, e.g., in Judg. 8:14, 16.

could be expected to know the Word and to speak according to it. The "counsel of the elders" gave leadership and direction, and this counsel is mentioned along with the vision of the prophets and the teaching of the priests (Ezek. 7:26; Jer. 18:18).

With the elders' leadership functions came a great responsibility. Failure to provide godly leadership resulted in great injury to the people. We see such devastating consequences in the corruptness of society in the days of the judges (cf. Judg. 2:7), and in the loss of the ark (1 Sam. 4:3–11). The unfaithfulness of the elders in not reading the law every seven years with the priests, and apparently being party to the law's being lost through neglect, had a devastating effect on God's people (2 Kings 22:8–23:27). The elders' worshiping idols in Jerusalem was an additional reason for the city's destruction (Ezek. 8, 14, 20).

As leaders, elders also had the general duty of helping to "carry the burden of the people" (Num. 11:17). Such a comprehensive task would have included spiritual oversight for which knowing and acting on God's Word were essential. Such leadership was seen in the elders' accompanying Joshua when he mourned the defeat at Ai and pleaded with the Lord. This action gave an example for the people to follow and undoubtedly helped to set the national mood of repentance (Josh. 7:6–8). Elders also joined David when he humbled himself before God for his sin of the census and pleaded for the people (1 Chron. 21:16). Significantly, the elders appear to have proclaimed fasts for God's people in times of supplication before God (cf. 1 Kings 21:8–9; Joel 1:14). Such leadership would have had a salutary effect on the nation.

Having considered the political and spiritual leadership of the elders, we can now turn to their position as judges in Israel.

Elders as Judges in the Old Testament

JUST AS THE TASK of leadership that was entrusted to the elders of Israel was at one time, before nationhood, the responsibility of the father in the family unit, so also was the task of judging. In the patriarchal family unit, the head of the household had far-reaching powers over those under his care. Judah even condemned Tamar, his daughter-in-law, to death when he found out that she was guilty of prostitution and was pregnant as a result (Gen. 38:24). The death sentence was, however, never carried out, and it is questionable whether we can deduce from the outburst of Judah ("Bring her out and have her burned to death!") that the head of the household indeed had juridical powers of life and death over his charge. In any case, as the patriarchal family became a nation in Egypt, one never reads of such an instance again (cf. Deut. 21:18–21), and it can be assumed that the more far-reaching aspects of the judicial power of the head of the household fell to the leading men of the clan, the elders.

The head of each family, however, still retained all the judicial authority necessary for the proper running of his household so that sin could be punished and obedience to God be blessed. Indeed, the maintenance of justice in Israel in a real sense started with the heads of the families, and this principle remained vital for the well-being of the nation. Being in charge of one's own home was so important that the law specifically forbade a creditor to enter the home of the debtor to secure his pledge. He would have to wait for it to be brought to him (Deut. 24:10–11). Similarly, Joash as head of his household could refuse to surrender for judicial execution Gideon as the prime suspect in the destruction of Baal's altar (Judg. 6:29–31). When we consider the duties of the elder as judge, we must therefore realize that his authority would not jeopardize the internal jurisdiction that the heads of the households in Israel retained over those in their care. In a certain sense, the work of judging never really left the family circle since Deuteronomy stresses that the Israelites are all brothers of each other, forming as it were one large family. Thus the charge given to the elders in Deuteronomy 1 reads in part: "Hear the disputes between your *brothers* and judge fairly" (v. 16).

In this chapter we will consider the elder's responsibility to judge. We will consider:

- A historical outline
- Representatives of God
- The involvement and responsibility of the people
- The administration of justice
- Summary and conclusions

Elders and Courts: A Historical Outline

Judges are first mentioned in the account of Jethro visiting Moses, his son-in-law, after the exodus from Egypt. When Jethro saw how busy Moses was from morning to evening with judging cases the people brought to him, he asked Moses why he did this. Moses answered: "Because the people come to me to seek God's will. Whenever they have a dispute, it is brought to me, and I decide between the parties and inform them of God's decrees and laws" (Ex. 18:15–16). Jethro advised Moses that this course of action had to change lest he be worn out. He suggested that Moses select men to "serve as judges for the people at all times, but have them bring every difficult case to you; the simple cases they can decide themselves" (Ex. 18:22). So Moses appointed "the heads" or "leading men of the tribes" (Deut. 1:15), who would most likely have been elders, to be judges. When Moses received difficult cases he could go to God with them (Ex. 18:19).

Those selected to be judges were set as officials over thousands, hundreds, fifties, and tens, ensuring ready access to justice for all (Ex. 18:21–26; Deut. 1:15–17).[1] The arrangement suggests a military organization, which would be quite appropriate for the wilderness period since Israel was organized as an army of the Lord (Num. 1–2; 31:14). How exactly this judicial system functioned is not stated. The choosing of these judges was so important that this event is mentioned right at the beginning of Deuteronomy (1:9–18). In this way, already during the wilderness wandering the essentials of local judges and a court for the difficult cases were in place for the maintenance of justice.

In anticipation of the entry into the Promised Land, Israel was told to "appoint judges and officials for each of your tribes in every town the LORD your God is giving you" (Deut. 16:18). If, however, a case was too difficult for the local judges, it was to be taken "to the place the LORD your God will choose. Go to the priests, who are Levites, and to the judge who is in office at that time. Inquire of them and they will give you the verdict" (Deut. 17:8–9; 19:17). This is usually understood as referring to a central court at the place where the tabernacle or temple was. Just as Moses had to deal with the difficult cases, so also provision was made for a special court in Canaan for such eventualities. The presence of the priests would ensure that specialists in the law would deal with such difficult cases. If God's revelation was not sufficiently clear and the case was of national significance, it is possible that the high-priestly means of receiving divine revelation, the Urim and Thummim, could have been used (Ex. 28:30; Num. 27:21).

---

1. The officials (*sarim*) mentioned in Ex. 18:25 and Deut. 1:15 whom Moses appointed to have authority and to judge are not always clearly distinguished from the elders from whom they were apparently chosen. Due to the nature of the case, with the elders being the prominent men of the community who would readily qualify for specialized positions of leadership, such a lack of consistent and clear distinction is understandable. See for more detail John L. McKenzie, "The Elders in the Old Testament," *Biblica* 40 (1959): 527–28.

In the tumultuous days before kingship, the judges seem to have settled difficult cases (e.g., Deborah, Judg. 4:4–5) as Samuel did later (1 Sam. 7:16). The elders themselves did retain great influence in executing justice both in the city gate (Ruth 4:1–12) and even among the tribes, as the (badly flawed) retribution for the crime at Gibeah in the war with Benjamin shows (Judg. 20–21). With the coming of the office of king in Israel, the king became involved. Israel asked for a king "to judge" them (1 Sam. 8:5, 20 NASB; 2 Sam. 8:15; Prov. 20:8). Difficult cases could go directly to the king (2 Sam. 15:2). David designated six thousand Levites as "officials and judges" in his realm (1 Chron. 23:4; 26:29). In all likelihood they assisted the local elders in the larger centers with their expert knowledge of the law. Solomon's involvement as judge in a difficult case involving two prostitutes and a dead baby is well known (1 Kings 3:16–28). This king also had a hall of judgment built (1 Kings 7:7) where he administered justice (Ps. 72).

We may assume that local courts continued to function throughout Israel's history (1 Chron. 23:4). The royal palace could, however, influence the local administration of justice. This influence could be negative and promote injustice, as the case of Naboth's conviction and death on the basis of false witnesses shows (1 Kings 21:1–13). The prophets complained bitterly that justice was corrupted, in both the northern kingdom (Amos 5:12; 6:12) and in Judah (Micah 3:11; Isa. 1:23; 3:14; 10:1–2).

Influence from the royal palace could also be positive. In Judah, the name of Jehoshaphat stands out as one working for judicial reform in the face of widespread injustice and corruption. This king commissioned officials, Levites, and priests to teach the people from the book of the law of the Lord (2 Chron. 17:7–10). Such education in the norms of true justice would have benefited the local administration of the law. Jehoshaphat also appointed judges in each of the fortified cities. In Jerusalem he appointed "some of the Levites, priests and heads of Israelite families to administer the law of the LORD and to settle disputes" (2 Chron. 19:8). The "heads of Israelite families" would have been elders.

At the Jerusalem court, the king appointed the chief priest as head over the matters concerning the Lord, and the leaders of the tribe of Judah as head over matters concerning the king (2 Chron. 19:11). This court probably functioned as the central place of justice that would deal with matters too difficult for the local magistrates (Deut. 17:8–9).

Since only fortified cities are mentioned in Jehoshaphat's reforms, one can assume that the local courts in the small communities would have been free to continue to function on their own. Jehoshaphat, however, apparently wanted to strengthen his control over the judiciary by appointing his own judges in the key cities. Since Jehoshaphat wanted to turn the people back to the Lord, his desire for control through godly judges is understandable (2 Chron. 19:4, 6–7). The Jerusalem appointments can be explained similarly (2 Chron. 19:9–10). We are not told whether the king appointed elders as judges in the fortified cities. We may assume he did if his appointment of elders in the Jerusalem court and the continuing importance of the elder in subsequent history are any indications. Indeed, elders are mentioned as an example of people working injustice (Isa. 3:14). They had a place of honor (Isa. 24:23) and were prominent in the covenant renewal under King Josiah (2 Kings 23:1; 2 Chron. 34:29). Furthermore, as could be expected, elders were present at the trial of Jeremiah in Jerusalem and spoke up in his defense (Jer. 26:17–19).

The exile into Babylon meant that the elders had gone from the city gates (Lam. 5:14) and were thus no longer able to administer justice in the Promised Land. Although they may have carried out judicial functions in exile, there is no record of this. After the exile, the elders again participated in judicial matters as is evident from their involvement in resolving the issue of intermarriage (Ezra 10:8, 14). The elders likely resumed their normal judicial duties in postexilic Israel, given the fact that the elders had these responsibilities in New Testament times. It was, for instance, the council of the elders or Sanhedrin that condemned Jesus to death (Luke 22:66–71).

Representatives of God

When Moses on the advice of Jethro chose able men out of all Israel and made them judges, Moses selected these judges from the elders, heads of the tribes (Ex. 18:21, 25; Deut. 1:15). This is significant for a number of reasons. As elders, these men would be men of ability, experienced and seasoned leaders who would stand in the midst of life. They were not theoretical legal experts, but they would have had down-to-earth wisdom and insight into real life. Judging for them would never be a hypothetical but a practical exercise, with implications and consequences they were familiar with. Furthermore, as elders these men would enjoy the respect and confidence of the people. Finally, as heads of hundreds and thousands, these men would in all likelihood be physically related to the people in their care and they would thus be judging their own kin. As elders in positions of leadership functioned within the tribal or family setting, so the elders as judges were to function as well.

In order for judges to function as intended, however, they had to be conscious that they were representatives or deputies of God. Through the human judge, God's will had to be done. Not what the humans involved in the case might desire, but what God had stated in his law was decisive. After all, God is the judge of all the earth.[2] For this reason Moses charged the judges to judge fairly, not to show partiality, and not to be afraid of any man, "for judgment belongs to God" (Deut. 1:17). Comparable words were spoken when Moses instructed the people to appoint judges in their towns (Deut. 16:18–20). Much later, Jehoshaphat recalled the injunction of Deuteronomy 1 by telling the judges, "Consider carefully what you do, because you are not judging for man but for the LORD, who is with you whenever you give a verdict" (2 Chron. 19:6).

The fact that the elder judge—that is, the elder who functioned as a judge—spoke for God also determined the qualifications for the judge. The judge had to therefore fear God (Ex.

2. Gen. 15:14; 18:25; 1 Sam. 2:10; Ps. 76:8.

18:21; 2 Chron. 19:7), knowing that he is the final authority in life. The people were to submit to him always, regardless of the consequences (Ex. 1:17).

Connected with the need to fear the Lord was the requirement that the judge must know the law and be wise in the Lord. For this reason Moses was to teach the law to the judges (Ex. 18:20). Indeed, as we have seen, the elders were to know the law and to be able to teach it themselves (Deut. 31:12; 32:7).

Wisdom and insight were required to apply the general rule of the law to the specific circumstances of a particular case. Such application implies a thorough understanding of the problem at hand. For that reason, the judges were to be wise and understanding (Deut. 1:13), possessing life wisdom, and having insight with sensitivity to each situation—in short, men who were capable (Ex. 18:21). The judges were also to be trustworthy men on whom others could rely and who hated dishonest gain (Ex. 18:21). Those who fell for bribes and were easily corruptible would be out for themselves and would bend the demands of the law to suit their persons. They were not sensitive to true justice and would not do what was right (Jer. 22:17; Hab. 2:9). Only those who were completely unselfish could do so (Prov. 15:27; 28:16). Of course, only those who were familiar with a person could judge whether one was "respected" and of proven character and ability (Deut. 1:13). Those judges who qualified would reflect something of the truth, justice, and wisdom of God.

Since the judge represented God, he was to "hear out" and listen patiently to all that was said by both parties, to "judge fairly" and "not show partiality in judging" (Deut. 1:16–17). It could be tempting to take a person's status into consideration in giving judgment, but then one judged as the wicked (Prov. 24:23) and no longer administered justice on behalf of God who does not have regard for persons' status (Deut. 10:17). A judge was not to take bribes, for "a bribe blinds the eyes of the wise and twists the words of the righteous. Follow justice and justice alone" (Deut. 16:19–20; 10:17). To that end, the judge was to do his work carefully (2 Chron. 19:6–7). Jehoshaphat reminded the judges in Jerusalem that as representatives of God they were to warn their brothers not to sin against the Lord lest his wrath come upon them (2 Chron. 19:10). This indicates a pastoral dimension to their task.

Finally it should be noted that the concept of the judges representing the Lord and administering justice on his behalf was so important that appearing before the judges could be described as appearing before God. For example, if a man had given his neighbor goods for safekeeping and they were stolen, a judicial determination would be necessary to ascertain whether the goods had indeed been stolen and the neighbor himself had not laid his hands on them. His going to court or to the judges is literally described as appearing "before God," which in the context means "before the judges" (Ex. 22:8).[3] Similarly, when the people came to Moses to have a dispute judged and settled, they came "to inquire of God" (Ex. 18:15 NASB).

The Involvement and Responsibility of the People

Although the judges spoke for God in executing justice, yet their position as judges involved the active participation of the people in at least three ways.

First, the people were involved in choosing and appointing the elders to serve as judges both in the wilderness and in Canaan. When Jethro advised Moses to get help to relieve his onerous task of judging the people in the wilderness, Jethro said to Moses: "Select capable men from all the people" (Ex. 18:21). Now the Hebrew term for "select" is one that stresses a very careful choice based on thorough investigation.[4] But how could Moses have done that? He could not possibly have known all the best candidates for this task. His task of leadership and judging took all his time, and the number of leaders of tens, hundreds, and thousands would have been in the thousands.

---

3. Also verse 9 and Ex. 21:6. See NIV text notes.
4. See Cornelis Houtman, *Exodus*, 3 vols., Historical Commentary on the Old Testament (Kampen/Leuven: Kok/Peeters, 1993, 1996, 2000), 2:418.

When Moses later recalled this event in more detail, he clarified the very brief description of what took place as related in Exodus. In Deuteronomy we read that he had said to "all Israel" (Deut. 1:1): "Choose some wise, understanding, and respected men from each of your tribes, and I will set them over you" (Deut. 1:13). The vital role which the people played is now obvious. They had to do the choosing and that made sense. They would have known who the best qualified candidates were. The selecting that Moses had to do was done by means of the people putting forward their choice of the most capable elders. Something else can be noted as well. What is translated as "choose" is literally "give for yourselves" or "give for your advantage." In other words, one could say that Moses announced the office of judge as a gift that Israel could give herself. Israel was not to be burdened by having judges. This office was to be a blessing.

With an eye to the upcoming situation in Canaan, Moses told the people: "Appoint judges and officials for each of your tribes in every town the LORD your God is giving you" (Deut. 16:18). As in Deuteronomy 1:13, here as well the first words of the original can be rendered "give for yourselves" or "give for your advantage." The word rendered "town" is literally "gates," which is the place where the judges did their work. In Canaan also, the people were to make the appointments. How this was to be done is not specified, but it is important to note that the people had responsibilities and were involved.

A second area in which the people participated in the work of the judges was to watch for and fight against corruption in the courts. It is remarkable that Moses spoke to the people as a whole when he said concerning the judges: "Do not deny justice to your poor people in their lawsuits. Have nothing to do with a false charge and do not put an innocent or honest person to death, for I will not acquit the guilty. Do not accept a bribe, for a bribe blinds those who see and twists the words of the righteous" (Ex. 23:6–8). Later, before entry into the Promised Land, Moses struck that theme once more, and again in the presence of all the people: "Do not pervert justice or show partiality. Do not accept a bribe, for a bribe blinds the eyes of the wise and twists the words of the righteous. Follow justice and justice alone, so that you may live and possess the land the LORD your God is giving you" (Deut. 16:19–20).

Clearly the people were not to tolerate any injustice. It is not specified how the people were to act in these particular instances if they noticed abuse. Since the judges were to act with righteous judgment, that is, fairly, and follow justice and justice alone (Deut. 16:18–19), the people could presumably refuse to honor those judgments that were not righteous. Later in this chapter we will consider what constituted a fair and righteous judgment.

In a more positive sense, justice was to be promoted and obedience to the law encouraged, through widespread knowledge of the law. Generally speaking, the more widely the law was known, the less opportunity there would be for corruption to go unchallenged. It is very significant that in Israel knowledge of the law, even law that was specifically relevant for the priests, was not to be the privilege of the priests or an intellectual elite as was the case elsewhere in the ancient Near East. Everyone was to be familiar with the law. After all, the nation was to be a priestly kingdom and the people had pledged to uphold and do the law (Ex. 19:5–8; 24:3–8). The responsibility to maintain the covenant law was placed upon the people as a whole, and the future blessing or curse depended on their obedience, collectively and individually. The fact that the law was addressed to them in both the singular and the plural underlined this point.[5] Many years later, King Jehoshaphat understood this and ensured that the entire nation was instructed in the law as part of his reformation (2 Chron. 17:7–9).

As we saw earlier, in the preceding chapter, the priests and elders had the duty to instruct the people in the law, but it was primarily the responsibility of the parents to pass this knowledge on to the children.[6] This knowledge was not to remain theoreti-

---

5. So, e.g., in Deut. 12:1–12 the people are mainly addressed in the second person plural, whereas in Deut. 12:13–25 they are mainly addressed in the second person singular.

6. Deut. 31:19; 4:10; 5:31. Both father and mother participated in this responsibility (Prov. 1:8; 3:1; 4:1–2).

cal. Parents were expected to teach the meaning of justice by example and punish sin in the family. If necessary, wrongdoing that could not be resolved within the immediate family circle had to be taken to the elders for adjudication (Deut. 21:18–21). With respect to injustice outside the inner circle of the family home in society at large, Israel was to be vigilant as well and seek righteousness and justice. There was no police force in Israel. The people themselves were to ensure that the community of God's people would remain holy to the Lord. Knowledge of the law was a key element in fulfilling this obligation.

The community was also involved in the maintenance of justice by their passive or active involvement in the actual trials. Because court sessions took place in the city gate, a very public place, the entire population could witness them. The court of the elder judges was convened as necessary. Anyone could become involved in bringing someone to trial, being a witness, and even in executing the guilty (Deut. 17:7; 21:21; 22:21). With respect to being witnesses, God warned his people: "Do not spread false reports. Do not help a wicked man by being a malicious witness. Do not follow the crowd in doing wrong. When you give testimony in a lawsuit, do not pervert justice by siding with the crowd, and do not show favoritism to a poor man in his lawsuit" (Ex. 23:1–3).

This participation of the community in the work of the judges was very important. The gross injustices that later plagued Israel did not occur overnight and would have been unimaginable if the people had remained faithful to the divine demands not to pervert justice, take bribes, show partiality, and tolerate false witnesses (Deut. 16:19–20; 19:16–21). It is telling, for example, that Jezebel apparently had little difficulty in getting the cooperation of elders and false witnesses for the perversion of justice in the judicial murder of Naboth (1 Kings 21:9–13). Such violations of the law were sins against God and as such had to be dealt with. If the community did not punish the offenders, God would punish the community and fulfill his covenant curses (Lev. 18:26–28; 26:14–45; Deut. 28). This threat alone would have

71

provided considerable motivation for the believing Israelites to safeguard the integrity of the judicial process. After all, "the eyes of the LORD are everywhere, keeping watch on the wicked and the good" (Prov. 15:3). Thus the Lord repeatedly reminded Israel that the people as a whole had the responsibility to purge the evil from among them by using the means available (e.g., Deut. 13:5; 19:19; 24:7).

A third way in which the people were involved in the maintenance of justice was by means of the elders serving as their representatives. To be sure, the elders were to speak for God and render his judgment (Deut. 1:17; 2 Chron. 19:6). On the other hand the elders were also in a sense acting for the people who had chosen them when they did their judicial task. An example of that is found in Deuteronomy 21. The elders of the town nearest to an unsolved murder represented their town when they washed their hands over a heifer whose neck had been broken and declared their innocence of the crime. In this way the guilt of shedding innocent blood was purged from the community (vv. 1–9). Elders in their judicial capacity also represented the people when admitting a fugitive to a city of refuge (Josh. 20:4–5). Elsewhere the elders are seen as representing the people as a whole. For example, when Moses had to tell the whole community about the Passover, he told their representatives, the elders (Ex. 12:3, 21). Also when the elders asked for a king, God said to Samuel, "Listen to all that *the people* are saying to you" (1 Sam. 8:4–5, 7).

In a somewhat different way, the fact that the elder judges represented the people is seen in their being accountable to the people. This accountability is assumed in the people's involvement in choosing the elders who are to judge (Deut. 1:13; 16:18) and their responsibility to fight any corruption of justice (Deut. 16:19–20). This accountability becomes explicit in the somewhat analogous situation of Samuel defending his judging of Israel before the people. He asked them to testify against him if he had ever been unfaithful as judge (1 Sam. 12:3–4). If someone of the stature of Samuel felt constrained to give a public accounting (even if the circumstances of his action were special), one can be sure that the onus was no less on the elder judges to be fully answerable to the people that they have acted according to God's will.

The Administration of Justice

To properly appreciate the elders' role in the administration of justice, we need to see how they functioned in the maintenance of justice in Israel. The most basic institution for the upholding of the law of God was the family unit. There parents passed down to the next generation knowledge of the law (Deut. 6:6–9) and disciplined in its most basic sense (Ex. 20:12). Furthermore, the closest relatives had the responsibility to redeem family property and their next of kin in case of financial difficulty (Lev. 25:25–34, 47–49). In the event of murder, the responsibility for punishing the killer lay with the "avenger of blood" who was probably the nearest male kinsman of the deceased (Deut. 19:4–13; 2 Sam. 3:26–30), and the whole clan could get involved (2 Sam. 14:5–11). The primary importance of the family was also evident in the obligation of a brother to marry his brother's widow if she had no son. The first son born from that union would carry on the name of the deceased (Deut. 25:5–10).

Matters that could not be resolved within the family circle were normally brought to the elders in the gate (Deut. 21:18–21). Besides the local elders, there was eventually the court in Jerusalem, which would deal with matters too difficult for the local judges. Priests and Levites were part of that court (Deut. 17:8–9; 2 Chron. 19:8–11). The priests and Levites also dealt with legal matters that pertained to ritual law such as legislation delineating what was clean and unclean (Lev. 11–15) or with assuring the veracity of a case in the presence of the Lord (Num. 5:11–31). The king played a role in maintaining justice too (1 Chron. 23:4; Ps. 72; Prov. 31:8–9). Yet the family and clan circle with its elders would have been the most pervasive court forum.

73

The City Gate

The local elders usually administered justice in the city gate.[7] Since most cities were not large, they generally had but one gate with an adjoining square. This was in effect the center of town where the life of the community found a focus. People would need to pass through the gate in order to leave the city for whatever reason, and so this was a place where one was likely to meet people (e.g., Ruth 4:1), hear the latest news (Ps. 69:12), and conduct business (e.g., 2 Kings 7:1). The gate was the social and economic center for the population. It was also here that the local elders met to dispense justice. The judiciary was a decentralized one in which the local elders and people were involved in the legal process.

One gets the impression that the judgment of the elders could be received at a rather short notice. Boaz, for example, went to the city gate and gathered together ten elders so that the legal proceedings for the redemption of Naomi's land could begin immediately (Ruth 4:1–2).[8] Of course there were doubtless situations where a trial date would be set for some time in the future so that witnesses could be summoned and a prosecution prepared, as apparently happened with the sham trial of Naboth (1 Kings 21:8–14). But on the whole, justice seems to have been readily available at the gate within a relatively short time.

The elders as judges in the city gates could settle a wide variety of issues such as a stubborn and rebellious son (Deut. 21:18–20), disputed virginity (Deut. 22:13–21), or noncompliance with levirate marriage law (Deut. 25:7–9). They could also hear the case of an apparent unintentional killing and decide either to admit the one involved into a city of refuge (Josh. 20:4) or give him up to the avenger of blood (Deut. 19:12). Indeed, virtually any dispute could be brought before the judges (Deut. 25:1).

7. Deut. 16:18 literally reads that the judges are in the city gates (see NASB note). Also Deut. 21:19; 25:7; Amos 5:15 (NASB).

8. Also, e.g., Jeremiah's trial for prophesying against Jerusalem could be arranged quickly (Jer. 26).

A Typical Trial. We can imagine how a typical trial was conducted. Since the normal place for a trial was the city gate, it did not take place in secret, but in public for all who wished to observe. When the trial commenced, the elders would be seated (Ruth 4:2; Job 29:7), but probably stood to pronounce judgment (Isa. 3:13). The plaintiff, who would be well prepared (Job 13:18; 23:4), would state his case (Deut. 21:20; Jer. 26:11). Naturally he would try to be as convincing as possible, although he could be questioned and challenged.[9] After the plaintiff had spoken and the defendant had the opportunity to defend himself (Deut. 1:16), witnesses from both parties were called. They would rise to give their testimony (Deut. 19:16; Ps. 35:11). Two witnesses who agreed were needed to sustain a charge (Deut. 19:15), especially for a capital offense (Num. 35:30; Deut. 17:6). The judges were to inquire diligently, and a false witness was to have done to him as he wanted done to his brother (Deut. 19:16–21). In the case of parents with a recalcitrant son, their joint complaint was sufficient evidence (Deut. 21:18–21). In other cases the simple exhibition of the evidence, such as an injured animal (Ex. 22:13) or proof of virginity (Deut. 22:15), was sufficient.

It is conceivable that the defendant received a final opportunity to clear himself.[10] The elders would then confer (Deut. 25:1), paying particular attention to those with a reputation for wise and judicious decisions (Job 29:7–25; Jer. 26:16–19). When the judges reached agreement, they would give the verdict. If guilty, the punishment was specified and carried out immediately (Num. 15:35–36; Deut. 22:18). If the specified punishment was beating, the guilty one was to lie down before the judge and be beaten in proportion to the nature of his offense. As an act of mercy there were in any case to be no more than forty lashes, as one had to remember that the guilty one was still a brother (Deut. 25:2–3). Sometimes the punishment included a fine (Deut. 22:18–19). If the

9. "The first to present his case seems right, till another comes forward and questions him" (Prov. 18:17).
10. It is possible to derive such a practice from the way Job had the last word against his accusers (Job 29–31).

punishment was death, the witnesses were to cast the first stones and the rest of the people would join in (Deut. 17:5; 22:21; Lev. 24:14). Punishment by death was in essence the Old Testament form of excommunication from the people of God. In this way Israel purged the evil from their midst (Deut. 17:7; 19:19; 21:21; 22:21, 24; 24:7), and the guilty one was definitively excluded from the covenant nation, Israel.

Special Circumstances. Sometimes the situation was such that no evidence could be produced. In such cases an oath would be administered to conclude the matter before God who sees and knows all things (Prov. 15:3). For example, an oath could be accepted as evidence (1 Kings 8:31–32) when property was in dispute, such as when an animal given for safekeeping was harmed. Then the one to whom the animal was given could swear before the Lord to his innocence if he did not lay his hands on it. Such an oath, which was probably made before God's representatives, the judges, would conclude the matter (Ex. 22:10–11; Heb. 6:16). Another example is the self-imprecating oath that a wife suspected of adultery swore before the officiating priest at the sanctuary. This too would settle the issue, for God would respond to the self-maledictory oath if the one who took it swore falsely (Num. 5:11–31). Elsewhere, the Lord reminded his people that he could punish sin without the intervention of the courts by cutting off the guilty (Lev. 17:10).[11] Such an awareness of the Lord's prerogative would have helped maintain respect for God's law in spite of the inherent limitations of a human court in enforcing it.

If a case was too complex for the local court with its limited resources to deal with, the elders were to take the matter to the central court with its priests and judge who would give them the verdict. The local elders would be bound by their judgment (Deut. 17:8–13). This manner of dealing was analogous to the elders' going to Moses with the most difficult cases (Deut. 1:17).

11. "To cut off" (Hebrew *karat*) someone probably included the death of the person involved, judging from the parallelism of "cut off" with the death penalty in Ex. 31:14 and Lev. 20:2–3.

Jehoshaphat's establishing a court in Jerusalem that consisted of Levites, priests, and heads of families would have made such a resource available to the local elders (2 Chron. 19:8–10).

Through the administration of justice as sketched above, justice and righteousness were to be upheld in the land among the people of God. We need to consider more closely the meaning of judging, justice, and righteousness. This will help us to understand more fully the rationale for the way justice was administered in Israel and will also help us understand the basic principles which elders today need to keep in mind.

Judging and Righteousness

Two preliminary comments are necessary to place the concepts of judging and righteousness in a proper context. In the first place, the nation of Israel was a people whose identity was largely shaped by God's delivering them from the bondage of Egypt in the exodus. This foundational event meant that Israel's very existence was a direct result of God's intervening in justice and righteousness. God condemned the injustices of Egypt over against his people by judging Egypt with the plagues (Ex. 9:27), and he restored his people to a renewed relationship of peace and righteousness with himself as their covenant Lord (Ex. 19:3–6). It was this relationship of peace and rightness with God and with each other that Israel's elders had to safeguard and promote. They did not need to establish righteousness among the people. God had already done that. They needed to maintain it and so do justice.

In the second place, since God had given the law to Israel, any transgression of this law was not simply an offense against society or one's fellow man, but against God himself (Ps. 51:4). This serious nature of breaking the law added weight and urgency to the judging task of the elders. God was always intimately involved.

When the elders met in the gate to judge, they did so because of unresolved conflicts in the community of God's people. Such discord could have originated in the privacy of the home, as with

77

the dishonoring son, or have immediate public impact, as in a sudden death. It is important for understanding the role of the elder judges to realize that the Hebrew verb "to judge" (*shapat*) used in these contexts designates restoring the disturbed order of a community to a state of peace.[12] The goal was to remove the conflicts because they dishonored God and threatened the well-being of God's people and therefore needed to be taken away. The judging in the gate, therefore, did not in the first instance have the character of imposing a sentence, but of helping to resolve difficulties. It is remarkable in this context that when the Lord gave guidelines for being a witness at a trial and being a judge (Ex. 23:1–3, 6–8), he admonished those antagonistic to each other (and surely protagonists at a trial are in view here) to help each other by, for instance, returning a lost donkey or helping the person's donkey that had fallen under a load get up (Ex. 23:4–5). Such brotherly attitudes would have gone a long way to work reconciliation. Such a disposition would also have been consistent with the ultimate aim of the court sessions in the gate, namely to restore the good relationships between members of the community so that there could be peace. There were of course occasions where the peace could be restored only by severing the relationship from the family, tribe, or nation completely. This would be the case, for instance, with the death penalty.

If the basic meaning of "to judge" is to restore the disturbed order and relationships of a community to peace, this verb should be understood accordingly. When David prayed: "Judge me, O LORD" (Ps. 26:1 KJV), he did not necessarily mean that God should punish him because he was guilty. Rather the intent could have been: "Give me justice" (NEB) or "Vindicate me" (NIV). When God exhorted Judah through Isaiah: "Judge the fatherless" (Isa. 1:17 KJV), this did not mean "condemn him," but "defend the fatherless and assist them to get their rights" (cf. NIV). Of course when

12. See, e.g., G. Liedke, "*spt* to judge," in Ernst Jenni and Claus Westermann, *Theological Lexicon of the Old Testament*, trans. Mark E. Biddle, 3 vols. (Peabody, MA: Hendrickson, 1997), 3:1393.

the severing of a relationship was in view so that peace could be restored, the meaning of "judge" could be "to punish" as when the Lord was going to "judge," that is, "punish" the house of Eli for their sins by killing the two sons of Eli, Hophni and Phinehas (1 Sam. 3:13; 4:11).

In sum, the task of judging by the local elders was to serve the internal peace and well-being of God's people as well as their peace with God according to the norms of the covenant.

This brings us to the next point—the meaning of "justice" (*mishpat*) and "righteousness" (*tsedaqah*) in the context of judging. The elders were to judge righteously, that is, in righteousness (Deut. 1:16; 16:18). What does that mean? It means to act in accordance with the law and revealed will of God. However, the concept of righteousness is not merely acting in accord with the letter of the law, as one might be inclined to interpret it. In other words, righteousness is not a legalistic concept. Rather, righteousness and justice always include the idea of promoting fellowship and communion—be it between humans or between God and his people. After all, to take heed to the entire law of God in judging is also to take into account the basic underlying demand of loving God and one's neighbor (Deut. 6:5; Lev. 19:18; James 2:8). On this demand all the law and prophets depend (Matt. 22:37–40).

There is, therefore, no tension between justice and love in God's law. Seeking righteousness and justice in God's way includes reckoning with the injunction to love God and the neighbor. To put it differently, it would have been impossible, according to the norms of God's revelation, that a judge be called righteous in Israel who strictly and without wavering simply applied the law in a cold, mechanical, and unmerciful way. Justice and love belong together. As a matter of fact, "righteousness" often has the meaning of "benevolence going beyond strict justice" and "mercy" and is then rendered that way in the ancient Greek translation of the Old Testament.[13] We see the close relationship of righteousness

13. Edwin Hatch and Henry A. Redpath, *A Concordance to the Septuagint and Other Greek Versions of the Old Testament (including the Apocryphal Books)*, 2 vols. with Supplement

on the one hand and mercy and love on the other in passages such as Isaiah 30:18:

> Yet the LORD longs to be gracious to you;
>   he rises to show you compassion.
> For the LORD is a God of justice (*mishpat*),
>   Blessed are all who wait for him.

Or, think of the following passages where the parallelism shows the close association of righteousness with mercy and love.

> The LORD loves righteousness and justice;
>   the earth is full of his unfailing love. (Ps. 33:5)

> . . . break off your sins by practicing righteousness,
> and your iniquities by showing mercy. . . . (Dan. 4:27 ESV)

The justice and righteousness of the law reflect the love and grace of its author, God, who had entered into a covenant relationship with Israel. Israel therefore had the obligation to follow the commands and decrees of the Lord (Deut. 7:7–11). The law was not to be a burden, but was a gift of life from God. God's righteousness was to be a source of joy to the godly and a terror to the wicked. Therefore "righteousness" can also be used as a synonym for "salvation" (Isa. 45:8; 46:13).

Obviously all this was of great importance for the elder judging in the city gate. He was to be unswerving in justice, but his justice was at the same time to be full of mercy and pity for the poor and downcast, just as the Lord God was toward his people. There was no true discipline of the law without compassion. The application of the law was to be governed by the grace of God who had first chosen his people and given them his good law.

The Lord himself gave indications in his law concerning how his punishments were tempered by his mercy because the

---

(Oxford: Clarendon, 1897, 1906), 1:450–52; see also Norman H. Snaith, *Distinctive Ideas of the Old Testament* (London: Epworth, 1944), 71.

ultimate aim was to restore relationships. Punishment was necessary and obviously just. One who committed an offense must be held to account and receive his just desert (Deut. 19:19). But the punishment given needed to conform to certain criteria. The normal physical punishment was beating and the number of lashes depended on the nature of the offense. But as already noted, there were to be no more than forty lashes. The offender was still a brother, and he should not be degraded before others (Deut. 25:2–3). In this way his restoration in the community was facilitated.

Also, restitution was never made to the state but to the injured party. In this way, the restoration of the relationship between the offender and the injured would have been expedited. Furthermore, the amount of the restitution depended on the degree of penitence shown by the thief. If someone, for example, stole an animal and had already sold it, he would need to pay back at four or five times the value. Compensation was less in other cases (Ex. 22:1, 7–15; Lev. 6:1–7). God prevented vengeful and excessive punishment by the principle of "an eye for an eye" (Ex. 21:23–25; Lev. 24:17–22; Deut. 19:18–21). This was a limiting law, and compensation was probably not given in kind but in monetary terms unless the offended party insisted otherwise.[14] Again, matching the punishment to the offense so that the penalty was transparently fair would have facilitated the restoration of relationships within the covenant community.

God's love in demanding punishment is also evident from two further considerations. First, by punishing the wrongdoer, evil was purged from the midst of the people. As the law says: "if the witness proves to be a liar, giving false testimony against his brother, then do to him as he intended to do to his brother. You must purge the evil from among you" (Deut. 19:18–19). "The evil" cannot refer to the offense being punished, for what is done cannot be undone. Rather it refers to the guilt because of the offense that rests on the land and the people. If the guilt was not

14. Ex. 21:30; W. H. Gispen, *Exodus*, Bible Student's Commentary, trans. Ed van der Maas (Grand Rapids: Zondervan, 1982), 213.

81

removed, God's wrath would come upon them (Deut. 21:1–9; Lev. 18:24–28). Second, punishment would deter others. "The rest of the people will hear of this and be afraid, and never again will such an evil thing be done among you" (Deut. 19:20; similarly 13:11; 17:13; 21:21).

By following these and similar principles, the elders were to reflect God's justice and compassion. The Lord specifically stated that the judgment to be rendered was to be the Lord's. "Do not show partiality in judging; hear both small and great alike. Do not be afraid of any man, for judgment belongs to God" (Deut. 1:17). God was the one who was giving his judgment through his elders. As Zephaniah 3:5 informs us, "Morning by morning" (when the elders normally sat in judgment in the city gate) the Lord "dispenses his justice." God is the one who had to have the say when justice was meted out. His law and will had to be reflected.

With such a high calling, it is small wonder that God's standards for being an elder in Israel were very high. Elders were to be "wise, understanding and respected men" (Deut. 1:13) who therefore had life-wisdom and insight. They needed to be able to see the issues involved in all the situations that came up so that the Lord's will would be done. These elders were not to be rigid legalists who mechanically followed the letter of the law. Not only the letter, but also the spirit of the law had to be followed so that the love for God and the neighbor found expression in true justice and righteousness, both in wrath and mercy. To that end, the elders had to be able to discern the nature of the sin and to understand the intent of the law.

Distinctions in Sin and Consequences

When two people commit the same sin, it is not necessarily the same. We need to distinguish carefully whether the sin was done "in weakness" (NIV "unintentionally"; RSV "unwittingly") or "defiantly" (lit. "with a high hand"). These are the two categories of sin that Scripture recognizes (Num. 15:28–31).

The first category is best described as sin done in weakness rather than done unintentionally since intention is not necessarily the issue and confining the meaning to this sense can be too restrictive. Rather the Hebrew phrase in question speaks of human weakness as wandering away from the demands of God because of one's fallen condition as a sinful creature. Sins done in weakness include all transgressions that are not done defiantly. In the Old Testament such sins could be atoned for by sacrifices (Lev. 4–5; Num. 15:22–29), and they did not exclude one from the covenant community. In other words, sins of weakness were done by the righteous who wanted to walk in the ways of the Lord but were not always successful. This desire to serve God set the righteous apart from the wicked, to mention the two categories described in Psalm 1.

By contrast, the wicked sinned defiantly as a way of life. Their sins could not be atoned for because they were characterized by open and unrepentant rebellion against God. Such iniquity threatened the covenant peace. It was therefore to be punished by being cut off from God's people since their guilt remained on them (Num. 15:30–36). Either the people or God acting directly could bring about this cutting off with the death penalty (Ex. 31:14; Lev. 17:10; 20:2–6).

The elders therefore had the duty to discern carefully the nature of the sin before them and act accordingly. Any sin could be or could become a sin done defiantly and thus demand the extreme remedy of taking the life of the perpetrator. All the Words of the Covenant that could be enforced by human agents (the first nine commandments) carried the maximum penalty of death if the disobedience constituted open and persistent rebellion against God.[15] With such a sin, one in effect placed oneself outside the covenant communion of life with God and his people. The death penalty was in essence excommunication by death from the people

15. For the death penalty on each of the first nine commandments see on I—Ex. 22:20; Lev. 20:2–3; Deut. 6:14–15; II—Deut. 4:15–31; III—Lev. 24:15–17; 1 Kings 21:10; IV—Ex. 31:13–14; 35:2; Num. 15:32–36; V—Ex. 21:15–17; Lev. 20:9; Deut. 21:18–21; VI—Ex. 21:12; Lev. 24:17, 21; VII—Lev. 20:10; Deut. 22:22; VIII—Ex. 21:16; Deut. 24:7 (stealing property did not entail the death penalty in Israel); IX—Deut. 19:16, 19, 21.

of God. It graphically showed what had already taken place spiritually with unrepentant sinful defiance. As such, being cut off for such sins was surely not only done in justice but also in love, for in this way God showed his people very clearly the radical consequences of their actions. The horror of physical death would have underlined the absolute seriousness of unrepentant disregard for God's will, and it would have given cause for reflection by the weaker members of the people who were in danger of becoming defiant of God and his will. Israel had to remember that they had a covenant with God, the Holy One! He yearned for the obedience of his people. God guarded the judicial process with stringent safeguards. For instance, one "who shows contempt for the judge or for the priest who stands ministering there to the LORD your God must be put to death. You must purge the evil from Israel" (Deut. 17:12). God also reminded his people that if the elders and the people did not punish such a person, he himself would cut him off (Lev. 20:4–5).

With respect to the sins done in weakness, the elders needed much wisdom and insight in dealing with them so that God's will, justice, and love would be reflected in the decisions they made. A sin done in weakness could become a sin of defiance against God and a rejection of the covenant. The elder had to determine when the maximum penalty of death was warranted. This was an awesome responsibility. After all, with one exception, any sin for which there was godly sorrow could be forgiven and the death penalty averted.[16] The one exception was the sin of willful murder. The one guilty of this sin could have true remorse and be right with God, but the death of the murderer was still required (Gen. 9:6; Ex. 21:12; Num. 35:31).[17] Even if such a person fled to a city of refuge, he would have to be delivered up to the elders of his

16. Note how on the Day of Atonement "all the wickedness and rebellion of the Israelites—all their sins" were placed on the head of the scapegoat and removed from Israel (Lev. 16:21).

17. The fact that God did not punish David with death for the murder of Uriah (2 Sam. 12:13) is not fully explained. However, the consequences of this murder were with David to the end of his life. The sword never departed from his house (2 Sam. 12:10–12), and the child Bathsheba bore to him died (2 Sam. 12:14–18).

city for justice (Deut. 19:11–12). This is an example of how the consequences of sin done in a moment of weakness still needed to be shouldered.

But apart from this exception, the elders had to carefully weigh and evaluate the nature of each sin brought before them for judgment so that the appropriate punishment could be determined. God's justice had to be reflected. For example, did the case of adultery before the elders warrant the death penalty or not? The fact that the wronged husband, whose wife committed adultery, had the option of not showing mercy and not accepting any compensation (Prov. 6:34–35) suggests that the death penalty was not always applied. Furthermore, the principle of lighter restitution, if remorse and repentance were shown, would also argue against an automatic death penalty for the sins that could require it. Indeed, after David's adultery with Bathsheba, God accepted his remorse as true repentance and told David through Nathan the prophet: "The LORD has taken away your sin. You are not going to die" (2 Sam. 12:13). The principle is that the death penalty was the maximum punishment for sin done with defiance and with no remorse.[18]

The elders had to execute the justice and righteousness of God to the best of their ability. In determining how to apply the law to a particular situation, the elders would have needed to be sensitive to two related aspects of God's law: the flexibility that was inherent in the law and the impossibility for humans to actually do the full intent of the law as God desired. We will consider these in turn.

Divine Flexibility

The Mosaic law is often caricatured as being rigid with absolutely no exceptions in its application. The reality is, however, somewhat different. There was a certain flexibility with respect to the law which showed that God is not legalistic and

18. See, e.g., Gordon J. Wenham, *The Book of Leviticus*, New International Commentary on the Old Testament (Grand Rapids: Eerdmans, 1979), 285–86.

rigid and therefore neither should his representatives the elders be when they judge.

For example, in Exodus 12 the Lord set the date for the Passover. This important law had to be maintained. However, in the second year after leaving Egypt, it appeared that some were unclean and could not keep the Passover on that day. In order to accommodate these people then and for similar cases in the future, the Lord set a date for a second Passover a month later (Num. 9). God did not strictly insist that the original date be maintained at all costs but kept in mind the needs of his people. It is remarkable that godly King Hezekiah made use of this second date because the people simply could not get ready on time (2 Chron. 30:2–3). In spite of the fact that Hezekiah's reason for delaying the Passover was different from that which originally prompted the Lord to fix a second date, there is no hint of divine disapproval of Hezekiah's action. To the contrary, although many of the participants at this Passover were actually unclean, the Lord heard Hezekiah's prayer and healed the people (2 Chron. 30:20). The Lord approved of this Passover for he saw it in its total context. It was an act of reformation after much religious decline in Israel, and it was celebrated in the spirit of the law, in love to him. Here was clearly a situation in which ritual law took second place to faith and a desire to obey God (cf. Isa. 1:11–13; Jer. 7:21–23; Amos 5:21–26).

Two other examples of the Lord's patience and mercy illustrate divine flexibility. The Lord had clearly stated that his people were not to eat an animal that was found dead (Deut. 14:21). However, knowing the weaknesses of his people, the Lord reckoned with the fact that his people might nevertheless do so. God in his mercy therefore made provision for disobedience to this ordinance. "Anyone who eats some of the carcass must wash his clothes, and he will be unclean till evening" (Lev. 11:40). Another example: God hated divorce (Mal. 2:16), but he did not demand the removal of divorced individuals from his holy nation. God did insist that a priest was not to marry a divorcée (Lev. 21:7, 14), but for the rest exhibited considerable tolerance for this evil due to the hardness of men's hearts (Matt. 19:8; cf. Deut. 24:1–4). He made provision that a priest's daughter who was divorced could partake of the sacred food of her father (Lev. 22:13). Divorced women could also make a binding vow (Num. 30:9).

The Lord's patience for the weakness of his people is additionally evident in the often positive evaluation of imperfect and sinful leaders such as Samson (Heb. 11:32–34; cf. Judg. 14–16), David (1 Kings 15:5), Jehoshaphat (1 Kings 22:43), and Hezekiah (2 Kings 18:3). These men were far from perfect, but the Lord was pleased to use them for his work, and he reckoned them with the righteous who furthered his cause.

Israel's leaders were also not rigid over against the law of God. For example, during the desert wandering, Nadab and Abihu, sons of Aaron, had died because they had brought unauthorized fire before the Lord. Soon thereafter, Moses confronted Aaron and his remaining sons, Eleazar and Ithamar, with the fact that they had not followed the law by neglecting to eat the sin offering in the sanctuary (Lev. 10:17–18) as was required (Lev. 6:26). However, Aaron explained that they had been diligent in following the ritual requirements, but the death of Nadab and Abihu had intervened. Would eating a sin offering after this judgment have been pleasing to the Lord? In view of this special circumstance, Moses acquiesced (Lev. 10:19–20). The Lord did not punish this conscious neglect of his law. He took the circumstances into consideration.

Other examples concern the breaking of an oath. Even though King Saul had put the army under an oath not to eat on pain of death, the people saved Jonathan who had eaten in spite of this oath (1 Sam. 14:24–45). Abigail kept David from carrying out his oath to kill Nabal and all his men (1 Sam. 25:22–35). These instances are noteworthy because an oath was an extremely serious matter (2 Sam. 21:1–7), but in the above cases it was broken without the Lord intervening in wrath because of the extenuating circumstances and the need to do justice in love to God and the neighbor.

One final example should suffice to illustrate that the law is not an end to itself. Its underlying demand is to love God and the neighbor. When David asked Ahimelech the priest for bread, "the priest gave him the consecrated bread, since there was no bread there except the bread of the Presence that had been removed from before the LORD and replaced by hot bread on the day it was taken away" (1 Sam. 21:6). This action of Ahimelech was in direct violation of the law of God, which specified that this bread was only for Aaron and his sons (Lev. 24:9). Yet Ahimelech dealt rightly because not rigid legalism, but love and mercy is the fulfillment of the law (Rom. 13:10). The Lord Jesus even appealed to this incident when the Pharisees accused his disciples of desecrating the Sabbath on the basis of their rigid interpretation of the law. Christ quoted Hosea 6:6 when he said: "If you had known what these words mean, 'I desire mercy, not sacrifice,' you would not have condemned the innocent" (Matt. 12:7).

Now if God's law was not meant to be the rigid unchangeable law of the Medes and Persians (cf. Esth. 1:19; 8:8), the question arises: where does a flexible approach to the law stop and disobedience begin? A very important question. This is why the elders in the gate needed to be consecrated and full of wisdom, understanding, and insight. They needed to understand that God's justice and love are not opposites but come together in the self-revelation of his will in the law. With that realization, they could distinguish between God's will and an insensitive legalistic approach which completely lacked compassion and mercy. The traditions of men, as well intentioned as they may have been, could then be differentiated from the wishes of holy God.

Human Inability

We now need to consider the second aspect that elders were to be sensitive to, namely, the inability of humans to actually do the full intent of the law as God desired. The outward obedience of at least the first nine of the Ten Commandments would have been achievable.[19] However, the fact that one does not, for instance,

19. The tenth commandment concerns one's thoughts and can hardly be policed by others.

worship another god, does not commit adultery, or does not steal does not mean that one has done the full intent or underlying *positive* demand of the law. After all, Israel was enjoined to love the Lord their God with all their heart, mind, and soul and their neighbor as themselves (Deut. 6:5; Lev. 19:18). Such love is more than a simple outward obedience. And so "the law represents the floor below which human behavior must not sink. The ethical ceiling is as high as heaven itself. . . . 'Be holy, for I the LORD your God am holy' (Lev. 19:2)."[20] There is, in other words, quite a disparity between how God wanted his people to behave and what he was prepared to tolerate before punishing.

God wanted his people to be as he is, that is, to reflect his image and so mirror his holiness, righteousness, justice, love, and mercy. On the other hand, God knew what was in man and how he stumbled in his weakness as a fallen creature. It was not because Israel had such desirable qualities that God chose them, but because he loved them (Deut. 7:7–8). God was merciful and very patient with his people. The minimum requirement was obedience to the letter of the law, a requirement that was attainable, certainly in the ritual law. But the real goal that needed to be kept in view was to respond to God's mercy with undivided love and affection for God (Deut. 10:12). Such obedience was not attainable.

All this was relevant for the Old Testament elder in his judicial capacity. He was there as God's representative and his judgment had to be the Lord's (Deut. 1:17). He had to keep in mind that the Lord is "the compassionate and gracious God, slow to anger, abounding in love and faithfulness, maintaining love to thousands, and forgiving wickedness, rebellion and sin. Yet he does not leave the guilty unpunished" (Ex. 34:6–7). So on the one hand, the judges were to be merciful and give the benefit of the doubt where possible, but on the other hand they were to be unremitting in punishing the guilty. No pity was to be shown to those who persisted in transgressing (Deut. 13:8–9). In practice,

20. G. J. Wenham, "The Gap between Law and Ethics in the Bible," *Journal of Jewish Studies* 48 (1997): 25–26.

this meant that there was to be considerable tolerance towards those who kept the letter of the law, but fell considerably short of God's expectations for their life, namely, to be holy as God is holy. There was to be a realism in dealing with human sinfulness, as God was also realistic. In summary, the Old Testament "encourages the righteous to aim at ethical perfection like God's, but to be long-suffering and tolerant towards those who fail to achieve it. Only the gravest offenders must face the law's sanctions."[21] The distinction between the righteous and the wicked within God's people (Ps. 1) needed always to be kept in mind.

The Unique Character of God's Law

We have seen that the administration of justice by the elders had several special features. Their first duty as God's representatives was not to impose punishments, but to restore peace to the community by judging rightly. In their judicial work they had to be sensitive to the nature of the transgression and God's own patience in dealing with sinners. Furthermore, they needed a measure of tolerance because of the impossibility of perfect obedience to the full intent of the law. It now remains to pull some of these different elements together by noting briefly some aspects of the unique character of Israel's law. Noting something of the uniqueness of Israel's law will also enable us to see more easily some of the essentials of the administration of justice by the elders in New Testament times.

In the ancient Near East, law codes were highly developed juridical documents that listed as completely as possible all the conceivable crimes and the corresponding punishments. Little was left to the imagination. This meant that knowing all the ins and outs of the law became the privilege of an elite group within society. Biblical law on the other hand does not have a comprehensive system of case laws, although many similarities in ancient Near Eastern and biblical law can be pointed out. Unlike ancient Near Eastern law codes, which were often elaborate and complicated,

21. Ibid., 28.

God's law and will were characterized by simplicity and clarity. Key principles were given and then applied by way of example. No exhaustive treatment was attempted. As a result, all Israel could know God's law and be held responsible for it.[22]

The simplicity of biblical law is evident from the fact that God summarized his entire will for his people in the Ten Commandments. These are the only laws that God himself spoke directly to his people (Ex. 20:1–17; Deut. 5:4–28). They are the core legislation that form the basis of everything else. Indeed, it has been argued that Deuteronomy is structured on the Ten Commandments and is in effect a commentary on them, providing examples of how to deal with violations of God's will in different areas of life. No attempt at a comprehensive treatment is made.

Considering the importance of the Ten Words of the Covenant, let us take a closer look at the character of this law. In the first place, as already mentioned, Israel received from God's own mouth this revelation of his will. In ten clear foundational statements God revealed his commands for all of life. The centrality of such a simple formulation should have cautioned all those concerned with upholding God's will among his people against making new laws and decrees and requirements for the holy nation in an apparent attempt to cover all sorts of situations. God could say it all in ten words, so to speak, and give the necessary application in other laws. What God gave was sufficient for the elders to work with. The profuse elaboration of rule on rule in later Judaism went against the original simplicity of God's law.

In the second place, it is noteworthy that the people were addressed as a redeemed people. Vital for understanding the import of the commandments that follow is the prologue. "And God spoke all these words: 'I am the LORD your God, who brought you out of Egypt, out of the land of slavery'" (Ex. 20:1–2). Here is proclamation of the gospel. God said as it were to his people, "You, my people, have been set free by the living God, your covenant

---

22. As a priestly kingdom (Ex. 19:6), Israel was expected to know God's will. Such knowledge is, e.g., presupposed by the admonitions of the prophets to the people, as in Amos 2:4.

LORD." *Therefore*, "have no other gods before me; do not make for yourself an image by which to worship me; remember the Sabbath day by keeping it holy," and so on. The fact that the law is preceded by the glad tidings of their release from slavery shows that the law was intended to be the means by which Israel would show their gratitude to God. In other words, the law was to be the rule of thankfulness. It was for this reason that God used the exodus as a strong motivation for Israel to love and obey him (e.g., Deut. 11:1–9) and to carefully follow his decrees (e.g., Deut. 15:15; 16:12; 24:18). By following this rule of thankfulness, Israel was assured of experiencing life with their God. And so the proclamation of the Ten Words by God himself to his people, and later the entire body of law through his servant Moses, was in a real sense gospel proclamation. God gave his law to his people with great love and care. It was not just a "cold" collection of rules, but the law was interspersed with admonitions and exhortations that Israel walk in God's ways and reap the benefits (Deut. 6:3; 7:11; 8:1; 11:22–25; 15:1–11). The law was not given dispassionately but with much affection, seeking to convince Israel of its merits. It was law preached. Those who accepted this law rejoiced in it for it showed the way of life. It was a lamp before their feet (Ps. 119:93, 105). It gave wisdom and understanding (Deut. 4:6; Ps. 19:7).

When we reflect on the law as a tremendous gift of God who has saved his people, then it becomes clear why God was not interested in giving Israel a law code listing every possible scenario for sin, complete with sanctions for every misdemeanor. Ultimately the purpose of the law was not to frighten Israel into obedience, but to provide Israel with God's will so that this redeemed nation could show her gratitude to her covenant Lord in a manner pleasing to him. This was covenant law and the relationship with their God was crucial.

God himself therefore gave the central commandments directly to his people and through Moses gave many examples of how that law could be further applied, as well as his detailed ritual law. Thus the Lord meticulously hedged in their life as a training school of obedience to teach Israel the basic principles of their relationship to God. The Lord considered that sufficient. On the basis of what he had given, the people could know enough by which to regulate their life in a manner pleasing to God. The elders could also know their duty in assisting the nation to articulate their gratitude to God. They did this as judges in the gates of the towns, but, perhaps just as significantly, they were expected to show Israel by example, exhortation, and other such means of self-discipline what God expected of them.

However, as is the nature of a life of gratitude and love to God, such obedience cannot be forced or legislated in detail. After all, God wanted Israel's heart and mind, their love, and not mere outward and ritual obedience. No human judge could see what lived inside another human heart. The inability of the elders to monitor the prohibition of coveting (the tenth commandment) illustrates in a dramatic way that it was impossible for them to fully oversee adherence to the law and its most essential requirements of love and dedication to God. Thus, if the people did not truly respond to their salvation in a manner pleasing to God, the Lord himself would ultimately intervene in judgment. On the other hand, the life of gratitude in obedience to God was possible since God had made his will known. Such a life would be blessed (Deut. 30:11–20).

Summary and Conclusions

As the role of the elders as leaders was rooted in the family circle, so too was their role as judges. The head of each family had the judicial authority necessary to lead his household into the ways of the Lord. It was evident, however, that judicial authority outside the immediate family was needed in situations that were beyond the competence of the head of each household to resolve. Initially all such problems came to Moses. Because Moses was not able to hear all the cases brought to him, he appointed judges to handle these (Ex. 18:14–24; Deut. 1:9–16). But even then, the idea of a family setting, although in a larger sense, was not really far behind. The judges were appointed according to the tribal units, and the charge given to the judges included: "Hear the disputes between your brothers and judge fairly" (Deut. 1:16). Moses would continue to hear the most difficult cases. This Mosaic regulation laid the basis for the later system of local judges and central court in the place where the tabernacle or temple was (Deut. 16:18; 17:8–9; 19:17).

The system of local courts seems to have functioned throughout Israel's history. Once the monarchy was established, the king became involved in promoting justice by hearing the most difficult cases (2 Sam. 15:2; 1 Kings 3:16–28), by providing resources for the local judges (1 Chron. 23:4), by promoting education in the law (2 Chron. 17:7–10), and by establishing a central court in Jerusalem (2 Chron. 19:11).

Since God is the judge of all the earth, the elder had to reflect God's judgment in his decisions (Deut. 1:17; 16:18–20; 2 Chron. 19:6). This responsibility also helped determine the qualifications necessary for a judge. He needed to fear God, have wisdom and insight into God's laws, and be of irreproachable integrity (Ex. 18:21; Deut. 1:13).

Noteworthy is the active involvement of the people in the judicial process in a number of ways. They were involved in choosing judges (Ex. 18:21; Deut. 1:1, 13; 16:18). The people had the obligation to be vigilant against corruption and fight it (Ex. 23:6–8; Deut. 16:19–20). This duty was partly realized by promoting knowledge of the law, starting in their homes (Deut. 6:6–9), as well as by participating in the actual trials, either as witnesses or in executing the guilty. Finally, the people were also involved in so far that the elders as judges represented them in their judicial acts (Deut. 21:1–9; Josh. 20:4, 6).

The local elders administered justice in the city gate, which was very much a public forum. Each side in the dispute would have their say, but two witnesses were needed to sustain a charge. A false witness received the punishment he had tried to impose on his innocent brother (Deut. 19:15–21). Verdicts were normally executed without delay, including capital punishment. If a matter was unclear, a self-imprecating oath could be accepted as evidence (Ex. 22:11).

In giving a just verdict, the judges were to restore peace between God and his people and within the community. The elders were to judge righteously, which is not the same as acting legalistically. Seeking God's justice included reckoning with the command of love. To achieve this high standard meant that the elders needed to be wise, understanding, and able to reflect God's justice and love in the given situation. They needed to be able to distinguish between an offense done in human weakness and one done defiantly against God with unrepentant rebellion (Num. 15:28–31). They needed to be flexible where God according to his revelation of himself would also be flexible and to be merciful where the Lord would be merciful. After all, there was the indisputable fact of human weakness in not being able to keep the law of God perfectly. In this context, it is therefore understandable that Old Testament law can be characterized as preached law that instructs and exhorts God's people in how to show their thankfulness for his salvation. The elders as judges needed to take all this into account.

Part 3

Continuity and Transformation

The Christian Congregation
Inherits the Office

IN MOST BIBLES a blank page separates the Old and New Testaments. As a result, it is very easy for us to make a sharp distinction between these two parts of Scripture. One consequence of stressing the discontinuity between the testaments is that it may be more difficult to appreciate fully that the very first Christians were mostly Jewish believers. For them the Hebrew Scriptures and the synagogue had long provided the basic orientation points for their worship of God. The office of elder was a familiar one in their religious landscape. Indeed, the Christian congregation inherited this office from their Jewish past. In the first and third chapters of this book we have seen some of this continuity when we considered basic elements of the office. The purpose of this chapter is to consider briefly how the New Testament church received the office of elder and the ramifications this has for our present day. We will deal with:

- The congregation of Christ
- The Jerusalem elders
- Elders in each church
- Distinctions among elders
- Summary and conclusions

The Congregation of Christ

Before we enter into specifics, it is important to underline that the offices of the church are the offices of the body of Christ. The risen Christ who has all authority in heaven and on earth (Matt. 28:18–20; Eph. 1:22) is the ultimate reason and source of authority for the ecclesiastical offices. They are his gift to the church (1 Cor. 12:27; Eph. 4:8–11). His authority was mediated through the apostles who had been his disciples and through whom he established his church (Matt. 16:18; 18:18; John 20:23).[1] The apostles in turn saw to it that the normal offices would function in the local churches (Acts 14:23). The offices have therefore been given to the church through the mediation of the apostles who had been chosen and instructed by Christ.

Regardless of the precise manner in which the Old Testament office of elder came into the Christian church, it is important to note that the risen Christ has given his authority to this office. He has done so by means of the apostles who ensured the establishment of the eldership in each congregation (Acts 14:23; Titus 1:5). The apostle Paul could therefore remind the Ephesian elders that the Holy Spirit, the Spirit of Christ, had made them overseers of the flock (Acts 20:28). This appointment by Christ's Spirit legitimized the office of elder and not its pedigree as such.

When we see that the Christian office of elder was mediated through the apostolic ministry and so given to the church, several things become more clear. We can better appreciate that the very first Christian congregation, the one in Jerusalem, apparently not only had elders but also apostles in their council (Acts 15:4).[2] Indeed, it even appears that the apostles in establishing normal church government in the various new churches consid-

---

1. In that sense the apostles form part of the foundation of the church of which Christ is the cornerstone (Eph. 2:20; Rev. 21:14). See further on Christ's establishing his church through the apostles, William Hendriksen, *Exposition of the Gospel according to Matthew*, New Testament Commentary (Grand Rapids: Baker, 1973), 647–49, 702.

2. Note how the delegation from Antioch was welcomed in Jerusalem "by the church and the apostles and elders," implying that the apostles and elders both served that church as office bearers.

ered themselves to be elders. Thus Peter, although identifying himself as an apostle (1 Peter 1:1), nevertheless spoke of himself as a fellow elder as well when addressing the elders (1 Peter 5:1). The apostle John also called himself an elder when writing his first and second letters (2 John 1; 3 John 1). And so through the apostolic office legitimacy was granted to the Christian office of elder, not only in the apostles' seeing to the establishment of the office in the various congregations, but also by their associating the office of elder with that of apostle.

The Christ who gives the offices also enables with his Spirit those who serve his congregation (1 Cor. 12:4–11). In that first critical phase, the risen Christ confirmed the proclamation of his Word with special signs and wonders (Mark 16:17–18).[3] Each new stage in the progress of the gospel was accompanied with miracles. The early preaching in Jerusalem was confirmed by miraculous signs of healing (Acts 3:1–11), as was the first proclamation to Samaria, to Gentiles, and beyond the eastern Mediterranean (Acts 8:5–7; 10:45–46; 19:6; 28:3–6).

The Jerusalem Elders

The Jerusalem church was, as mentioned, the very first Christian congregation, and it is apparent that the elders of this church stood in a class somewhat by themselves. These elders were closely associated with the apostles (Acts 15:2, 4) and with them judged concerning the problems that were brought to them by the church at Antioch (Acts 15; 16:4). They thus had considerable authority. Also indicative of the unique character of this church was the fact that the Jerusalem congregation was led by James, the brother of the Lord Jesus (Matt. 13:55; Acts 21:18; Gal. 1:19). James appears to have been among the believers before the day of Pentecost (Acts 1:14; 1 Cor. 15:7). Peter acknowledged him to be the leader of the Jerusalem church since it was to James that the account of his escape from prison had to be relayed (Acts 12:17). James

3. Matt. 10:1–8; Mark 6:12–13; Luke 10:8–9; Acts 1:8.

was one of the Jerusalem elders (Acts 15:6, 13), and he played a prominent part in resolving the difficulties that Antioch brought to Jerusalem for adjudication. His proposal was adopted as the solution (Acts 15:13–29). The apostle Paul called him a pillar of the church and mentioned him prior to Peter and John (Gal. 2:9), even though James was not an apostle (Gal. 1:19).[4]

The prominence of the Jerusalem elders in those early years was likely due to the fact that, like James, they too were part of the circle of believers before Pentecost and had probably been witnesses of Christ's public ministry. As a direct link to the Savior whom they had both seen and heard, they rose to prominence as elders in this congregation. We are not told how they became elders. They simply appear on the pages of Acts as a given (Acts 11:30; 15:2, 6, 23; 21:18). Although Luke mentions the choosing of the twelfth apostle in Acts 1, as well as the appointment of the seven (Acts 6), and the appointment of the elders in Asia Minor (Acts 14:23), nothing is said about how the elders in Jerusalem came to their office. This circumstance is somewhat remarkable to the modern reader, but not too much should be made of it since it would have been perfectly normal for a Jewish congregation to model itself after the synagogue and to have elders from the outset. There would have been no pressing need to record something deemed routine.

Since the Jerusalem elders were probably eyewitnesses of Christ's life and death, it is possible that they, along with the apostles, were given special power to do miracles for the sake of the gospel (Luke 10:8–9; Mark 16:17–20). Such special gifts could be in view in James 5 where those who are sick are told to call the elders to pray over them, anointing them with oil in the name of the Lord. "And the prayer offered in faith will make the sick person well; the Lord will raise him up" (James 5:15; cf. Mark 6:13). The letter of James, therefore, reflects the early period of the Christian church. Indeed, this letter appears

4. The NIV renders the intent of Gal. 1:19 accurately: "I saw none of the other apostles— only James, the Lord's brother." To be an apostle meant having been with the Lord Jesus from his baptism to his ascension (Acts 1:22), which James had not (John 7:5).

to be the earliest writing in the New Testament with a probable date of approximately A.D. 45.[5]

When James refers to the "elders of the church" (James 5:14), these elders would have included in the first place the church at Jerusalem, but the reference could also include elders who were scattered in new "daughter" congregations throughout Palestine and beyond (James 1:1; Acts 9:31).[6] These congregations came about due to the harassment and oppression that followed the killing of Stephen (Acts 8:1; 11:19).

In the year A.D. 70, in response to the Jewish revolt, the Roman legions under Titus took Jerusalem and razed it to the ground. Jerusalem's destruction also meant the end of the Jerusalem congregation.

Elders in Each Church

We may assume that the new Jewish congregations throughout Judea, Galilee, and Samaria would have had elders as a matter of course. However, *all* churches, including those originating with non-Jewish believers, needed this office. It was part of Christ's plan for the functioning of his church. And so during their first missionary journey, Paul and Barnabas saw to it that elders were found in every church, that is, in Derbe, Lystra, Iconium, and Pisidian Antioch (Acts 14:23). Later Paul instructed Titus to do the same for every town on the island of Crete (Titus 1:5). Elders were found wherever congregations were established. Elders are also specifically mentioned as existing in the churches of Ephesus (Acts 20:17), Philippi (Phil. 1:1),[7] and those in the provinces of northwestern Asia Minor, namely, Pontus, Galatia, Cappadocia,

5. See the discussion in Douglas J. Moo, *The Letter of James*, Pillar New Testament Commentary (Grand Rapids: Eerdmans, 2000), 9–27.

6. Interesting to note is that Acts 9:31 speaks of "the church" (singular) throughout Judea, Galilee, and Samaria, but the apostle Paul uses the plural in Gal. 1:22 and 1 Thess. 2:14. It is probably best to envision the singular as referring to the Jerusalem church in dispersion. But this church in dispersion formed new congregations.

7. The term *episkopos* is used, which is synonymous with elder. See chapter 3, near the end of the section "What's in a Name?"

Asia, and Bithynia (1 Peter 1:1; 5:1). The local council of elders was called the presbytery (*presbyterion;* 1 Tim. 4:14), a term which was also used of the highest Jewish council in Jerusalem (Luke 22:66; Acts 22:5).

As we saw briefly in chapter 1, the ordination of these elders could have included participation of the congregation. We do not read of any special miraculous gifts such as healing being specifically associated with these elders.

Distinctions among Elders

Different Offices

While the continuity with the Jewish elder is evident, the New Testament also uses the term "elder" in a more general, inclusive way. The term "elder" was probably appropriate for this more embracive usage because the core leadership function of an elder was also to be part of the responsibility of other ecclesiastical offices. For example, as we have seen earlier in this chapter, the apostles Peter and John on occasion called themselves elders as well (1 Peter 5:1; 2 John 1; 3 John 1). These examples illustrate that the term "elder" could include someone who was an apostle. However, although one person could hold both offices, it is undisputed that a clear distinction remained between the offices of apostle and elder.

But what if the term "elder" was used both of the ruling and of the teaching elder, as in 1 Timothy 5:17? There we read: "The elders who direct the affairs of the church well are worthy of double honor, especially those whose work is preaching and teaching." Here we have elders who direct the affairs of the church and elders who labor in preaching and teaching. Is this another example of the term "elder" being used to include more than one office? The analogy of the earlier example of apostles being called elders, as well as the distinction made between these elders in this passage, would suggest that they were indeed two different offices.

Not everyone, however, is convinced that such is the case. Some would argue that only the office of the so-called lay elder is warranted by Scripture and that this office includes the task of teaching. In other words, ordained ministers ("clergy") have no place in a biblically constituted church government.[8] Such a conclusion, however, does not sufficiently recognize that the term "elder" can encompass more than one task or office in the church. Furthermore, it must be noted that although an apostle could be an elder, that did not make every elder an apostle. To apply this logic to the matter of teaching elder and ruling elder means that one cannot simply assume that just because a teaching elder is an elder, every ruling elder is also a teaching elder or pastor. In light of the above, the affirmation that pastor and ruling elder are exactly the same office needs to be demonstrated.

Such a demonstration is difficult to achieve when one considers the manner in which the New Testament distinguishes the gift of ruling from other gifts that are important for the church. In Romans 12:7–8 and 1 Corinthians 12:28, the gifts are listed in such a way that diverse gifts are linked to different people employing these gifts. Put differently, nowhere is the gift of teaching or exhorting practically or officially linked to that of ruling or governing. They are mentioned separately. The apostle's point is that those who have the gift of teaching should be teachers and those who have the gift of ruling should be rulers. One's office in the church is determined by the gifts one has received. The gift of ruling belongs to the ruling elder; the gift of teaching belongs to the calling of one who focuses on teaching.[9]

The above considerations can lead to the conclusion that the ruling elder and the teaching elder are two distinct offices, to which different people who have the necessary specific gifts and calling can be set apart.

8. See, e.g., Alexander Strauch, *Biblical Eldership: An Urgent Call to Restore Biblical Church Leadership*, rev. ed. (Littleton, CO: Lewis and Roth, 1995), 101–17.

9. See for the above Robert S. Rayburn, "Ministers, Elders, and Deacons" in Mark R. Brown, ed., *Order in the Offices: Essays Defining the Roles of Church Officers* (Duncansville, PA: Classic Presbyterian Government Resources, 1993), 228–29; also Edmund P. Clowney, "A Brief for Church Governors" in Brown, ed., *Order in the Offices*, 56–62.

The Underlying Unity in the Elder Offices

On the other hand, although I would argue for two distinct offices, it should be noted that because both the ruling elder and teaching elder are called *elders*, their offices do have an underlying unity and purpose that must be acknowledged. For example, both the ruling and teaching elders are shepherds of the flock. Peter charged the elders: "Be shepherds of God's flock that is under your care" (1 Peter 5:2), and Paul enjoined the Ephesian elders: "Keep watch over yourselves and all the flock of which the Holy Spirit has made you overseers. Be shepherds of the church of God, which he bought with his own blood" (Acts 20:28). Exactly the same admonitions can and should be directed to the teaching elders, and Presbyterian and Reformed churches have recognized this in their forms for ordination.

One could say that although there is a difference in the manner in which the ruling and teaching elders function in their respective offices, yet there is no difference in the underlying character and nature of their task. Both the ruling and teaching elder are shepherds of the sheep who are there to serve the flock. Both derive their authority from the Chief Shepherd of the flock (1 Peter 5:1–4). The minister does not speak more authoritatively than the elder when ministering the Word of God, for the authority of the office bearer derives from the Word and not from the person or the office as such. Furthermore, the minister does not have a monopoly on the Word or the shepherding task. There is, in other words, an equality between the offices of the ruling and teaching elder—an important principle in a biblical view of the offices. Scripture does not teach a hierarchy in church government.

The underlying unity in the offices of teaching and ruling elders is also evident from the fact that ruling elders are expected to be able to teach as well, even though it is not the main emphasis of their office. An overseer, or elder,[10] must be "able to teach"

10. On treating *episkopos* ("overseer") as a synonym of *presbyteros* ("elder"), see chapter 3, near the end of the section "What's in a Name?"

(1 Tim. 3:2). "He [the *episkopos*] must hold firm to the trustworthy word as taught, so that he may be able to give instruction in sound doctrine and also to rebuke those who contradict it" (Titus 1:9 ESV). Indeed, the elders have to be on guard against the wolves or false teachers that threaten the flock (Acts 20:28–31; Matt. 7:15). A thorough knowledge of the Word of God is essential to the office of elder. Think of the crucial role of the elders who with the apostles had to make far-reaching decisions at the landmark Jerusalem meeting (Acts 15:1–6). This knowledge of the Word and the ability to teach others are not just theoretical exercises or "head knowledge"; such competence also has to be accompanied by a mature sensibility so that the elder is not quarrelsome (1 Tim. 3:3) or does not enter into senseless controversies (1 Tim. 1:3–4; 6:3–5). And so, while there are elders "whose work is preaching and teaching" (1 Tim. 5:17), this does not absolve the ruling elders of needing to be able to teach as the occasion arises in the execution of their office.[11]

In view of the underlying commonality of ruling and teaching elder, one might be inclined to ask at this point: is there then, after all, only one office of elder which includes both the teaching and the ruling functions? That is the view of some in an ongoing debate in Presbyterian circles. However, the classic Presbyterian and Reformed understanding is that there are three church offices: the teaching elder or minister of the Word, the ruling elder, and the deacon.[12] This classic position can continue to be upheld, because in addition to earlier arguments from the New Testament for maintaining the traditional distinction of two elder offices—ruling and teaching—one must not forget the Old Testament context from which the New Testament office of

11. See chapter 8, under "Elders Administering the Word."
12. See, e.g., the distinction between minister of the Word and ruling elder in the Cal-vinian "Ecclesiastical Ordinances" (1541) in Philip E. Hughes, ed. and trans., *The Register of the Company of Pastors in Geneva in the Time of Calvin* (Grand Rapids: Eerdmans, 1966), 35–42; "The Form of Presbyterial Church Government . . . Approved by Act of the General Assembly, February 10, 1645" in *The Confession of Faith; The Larger Catechism; The Shorter Catechism; The Directory for Publick Worship; The Form of Presbyterial Church Government with References to the Proofs from Scripture* (Edinburgh: William Blackwood and Sons, 1966), 172–74.

elder arose. A consideration of the Old Testament background will provide the overall basis for the position that the ruling elder and the teaching elder are two separate offices.

The Old Testament Testimony

In the Hebrew Scriptures one finds an overlap of specific responsibilities between different offices such as we have seen in the New Testament. Furthermore, one also finds in the Old Testament a clear distinction between the ruling and teaching offices, a distinction one would expect to continue in the Christian church. We will briefly consider both of these aspects.

First, let us see the overlap of specific responsibilities between different offices, including the office of elder. This phenomenon is found in ancient Israel, and what occurred in the early Christian church is somewhat analogous. In the Old Testament church the teaching task was shared to a certain extent between two distinct offices, namely, between the priests and the elders. Although the main teaching responsibility lay with the Levitical priests (Lev. 10:11; Deut. 33:10; Mal. 2:7), the elders were not excluded from the task of giving instruction to God's people. Both the priests and the elders participated in the reading of the law every seven years at the Feast of Tabernacles (Deut. 31:9–12). Moses also commanded Israel to go to their fathers and the elders who would explain to them the days of old (Deut. 32:7). Later in the kingdom of Judah, Jehoshaphat commissioned officials, who were probably elders, along with Levites and priests to teach the people from the book of the law of the Lord (2 Chron. 17:7–10).[13] It is clear that these various teaching offices were not the same but remained separate.

Now in these examples, the priests, who represented the teaching office, were not called elders. However, in postexilic Judaism, the Sanhedrin, which was composed of priests, scribes, and elders, could be referred to as "elders" and "elders of the

13. For the identification of the officials as elders, see chapter 4, under "The Role of the Elders as Leaders."

court." In other words, the term "elder" could be used as a generic term for all the members of the Sanhedrin. We see an example of this type of usage in Luke 22:66 where "the council of the elders of the people" included "both the chief priests and teachers of the law." We find a similar usage in Acts 5:21 where "the Sanhedrin" is referred to as "the full assembly of the elders of Israel." Furthermore, when Pharisees and teachers of the law came to Jesus and asked why his disciples broke "the tradition of the elders" by not washing their hands before eating (Matt. 15:2), they meant the tradition of the scribes.[14] As is evident from the above, although the term "elder" could be used for priests and scribes, yet the offices obviously remained distinct. Here too it appears that the word "elder" may have been chosen as a general descriptive term in view of the leadership and ruling qualities characteristic of the eldership.

In the second place, there was a clear distinction between the ruling and teaching offices in the old dispensation, even though there was some overlap. However, in the normal discharge of their respective duties, the elders did the ruling and the judging, but the tribe of Levi, especially the priests, did the teaching.

When Moses blessed the tribes of Israel before his death, he said of Levi that he teaches God's precepts and law to Israel (Deut. 33:10). Elsewhere we read that "the lips of a priest ought to preserve knowledge, and from his mouth men should seek instruction—because he is the messenger of the LORD Almighty" (Mal. 2:7). This instruction would include matters such as ritual law (e.g., Lev. 10:11; Deut. 24:8), worship (2 Kings 17:28), and judicial decisions (e.g., Deut. 17:8–11; Ezek. 44:24). With the Levitical cities spread throughout the tribal possessions (Josh. 21), the priests and Levites would have been able to discharge their teaching responsibilities effectively. After the exile, we read of Ezra, the priest, instructing the people in the law on the first day of the seventh month (cf. Lev. 23:24), with the Levites assisting (Neh. 8:1–12). "They read from the Book of the Law of God,

14. See R. T. France, *The Gospel of Matthew*, New International Commentary on the New Testament (Grand Rapids/Cambridge: Eerdmans, 2007), 575–79.

making it clear and giving the meaning so that the people could understand what was being read" (Neh. 8:8). Here Ezra and the Levites were administering the Word to God's people. This biblical account may very well be "a careful description of the liturgical ritual of public worship in the post-exilic times."[15]

A clear difference was maintained between the ruling and teaching offices. When the offices are mentioned together, they are characterized as being distinctive. Thus Ezekiel speaks of "the teaching of the law by the priest . . . the counsel of the elders" (Ezek. 7:26). Both give direction to the people, but in distinctively different ways.

Besides the priestly office, the office of prophet also had teaching responsibilities. As necessary, the Lord raised up prophets to guide and instruct his people in his ways. A band of prophets (1 Sam. 10:5, 10; 19:20) ministered in the dark days near the end of the time of the judges when the tabernacle in Shiloh was destroyed. These prophets, under the leadership of Samuel (1 Sam. 19:20), may very well have been used to rejuvenate the Levitical teaching in Israel. Similarly the Lord raised up "the sons of the prophets" in the spiritually decadent days when Elijah and Elisha ministered in the northern kingdom (2 Kings 2). The faithful priests had gone in droves to the southern kingdom after Jeroboam had introduced the golden calf worship at Dan and Bethel (1 Kings 12:28–33; 2 Chron. 11:13–16). It appears that these prophets were expected to take over the educational responsibilities of the priests in the northern kingdom.

But, also with respect to the prophetic office, a clear distinction was maintained between the offices of prophet and elder. When the Lord lightened Moses' task, he gave a portion of the Spirit that was on Moses to seventy elders so that they would help carry this burden (Num. 11:16–17). "When the Spirit rested on them, they prophesied, but they did not do so again" (Num. 11:25). In other words, this prophetic gift legitimized their being called to assist Moses, but this gift did not continue and these

15. F. Charles Fensham, *The Books of Ezra and Nehemiah*, New International Commentary on the Old Testament (Grand Rapids: Eerdmans, 1982), 215.

elders did not become prophets. They received the Spirit, but remained in their distinctive office as elders.

It is furthermore of interest to note that whereas the priests are grouped with the prophets because of their similar responsibilities in the teaching ministry (Jer. 6:13–14; 8:10–11; Mic. 3:11), the elders never have this type of association. We see the proximity of priests and prophets in different ways. Not only prophets, but also Levites and Levitical priests prophesied. Before battle, a priest could assure an obedient people of a coming victory and so act as spokesman for God (Deut. 20:1–4; 2 Chron. 20:14–19). Zechariah, the son of Jehoiada the priest, prophesied under the influence of the Spirit, condemning the people's sins (2 Chron. 24:20–21). Also, the people sought out both prophet and priest for the will of the Lord (Zech. 7:3). The close association of prophets and priests is evident as well in that they both apparently ministered in the area of the temple (Jer. 23:11; 26:7–8). Additionally, the sons of the Levites—Heman, Asaph, and Jeduthun, leaders of the temple song—prophesied (1 Chron. 25:1–5).[16] It is no coincidence that elders are not mentioned in the above contexts. Their office did not focus on teaching and prophesying.

Two Offices: Teaching and Ruling

If the offices of elder and teacher were clearly distinguished in the old dispensation, then one could expect this to be continued in the new dispensation, with a special teaching office in the Christian congregation. There would have been no need for something this obvious to be specified, and the New Testament should be read with this in mind. It may be asking too much to attempt to discover from only the New Testament whether there were separate teaching and ruling offices. The New Testament was not written to make that point clear. One must read the Scriptures in their unity and take into account the Old Testament

16. The prophesying here can best be understood as hymnic praise. One can also think of the prophecy of Miriam the prophetess (Ex. 15:20–21) and Deborah the prophetess (Judg. 4:4; 5:1–31) who sang God's great deeds in poem and song.

111

background of the offices, as we may assume the first Jewish Christian believers did.

It then becomes highly significant that the apostle Paul spoke of the task of "being a minister of Christ Jesus to the Gentiles with the priestly duty of proclaiming the gospel of God, so that the Gentiles might become an offering acceptable to God, sanctified by the Holy Spirit" (Rom. 15:16). Here we have the preaching of the gospel understood as a priestly task.[17] Given the Old Testament background of the priestly duty of passing on the Word of God, such a description of the office of administering the gospel is not unexpected. The apostle hereby indicates that the task of the Levitical priests has been taken over by the New Testament office of the proclamation of the Good News. Besides the special temporary offices such as the apostleship, the normal office for the proclamation is the teaching elder or minister of the Word. In this connection, it should be noted that the prophecy of Isaiah, which predicted the inclusion of the Gentiles into the church, included the promise that the Lord would select some of them to be priests and Levites (Isa. 66:19–21). That can only mean ministers of the gospel. These ministers are the priests and Levites of today.[18]

The preaching of the gospel as a priestly task can also be seen elsewhere. A priest administered reconciliation between God and his people. He did this by way of offering sacrifices, teaching the law, and giving the priestly blessing (Deut 10:8; 33:10). This ministry of reconciliation God gave to his apostles and their coworkers. The apostle Paul writes: "[God] gave us the ministry of reconciliation: that God was reconciling the world to himself in Christ, not counting men's sins against them. And he has committed to us the message of reconciliation. We are therefore Christ's ambassadors, as though God were making his appeal

17. See further John Murray, *The Epistle to the Romans*, New International Commentary on the New Testament, 2 vols. in 1 (Grand Rapids: Eerdmans, 1968), 2:210–11.

18. John Calvin, *Commentary on the Book of the Prophet Isaiah*, 4 vols. in 2, trans. William Pringle (Grand Rapids: Baker, 1984), 4:436–37; E. J. Young, *The Book of Isaiah*, New International Commentary on the Old Testament, 3 vols. (Grand Rapids: Eerdmans, 1965–72), 3:535. Isa. 66:21 is mentioned as a proof text (to show that the work of ministers of the gospel is analogous to that of the priests and Levites under the law) in "The Form of Presbyterial Church Government," 173.

through us. We implore you on Christ's behalf: Be reconciled to God" (2 Cor. 5:18–20).

Within our present context, three inferences can be drawn from this passage. First, as in the Old Testament, there is also in the New Testament church "the ministry of reconciliation." This ministry is the ministry of restoring peace between God and human beings, a peace that had been lost because of sin (Rom. 5:1, 10; Col. 1:19–20). Second, this ministry of reconciliation, entrusted to the priests in the Old Testament, has been committed in the New Testament church to Christ's ambassadors, such as Paul and his coworkers. Third, as the priests in ancient Israel not only acted, but also spoke for God when teaching and explaining his Word to the people, so the ambassadors in the New Testament church speak for God with the authority given by Christ. Such ambassadors speak not only on behalf of God, but also in his place ("as though God were making his appeal through us").

The enduring ambassadorial office in the church is that of minister or teaching elder. Those holding this office are charged to proclaim the Word of God. The term used in Greek indicates the proclamation of a herald (Rom. 10:14–15; 2 Tim. 4:2). The Word is central in this proclamation, and this centrality is evident from the way the apostles posed their dilemma in Acts 6:2: "It would not be right for us to neglect the ministry of the word of God in order to wait on tables." Preaching is officially ministering the Word, which is the Word of reconciliation (2 Cor. 5:19).

It has been well stated that "true proclamation does not take place through Scripture alone, but through its exposition. . . . God does not send books to men; He sends messengers."[19] The office of preachers who proclaim, teach, and expound the Scriptures is an office of tremendous responsibility that demands gifts over and beyond what is common to both teaching and ruling elders. They require special gifts of understanding Scripture, the time

---

19. G. Friedrich, *"kēryssō,"* in G. Kittel and G. Friedrich, eds., *Theological Dictionary of the New Testament,* 10 vols. (Grand Rapids: Eerdmans, 1964–76), 3:712.

and opportunity to dig into the riches of redemption,[20] and the ability to expound and teach Scripture. Preachers, in essence, function as the mouthpiece of God (2 Cor. 5:20).

It is little wonder then that the office of preaching and teaching the gospel, which essentially replaces the Old Testament priest in the official ministry of reconciliation, is mentioned in 1 Timothy 5:17 as a task or office to be distinguished from that of ruling and directing the affairs of the church. That the preaching and teaching office is separate from that of a ruling elder is underlined by the fact that this office is also mentioned separately elsewhere. In Ephesians 4:11, several offices are mentioned. The ascended Christ "gave some to be apostles, some to be prophets, some to be evangelists, and some to be pastors and teachers." It is probably best to see the reference to "pastors and teachers" as referring to one group, the teaching elders.[21] The ruling elder is not mentioned in this passage. Teachers are also mentioned as being present, along with prophets, in the church at Antioch (Acts 13:1). The apostle Paul mentions the office of teacher after apostles and prophets in 1 Corinthians 12:28.

James mentioned the teacher as well, but he did so in a context that alerts us to the gravity of the office. He wrote: "Not many of you should presume to be teachers, my brothers, because you know that we who teach will be judged more strictly" (James 3:1). By associating himself with the teachers, James clearly referred to a teaching office in the church, probably teaching elder, since he too was an elder.[22] For that matter, the apostle Paul also called himself a teacher (2 Tim. 1:11). This clear differentiation of the teaching office, with its own special responsibilities and accountability, sets it apart from the ruling elder. One needs to be endowed with the gift of teaching to do this task (Rom. 12:7).

20. When the teaching office is mentioned in 1 Tim. 5:17, the word *kopiaō* is used for "work" in "whose *work* is preaching and teaching." This term indicates strenuous labor, working until one is exhausted.
21. This is a very old and traditional interpretation. See for documentation and further exegetical discussion Harold W. Hoehner, *Ephesians: An Exegetical Commentary* (Grand Rapids: Baker, 2002), 543 note 6 and 543–45 respectively.
22. See earlier in this chapter, under "The Jerusalem Elders."

Now the qualifications for the elder or overseer are listed in various places (1 Tim. 3:1–7; Titus 1:5–9), and we will come back to these. However, it should be noted here that these qualifications count for both the teaching and the ruling elder. No distinction is made.[23] This seems to imply that beyond these basic qualifications, the teaching elder must have a special gift for teaching and exhortation. That seems to be the point of the apostle Paul when he combines different gifts with different people in Romans 12 where he writes: "We have different gifts, according to the grace given us. If a man's gift is prophesying, let him use it in proportion to his faith. If it is serving, let him serve; if it is teaching, let him teach; if it is exhorting, let him exhort" (Rom. 12:6–8; for "exhort" see ESV, NASB, RSV).

It is evident that in verses 7 and 8, the apostle speaks in concrete terms of the persons exercising their gifts. The one with the gift of teaching should use it as a teacher, and the one with a gift of exhortation, as an exhorter. These last two gifts are vital for the office of teaching elder or pastor.[24] Just as a priest in ancient Israel would have been specially trained for his task in the ministry of reconciliation, so also in the New Testament church only the best preparation possible would be sufficient to honor the responsibilities that the risen Christ gives to his ambassadors and messengers (2 Tim. 2:2). In light of the special demands and expectations for the teaching elder, beyond those of a ruling elder, it is understandable that a distinction was made between the teaching and ruling elder as two separate offices.

Some Consequences of the Distinctions

We will now note some important ramifications that flow from distinguishing two offices of elders: the teaching elder and

23. The distinction, however, does show itself in that the qualifications of those entrusted with preaching the gospel, such as Titus and Timothy, are addressed to them directly. See 1 Tim. 1:3–11, 18; 4:11–13; 2 Tim. 4:2. See further, G. I. Williamson, "The *Two and Three-Office Issue* Reconsidered," *Ordained Servant* 12 (2003): 5–6.

24. As the context makes clear, the tasks of teaching and preaching are the work of one person, Timothy, in 1 Tim. 4:13.

the ruling elder. We will consider briefly the implications for their respective tasks, support, and equality.

First, with respect to their task, in Old Testament times only the priests were ordained and designated by the Lord to function in the official service of reconciliation, be it by sacrificing, teaching, or blessing the people. Anyone else who attempted to do their specific task had to be put to death.[25]

Ministers of the gospel, the teaching elders, may function in the *fulfilled* ministry of reconciliation as spokesmen for God (2 Cor. 5:18–20). In this sense they are heirs of the Old Testament office of priest. As the priests of old, they may teach, exhort, and bless the congregation before God. The force of the analogy would seem to indicate that normally only the teaching elders may administer the Word officially as spokesmen for God in the public worship services, and only they would be able to bless the congregation in such services. A ruling elder should simply read the blessing as given in Scripture, but not raise his hands, as this has always been the prerogative of the priest and hence today is that of the teaching elder.[26]

It is a great tragedy in the history of the church that elders came to be called priests, in part because of the erroneous belief that the Lord's Supper was to be regarded as a sacrificial meal, thus denying the once-for-all character of the sacrifice of Christ.[27]

25. For the anointing of the priests for holy service see Ex. 28:41; 30:30; Lev. 8:30; for the exclusive privilege of the priests and the penalty of death for violating it, see Num. 3:5–10, 38; 16:40.

26. Synagogue services normally ended with the priestly blessing given by a priest with uplifted hands (Lev. 9:22; Num. 6:22–27). If there was no priest, no blessing was given (Deut. 10:8; 21:5); instead, the words of benediction were simply recited. See Emil Schürer, *The History of the Jewish People in the Age of Jesus Christ (175 B.C.–A.D. 135)*, 4 vols., rev. ed. by G. Vermes, F. Millar, and M. Black (Edinburgh: T&T Clark, 1973–87), 2:453–54. The duty of the minister of the gospel "to bless the people from God" is specifically mentioned in "The Form of Presbyterial Church Government," 173.

27. By A.D. 375 or earlier, the Latin term for priest (*sacerdos*) was used for *presbyteros*, the Greek word for "elder." It is thus not surprising that the later English word "priest" is in essence a contraction of *presbyteros* through the Latin "presbyter." See *The Compact Edition of the Oxford English Dictionary: Complete Text Reproduced Micrographically*, 2 vols. (New York: Oxford University Press, 1971), 2:2297. For the use of "priest" and "priesthood" for ecclesiastical offices, see Colin Bulley, *The Priesthood of Some Believers: Developments from the General to the Special Priesthood in the Christian Literature of the First Three Centuries* (Carlisle, UK: Paternoster, 2000).

The reality, however, is that the office of priest in administering reconciliation has been taken over by the herald of the glad tidings of the fulfilled sacrifice of Jesus Christ who was raised for our justification and ascended into glory (Rom. 4:25; Heb. 10:11–14).

Second, with respect to their support, because the priests and Levites were employed full-time in the ministry of reconciliation, the Lord guaranteed the livelihood of the tribe of Levi by granting them the tithe as their inheritance (Num. 18:21–24).

Full-time ministers of the gospel are likewise to receive their livelihood from the gospel (1 Cor. 9:9–14). As in Old Testament times, there is no general mandate for God's people to support the ruling elder. We do read in 1 Timothy 5:17–18, however, that "the elders who direct the affairs of the church well are worthy of double honor, especially those whose work is preaching and teaching. For the Scripture says, 'Do not muzzle the ox while it is treading out the grain,' and 'The worker deserves his wages.'" This would seem to indicate that it is especially those laboring in preaching and teaching, namely, the ministers of the Word, who are to be honored, and such honor should include wages. The ruling elder should also be honored, and financial support is not necessarily excluded in showing that honor.[28]

Third, with respect to their equality, although the teaching and ruling elders are distinct offices, both offices are elder offices and they are both called to serve the church (cf. Matt. 23:8). One could say that the minister of the Word is in essence a specialized elder. Recognizing this undercuts any idea of clericalism or ecclesiastical hierarchy in the church. Also, the ruling elder is a shepherd of the flock with all that this entails. There is to be no domineering of the one office over the other. The only "boss" in the church is the Lord Jesus Christ who rules the church as the head of the body (Eph. 1:20–22). As a matter of fact, the very term "ruling elder" can be somewhat misleading. Instead of the rendering "the elders that rule well" (KJV), the relevant Greek

28. See William Hendriksen, *Exposition of the Pastoral Epistles*, New Testament Commentary (Grand Rapids: Baker, 1957), 180–81.

117

term in 1 Timothy 5:17 could better be translated: "the elders who direct the affairs of the church well." They give leadership.[29] The relationship of both elder offices to each other as well as towards the congregation is one of serving (1 Peter 5:2–5).

Finally, to reject an ordained ministry of the Word and have ruling elders only to shepherd the church and to preach the gospel is not consistent with the biblical demands. Such a course of action amounts to a willful self-impoverishment. Christ has blessed his church with the gifts of his undershepherds, the teaching and ruling elders.

Summary and Conclusions

The risen Christ has given the offices to the church, and he is the ultimate source of authority for them. Also, the New Testament office of elder gets its legitimacy and authority from Christ as mediated through the apostles who ensured that this office would be a normal feature of a Christian congregation whether or not it had Jewish origins. Paul and Barnabas saw to it that there were elders in Asia Minor during their first missionary journey (Acts 14:23), and Titus was charged to do the same in Crete (Titus 1:5).

The eldership in the Jerusalem congregation was unique in the sense that the elders there were apparently eyewitnesses of Christ's public ministry. Presumably as a result of the persecution of the Jerusalem church and the subsequent destruction of the city itself, these elders would eventually have served in other congregations to which they had fled. These elders may have been given special power to do miracles, such as the healing of the sick, for the sake of the gospel (James 5:14–15).

The New Testament was not written to provide a neat codification of church government. The terminology of eldership

29. See, e.g., Johannes P. Louw and Eugene A. Nida, eds., *Greek-English Lexicon of the New Testament Based on Semantic Domains*, 2d ed., 2 vols. (New York: United Bible Societies, 1989), 1:465–66 (no. 36.1).

varies and does not always match our expectations for precision. Different terms for the office are used, such as *episkopos*, "overseer" or "bishop." But *episkopos* means the same as *presbyteros* ("elder"), a fact that is clear from the context (e.g., Acts 20:17, 28). The variety of names for the office is understandable given the formative period of the church that the New Testament describes. The term "elder" is also used of someone who is an apostle (e.g., 1 Peter 5:1).

A disputed issue is whether the references to "the elders who rule" (ESV) and "those whose work is preaching and teaching" (1 Tim. 5:17) relate to two distinct offices, the minister and the elder, or to one office, namely the ruling elder. The separate mention of the gifts of ruling and exhorting in Romans 12:8 and 1 Corinthians 12:28 would suggest that they are two separate offices. This understanding is strengthened by the fact that the second passage even specifically relates gifts to offices.

Although one must distinguish between the two offices of the ruling and teaching elder, one cannot deny the underlying unity between these offices. Both are elder offices that have the care of the flock at the center of their mandate (Acts 20:28; 1 Peter 5:2), and both offices require the ability to teach (1 Tim. 3:2; Titus 1:9). Data like this certainly raises questions about whether there really are two offices or one. Indeed, to do justice to this issue we need to include the Old Testament.

In ancient Israel, the people of God always had a teaching office along with the office of elder. This reality would argue for two elder offices in the Christian church: a teaching and a ruling one. The teaching elder would ultimately be heir of the priestly teaching task (Deut. 33:10), and the ruling elder would be a continuation of the Old Testament elder. It is, however, noteworthy that also in the Old Testament there was an overlap in the teaching responsibilities, since the elders needed to be able to teach God's people as well (Deut. 32:7). However, as with the New Testament ruling elder, this was not their primary duty.

With the Old Testament background in mind, the description of ministering the Word as being "the priestly duty of proclaiming

119

the gospel of God" (Rom. 15:16) becomes significant and shows the continuity of the office of teaching elder with key elements of the office of Old Testament priest. Preachers are the priests and Levites of today. This understanding is confirmed by God's giving "the ministry of reconciliation" to his ambassadors today (2 Cor. 5:18–20). These ambassadors can only be those who now preach the gospel as ministers. They have taken over the proclamation of the ministry of reconciliation from the priests of old.

The fact that there are two distinct offices of elder, teaching elder and ruling elder, has several consequences. First, they each have their specific task, and thus ruling elders normally do not officially bring the Word in public worship. They also do not give the blessing. Second, especially those engaged full-time as the "priests" and teaching elders of today should be supported monetarily by the gospel. Third, both offices are elder offices and there is to be equality, not hierarchy. Fourth, there is no biblical warrant for a church polity in which the ordained ministry is rejected in favor of only ruling elders who preach and shepherd the church.

Elders and the Keys
of the Kingdom

THE COMING OF THE SAVIOR and the subsequent outpouring of the Holy Spirit at Pentecost have important consequences for properly understanding the character of the elders' authority. As we saw at the beginning of the previous chapter, present-day elders have received their authority as office bearers from the Lord Jesus Christ. This authority is pictured in the image of the keys of the kingdom of heaven. Since the power of the keys lies at the heart of the Christ-given authority of the elders today, we need to take a look at what characterizes the authority of the keys and its use. In this chapter we will therefore consider:

- The power of the keys
- Developments after Pentecost
- From apostles to elders
- Laying on of hands
- The elders, the keys, and the congregation

The Power of the Keys

When Christ began his public ministry, he also started to gather together the New Testament congregation in the form of disciples who believed in him and followed him. What defined the group was the confession that Jesus of Nazareth was indeed the promised Messiah, the Christ, the Son of God. This, the gospel in a nutshell so to speak, was needed before any understanding of the keys was possible. The gospel and the keys of the kingdom are closely related.

At a certain point during his earthly ministry, Christ asked his disciples, "Who do you say I am?" Peter answered, "You are the Christ, the Son of the living God" (Matt. 16:15–16). Christ then called Peter blessed because the Father had revealed this identity to him. The disciples were now ready to hear about the keys of the kingdom. Christ therefore continued by saying: "And I tell you that you are Peter, and on this rock I will build my church, and the gates of Hades will not overcome it. I will give you the keys of the kingdom of heaven; whatever you bind on earth will be bound in heaven, and whatever you loose on earth will be loosed in heaven" (Matt. 16:18–19).

What does this mean? Christ addressed Peter as one who had just made the good confession, a confession indispensable for the future church. To him Jesus says that he is Peter (Greek: *Petros*) and that on this rock (Greek: *petra*) he would build his church. It is in a sense on Peter, then, as true confessor of Christ, along with the other apostles, that the church would be built. This truth is also articulated in Ephesians 2:20. God's people are built on "the foundation of the apostles and prophets, with Christ Jesus himself as the chief cornerstone" (cf. Rev. 21:14).[1]

The one who does the actual building of the church on this foundation is Christ himself and his work will stand. "*I* will build my church, and the gates of Hades will not overcome it" (Matt. 16:18). What does this signify? Hades here means the same as hell (cf. KJV). One finds a similar usage in Christ's parable of the rich man and Lazarus where Hades and the place of Abraham are contrasted (Luke 16:23–26). What is the force of "gates"? The verb used with "the gates of Hades" portrays them as a very aggressive power that seeks to overcome the church with the expectation of

1. R. T. France, *The Gospel of Matthew*, New International Commentary on the New Testament (Grand Rapids/Cambridge: Eerdmans, 2007), 620–23.

defeating it, but they will not be able. The word "gates" is therefore used figuratively of the hellish power that hates God's people and seeks to destroy them.

There are different possibilities in further interpreting how gates relate to this power of hell. One could interpret "the gates of Hades" as Satan and his legions storming out of hell's gates to assail and destroy the church. Or these gates are the gates of death that seek with all their might to swallow up the church (Isa. 5:14; Rev. 6:8).[2] It may very well be, however, that the gates should be understood as the place where the juridical and economic powers of an ancient city are concentrated. Here is where the elders and the important men met, made decisions, and sat in judgment. The gates of Hades would then be a figure of speech for the leadership, power, and authority of Satan. All his authority and everything at his disposal will be used against the church.[3] In any case, regardless of how one specifically understands "the gates of Hades," the Lord clearly assures his disciples that hell and Satan will never be successful in their attacks on the church. It is, however, obvious from the context that the spiritual battle against the forces of hell will be difficult (Eph. 6:12).

Within this context of city gates and war the Lord Jesus promises to give to Peter, the first among the other apostles, the keys of the kingdom of God.[4] In order to grasp the significance of this promise, we first need to understand the image of the keys.

This image calls to mind the steward of the house of David in the prophecy of Isaiah 22. Such a steward would be entrusted with all the matters of running the palace, including the much-desired access to the throne. The sinful pride that such a position could engender was the downfall of Shebna (Isa. 22:15–19). When the new steward, Eliakim, was appointed, the Lord clothed him with the garments of his office and said: "I will place on his shoulder

2. See respectively W. D. Davies and Dale C. Allison, *A Critical and Exegetical Commentary on the Gospel according to Saint Matthew*, 3 vols., International Critical Commentary (Edinburgh: T&T Clark, 1988–97), 2:632–34, and France, *Matthew*, 624.

3. See J. LoMusio, "Pylons of Power," *Archaeology and Biblical Research* 3 (1990): 2–7.

4. The kingdom of heaven is the same as the kingdom of God. Cf., e.g., Matt. 5:3 with Luke 6:20.

the key to the house of David; what he opens no one can shut, and what he shuts no one can open" (Isa. 22:22). He who had the keys had power and privilege. The steward basically decided who would be admitted to see the king. This meant that he determined, for example, who would get to benefit from the justice that the king might dispense to the poor and oppressed (Ps. 72:2–4, 12–14). The steward, after all, had the key to David's house and had the power to open doors. However, this office had to be conducted with the sensitivity and compassion of a father who seeks the best for those in his charge. "He will be a father to those who live in Jerusalem and to the house of Judah" (Isa. 22:21). Furthermore, such a steward was responsible to the one who appointed him, in this case, the Lord. He could go no further in his authority than the jurisdiction that the Lord had given him.

If all of this is the background of the image of the keys, then the import of Christ's words becomes clearer. Although the forces of hell will attack the church, they will not overcome it. The Lord promises to give Peter the keys of the kingdom of God so that he can open the doors and admit people into the kingdom where it is safe and where treasures are to be found, such as being right with God and being able to live in his loving presence. As a steward in the service of the Lord, Peter was promised the authority and responsibility to give the people of God access to such treasures of the kingdom. The keys are therefore of critical importance in the battle against Satan.

What is the key that unlocks and opens the way to the treasures of the kingdom? Simply put, it is the gospel which Christ had been teaching the people. The Lord Jesus had been announcing the coming of the kingdom and had been dispensing its treasures, especially by proclaiming the righteousness of God and the forgiveness of sins. This last treasure was strongly contested by the Jewish religious leaders. Was it not God's prerogative to forgive sins? Was it not blasphemous for man to do so? Yet Christ pardoned sins, and he gave life and righteousness to all who believed in him (Matt. 9:2–7; Luke 7:48–49). In this way he ushered those who believed in him into the peace with God that characterizes his kingdom (Luke 1:79; John 14:27; 16:33; Acts 10:36).

But now in the context of Christ building his church, he promised that Peter as his steward would be able to share in this glorious work of giving access to the treasures of the kingdom of heaven on earth. That the plural "keys" is used indicates a broad mandate and authority. But to exercise that authority Peter needed to know the gospel. It is no accident that immediately after the promise to Peter about the keys, the Lord Jesus taught his disciples about his coming death and resurrection and corrected Peter's lack of understanding (Matt. 16:21–28). Only in knowing the gospel of salvation in Christ will the promise of the keys of the kingdom find its fulfillment.

The significance of the keys as opening the way to the kingdom and its treasures was emphasized when the Lord promised Peter: "Whatever you bind on earth will be bound in heaven, and whatever you loose on earth will be loosed in heaven" (Matt. 16:19). With these words, the Lord gave Peter the necessary authority to do his work. "Binding" and "loosening" were common rabbinic expressions, which declared in a legally binding manner what was forbidden and what was permitted with respect to doctrine and conduct. Thus, when Peter proclaimed this gospel, it would be as God speaking from his throne; it would be legally binding. After all, the great Key Bearer, Jesus Christ (Rev. 1:18; 3:7), gave him the authority to preach God's salvation and the forgiveness of sins by way of faith in Christ. This gospel is the key that opens the way to the great treasures of the kingdom![5] If one does not believe this message, the door is closed, one is still bound in his or her unforgiven sins, and God's judgment will come. However, believing this proclamation means an open door to the treasures of God's grace and receiving, for example, the forgiveness of sins. That is the force of the binding and loosening. Peter was not the one who determined this, but the gospel he preached, the Word

5. Because the gospel is the key that opens the way, Peter and the others had to keep quiet about Christ's identity. They still needed to be taught what the gospel entailed (Matt. 16:20–23).

of God, which declared that the way to the treasure of forgiveness is open for those who believe, but shut to those who do not believe (John 12:47–50; Acts 3:23).[6]

Not only Peter, but also the other disciples were given the power of the keys. When Christ was teaching them the basics of church discipline, he said to all of them: "I tell you [plural] the truth, whatever you bind on earth will be bound in heaven, and whatever you loose on earth will be loosed in heaven" (Matt. 18:18). So Christ emphatically let all the disciples share in what was first promised only to Peter. All these promises were confirmed when the resurrected Christ commissioned his disciples with the words: "As the Father has sent me, I am sending you." Then he breathed on them and said: "Receive the Holy Spirit. If you forgive anyone his sins, they are forgiven; if you do not forgive them, they are not forgiven" (John 20:21–23). When the apostles proclaimed the forgiveness of sins for all those who believe the gospel, they could be sure that what they preached and promised on earth would be confirmed in heaven.

While the apostles received the authority to open the doors to the kingdom of heaven, those leaders and elders among God's people who denied the gospel of Christ would not be able to open the way to the treasures of the kingdom. Rather, their speaking in unbelief would shut the door to their hearers (Matt. 23:13, 15; Luke 11:52).

Developments after Pentecost

From Apostles to Elders

The fact that Peter had been the first to receive the promise of the keys was reflected in the period immediately following Pente-

6. For the keys as proclaiming the good news of the kingdom, see D. A. Carson in Frank E. Gaebelein, ed., *The Expositor's Bible Commentary*, 12 vols. (Grand Rapids: Zondervan, 1988), 8:373, and Davies and Allison, *Matthew*, 2:639. The Heidelberg Catechism identifies the keys of the kingdom as the preaching of the gospel and church discipline (Lord's Day 31). In essence, however, this is the one key of the gospel, as it is proclaimed (in the preaching) and applied (in church discipline).

cost. He was the first among the apostles. His primary importance in that early period is obvious. He had the prominent role in the election of Matthias (Acts 1:15–22), and on the day of Pentecost it was Peter who, empowered by the Holy Spirit, was able to explain what was happening. He proclaimed the gospel of Christ crucified and resurrected and urged his hearers to repent and believe (Acts 2:14–40). How this preaching of the Word functioned as keys opening wide the gates to the kingdom treasures of forgiveness and the renewal of life in Christ for all who believed! Through Peter's preaching that day, thousands came to faith (Acts 2:41).

After Pentecost, Peter remained in the forefront in preaching, teaching, healing, and building the church (Acts 4:8–12; 5:15; 8:20–23; 9:34, 40). When he was accompanied by John, Peter was always mentioned first (Acts 3:1–11; 4:1–23; 8:14–25; cf. 5:29). Peter was in charge when the integrity of the church had to be protected from Satan's attack through Ananias and Sapphira (Acts 5:1–11). In addition, it was to Peter that the Lord revealed that the gospel had to go to the Gentiles (Acts 10–11), and Peter was the first to order the baptism of a Gentile believer (Acts 10:47–48). Furthermore, Peter addressed the meeting in Jerusalem that was so important for the future direction of the church (Acts 15:7–11). It was also to Peter that Paul went after his conversion (Gal. 1:18).

However, besides Peter there were the other apostles, the remaining disciples who had likewise been with the Lord Jesus and were witnesses of his resurrection glory (Acts 1:21–22). Christ had specifically called these to be his apostles after spending the night in prayer to God (Luke 6:12–16). As the Father had sent the Son, so the Christ would send out these to be his apostles empowered by the Holy Spirit (John 17:18; 20:21–22; cf. Heb. 3:1). They too received the power of the keys (Matt. 18:18), as would also that special apostle, Paul (Acts 9:17–20; Gal. 1:1), who would have a place of prominence in the church (Gal. 2:11–14).[7] The office of

7. The term "apostle" is used in the restricted sense of the twelve who were eyewitnesses of Christ's work and ministry (Mark 3:14), as well as Paul. For Paul's apostleship, see Simon Kistemaker, *Exposition of the Acts of the Apostles*, New Testament Commentary

apostle formed part of the foundation of the church, a spiritual house, of which Christ is the cornerstone (Eph. 2:20; 1 Peter 2:4–9). The apostolic office was, however, a temporary one.

As can be expected, there was a time of transition from the extraordinary and one-time office of apostle to the postapostolic era when, for example, the office of elder or overseer was charged with the well-being of the church. This transition is evident from the fact that the apostles Peter and John could call themselves elders as well (1 Peter 5:1; 2 John 1:1). Although the office of elder appears to have come into being as a matter of course in congregations of Jewish origin,[8] the apostles were also actively involved in making sure that all the congregations had elders. The eldership was clearly crucial for the normal functioning of the church.

The apostles went about ensuring the eldership in local congregations in different ways. Where necessary, they appointed elders, as they did in Lystra, Iconium, and Pisidian Antioch (Acts 14:23), or they instructed others, like Titus, to appoint elders (Titus 1:5). We saw earlier how the congregation was probably involved in these appointments.[9] It is important in our present context to note that the apostles considered it their responsibility to make sure that elders functioned everywhere. By seeing to their appointment and by charging them with their duties (Acts 20:28), they were safeguarding the future of the church that had been entrusted to their care. After all, the apostolic office could not be repeated; it functioned as the foundation of the church. And so the normal functioning of the office of elder had to be secured. In light of the many different offices and gifts that functioned in the early church (such as prophets, evangelists, and healers; 1 Cor. 12:9; Eph. 4:11), the focus on the office of elder is noteworthy and underlines its great and abiding significance for the church.

(Grand Rapids: Baker, 1990), 341–42. The term "apostle" is, however, also used in a broader sense of people like Barnabas (Acts 14:14), Andronicus and Junias (Rom. 16:7), and Apollos (1 Cor. 4:6, 9).

8. The office of the elders in Antioch and Jerusalem is mentioned without any explanation, as one would expect of something considered normal (Acts 11:30; 15:2; 21:18).

9. See chapter 1, under "A Task Given by God."

Ordination to the office of elder seems to have taken place with the laying on of hands. The apostle Paul enjoined Timothy: "Do not be hasty in the laying on of hands" (1 Tim. 5:22). This exhortation probably refers to the ordination of elders in the congregation and thus shows how the apostle wanted to safeguard the holiness of this important office. The process that leads to ordination must not be rushed (see 1 Tim. 3:1–10) lest an office bearer be chosen against whom accusations could be made (1 Tim. 5:19–21) and Timothy become a participant in sin (1 Tim. 5:22; James 3:1).

Laying On of Hands

The matter of the laying on of hands, when one assumes the office of elder, raises another issue. Is there any special significance in this ritual for understanding the authority of an elder? Some affirm that the act of laying on of hands serves to pass on the gift with which God equips the office bearer.[10] What is the significance of the laying on of the hands? In answering this question it will be profitable to survey briefly the use of this ritual for ordination or induction into special service, and so come to some conclusions.[11]

The laying on of hands in the ordination to office is an ancient practice, which is attested already in the time of Moses. When the Levites were consecrated to special service, the Lord instructed Moses to make them ceremonially clean (Num. 8:5–8). After these rituals were done, Moses brought the Levites before the Lord and the Israelites laid their hands on them (Num. 8:10). The context indicates that this laying on of hands was similar to the placing

10. So, e.g., E. Lohse, *"cheir,"* in G. Kittel and G. Friedrich, eds., *Theological Dictionary of the New Testament,* 10 vols. (Grand Rapids: Eerdmans, 1964–76), 9:433–34.
11. David Daube correctly makes the point that not all laying on of hands is of the same nature or kind. In the Old Testament the Hebrew vocabulary differs. This feature is not apparent in the Greek translation of the Old Testament and hence also not in the New Testament. However, he has shown that the laying on of the hands to heal or bless needs to be distinguished from laying on of the hands in ordination. It is therefore justified to restrict our New Testament investigation to passages dealing with ordination and induction into special service. See David Daube, *The New Testament and Rabbinic Judaism* (New York: Arno, 1973 [1956]), 224–36.

of one's hand on a sacrifice (e.g., Lev. 1:4; 8:18). The Levites were being offered to God as a wave offering so that they could be totally committed to their task (Num. 8:11–14). They took the place of the firstborn sons of Israel (Num. 8:16–19). By laying their hands on the Levites, the Israelites indicated that the Levites were their gift to God instead of their firstborn. In this way the Levites were set apart and consecrated to the Lord's service.

Prior to the death of Moses, the Lord instructed him to "take Joshua son of Nun, a man in whom is the Spirit, and lay your hand on him. Make him stand before Eleazar the priest and all the congregation, and you shall commission him in their sight. You shall invest him with some of your authority, that all the congregation of the people of Israel may obey" (Num. 27:18–20 ESV). Moses then laid his hands on Joshua and commissioned him (Num. 27:22–23).

There are several things to note. Prior to his ordination, Joshua already had the Spirit, that is, he was equipped for the task and ready to lead. His suitability came from the Spirit of God. When Joshua took over the leadership, God filled him with the spirit of wisdom, "because Moses had laid his hands on him" (Deut. 34:9). He had been ordained to the office on God's command, and now the Lord who had gifted Joshua in the past would continue to provide what was necessary for his task.

At the time of Joshua's ordination, God had instructed Moses to give Joshua some of his "authority" so that Israel would obey him. The idea here seems to be that by laying his hands on Joshua, and by instructing and commissioning him in the presence of all the people, the nation would understand that they should now obey him as they had obeyed Moses. At the same time, since only "some" of Moses' authority was being transferred to Joshua, it is evident that his leadership would not be fully comparable to that of Moses. And so with the ordination or induction of Joshua by the laying on of hands and the commissioning, authority was transferred to Joshua, and he was set apart for a special office of leadership. It could be argued that the actual transference of authority took place

with the words of commissioning that explained the laying on
of hands in the hearing of the people.

There are no other relevant examples in the Old Testament
concerning the laying on of hands that could be seen as ordaining or inducting into special service. Coming to the New Testament, we read in Acts 6 that because of the apparent neglect of
the Grecian Jewish widows in the daily distribution of food, the
Twelve, that is, the apostles, decided that rather than neglect the
ministry of the Word entrusted to them, others should be chosen
to wait on the tables. So the Twelve said: "Brothers, choose seven
men from among you who are known to be full of the Spirit
and wisdom. We will turn this responsibility over to them and
will give our attention to prayer and the ministry of the word"
(Acts 6:3–4). Seven men were chosen. And then we read literally:
"they [i.e., 'the whole multitude' of v. 5] presented these men to
the apostles, and praying they laid their hands on them" (Acts
6:6). Two things should be noted. First, although the Greek text
is somewhat ambiguous, the larger context indicates that the
apostles were the ones who laid their hands on the designated
men. After all, they would be putting those elected in charge of
their new task (Acts 6:3). Also, the prerogative to lay on hands
was not a general privilege.[12] Second, prior to the laying on of
hands, these men apparently already had the gifts necessary for
the task that awaited them. That is why they qualified for ordination. The laying on of hands was then accompanied by prayer.
Thus their ordination took place, and these men were set apart
with particular responsibilities.

An ordination with the laying on of hands also occurred in
Antioch. While the prophets and teachers were performing their
service to the Lord and fasting, "the Holy Spirit said, 'Set apart for
me Barnabas and Saul for the work to which I have called them.'
So after they had fasted and prayed, they placed their hands on
them and sent them off" (Acts 13:2–3). Barnabas and Saul (or Paul;

12. The NIV reflects the general consensus that the apostles were the ones who did
the laying on of hands when it translates: "They presented these men to the apostles, who
prayed and laid their hands on them."

Acts 13:9) had been teaching the gospel (Acts 11:26; 13:1), but now they were officially commissioned as missionaries. Note that the laying on of hands by the prophets and teachers was preceded by fasting and prayer, and this action gave neither Barnabas nor Saul any gift that they did not already possess. The laying on of hands was apparently done to set these men apart as missionaries according to the will of the Holy Spirit (Acts 13:2). Since all this happened in the context of the prophets and teachers ministering, we may assume that the congregation was gathered together and was thus present when the laying on of hands took place.

Another example of the laying on of hands concerns Timothy. He had been designated for the work of ministry by the Holy Spirit through prophecies (1 Tim. 1:18). The apostle Paul later referred to this when he wrote Timothy: "Do not neglect the gift you have, which was given you by prophecy when the council of elders laid their hands on you" (1 Tim. 4:14 ESV). What was the gift that was being referred to and how did it relate to the laying on of hands? The word used for gift, *charisma*, indicates that this God-given gift was one given by grace alone. The gift is best understood as the necessary endowment for the office to which Timothy was called (1 Tim. 1:18). For that reason the elders laid their hands on Timothy and ordained him to his office. Thus, the literal Greek phrase "with [*meta*] the laying on of hands by the council of the elders" (1 Tim. 4:14) expresses accompanying circumstances, rather than instrument. That is, the elders did not give these gifts to him by the laying on of their hands—Timothy had these gifts already. The laying on of hands was an acknowledgment of the gifts that marked Timothy for ordination to special service. The passage in question can therefore best be rendered, and in part paraphrased, to read: Do not neglect the gift that is in you and was testified by prophetic words and obediently accompanied by the laying on of hands by the council of the elders (1 Tim. 4:14). The situation here is thus analogous to that of Barnabas and Saul whom the Holy Spirit had first equipped and then indicated needed to be set apart and commissioned as missionaries by the laying on of hands (Acts 13:1–3).

132

When the apostle Paul later wrote Timothy from a Roman prison (2 Tim. 1:16–17), he encouraged his son in the faith (1 Tim. 1:2) and said: "I remind you to fan into flame the gift of God, which is in you through the laying on of my hands" (2 Tim. 1:6). This gift is a gift associated with the Spirit, for the apostle continued: "For the Spirit that God has given us does not make us timid; instead, his Spirit fills us with power, love and self-control" (2 Tim. 1:7 TEV).[13] This apostolic reminder of the gift of God and the laying on of hands should therefore be understood along the lines of the similar exhortation in 1 Timothy 4:14. The phrase "through the laying on of hands" does not signify that it was the act of the laying on of hands as such that conveyed the gift of God. Rather, the apostle used the laying on of the hands as a figure of speech, a synecdoche, by which a part (the laying on of hands) is mentioned for the whole (the entire process of Timothy receiving the gifts from God and being inducted into a special service).[14]

In surveying the above examples of the laying on of hands, the following observations can be made. First, in no case is there an indisputable instance of the gifts for the office being given with the laying on of the hands for ordination. Second, the common underlying element in all the examples relating to ordination is that the person involved is separated for special service. One could therefore say that the laying on of hands was a sign of consecration, of being offered up in holy service to God.[15] Third, in two of the three New Testament instances prayer is specifically

13. For the gift being the Holy Spirit, see I. Howard Marshall, *A Critical and Exegetical Commentary on the Pastoral Epistles*, in collaboration with Philip H. Towner, International Critical Commentary (Edinburgh: T&T Clark, 1999), 698–700; also New American Bible, New Jerusalem Bible, and Today's New International Version.

14. For the laying on of hands as such not conveying the gift of God, see Marshall, *The Pastoral Epistles*, 697, and for the use of synecdoche, John Calvin, *The Second Epistle of Paul the Apostle to the Corinthians and the Epistles to Timothy, Titus and Philemon*, ed. D. W. Torrance and T. F. Torrance (Grand Rapids: Eerdmans, 1964), 293.

15. On Acts 6:6 and Acts 13:3, see John Calvin, *The Acts of the Apostles*, 2 vols., ed. David W. Torrance and Thomas F. Torrance (Grand Rapids: Eerdmans, 1965–66), 1:163, 355. For separation for special service, see Frank Thielman, "Laying On of Hands," in Walter A. Elwell, ed., *Evangelical Dictionary of Biblical Theology* (Grand Rapids: Baker, 1996), 472–73.

mentioned as preceding the laying on of hands. This suggests that prayer was normally part of the procedure. Prayer would be offered in recognition that it was not the laying on of the hands, but God alone who would be able to give the necessary gifts and authority. Such gifts are not at man's disposal (Acts 8:18–20).[16] Fourth, different parties participated in the laying on of hands: the apostles (Acts 6:6), prophets and teachers (Acts 13:1–3), and the elders (1 Tim. 4:14). This variety of participants indicates that the right of ordination was not restricted to the apostolic office. Furthermore, it is clear from this variety that there is no conveyance of a particular quality necessary for office from one office bearer to another with the idea of succession, such as the apostolic succession championed by Rome. This is unknown in the New Testament.

In conclusion, the laying on of hands in itself does not confer any special gift or authority, as if the one office bearer gives something to the one being ordained. Rather, the laying on of hands signifies that the one ordained into the office is being separated for holy service. The prayer that precedes this ritual indicates that not man, but only the risen Christ and the Holy Spirit can equip his office bearers with the spiritual gifts necessary to execute the office. Even though the congregation and church leaders were involved in the ordination of elders (Acts 14:23; 1 Tim. 4:14; 5:22; Titus 1:5), it was not they, but the Holy Spirit, who had made them overseers (Acts 20:28).

Because the churches of the Reformation rejected Roman Catholic notions associated with the laying on of hands, they showed some ambivalence to the practice. On the European continent, the first edition of Article 31 in the Belgic Confession (1562) stipulated laying on of hands in the ordination of ministers and elders; however, this stipulation was left out in subsequent editions. Conversely in Scotland, the Scottish *First Book of Discipline* (1560) did not consider laying on of hands necessary for ordination, while *The Second Book of Discipline* (1578) mandated

16. See, e.g., Calvin, *Acts*, 1:163, 355.

134

the practice of laying on of hands (Chapter 3.6).[17] Currently both Presbyterian and Reformed churches ordain ministers or teaching elders with laying on of hands, but the practice is not consistent with respect to the ruling elder. While found in Presbyterian churches, the practice is not uniform and it is basically unknown in Reformed churches. However, since the office of minister (or teaching elder) and that of ruling elder are both elder offices, there is a certain inconsistency in using the laying on of hands with the teaching elder and not the ruling elder. It would be good if a more consistent use of this ritual could be achieved.[18]

The Elders, the Keys, and the Congregation

As those sent and authorized by the Lord Jesus, the apostles saw to it that elders were functioning in every church. They realized that this was part of their commission from the risen Savior. After all, they understood that the office bearers whom they were instrumental in appointing were in fact set over the flock by the Holy Spirit (Acts 20:28), the Spirit of Christ (Rom 8:9), in order to ensure the continued functioning of the apostolic Word after their departure (see, e.g., 1 Cor. 15:1–2). This Word is the gospel of the triumphant Christ. It is the key that opens the doors to the treasures of the kingdom of heaven. By passing on this apostolic Word to the teaching and ruling elders, the apostles also passed on to the elders the power of the keys. The Word is a mighty weapon in the hands of the elders in their struggle for the well-being of the church against the onslaughts of Satan. This Word

17. For the Scottish church, see D. B. Forrester, "Ordination," in Nigel M. de S. Cameron, ed., *Dictionary of Scottish Church History and Theology* (Downers Grove, IL: InterVarsity, 1993), 635–36. For the texts, see *The First Book of Discipline*, introduction and commentary by James K. Cameron (Edinburgh: Saint Andrew, 1972), 102, and James Kirk, ed., *The Second Book of Discipline with an Introduction and Commentary* (Edinburgh: Saint Andrew, 1980), 67–68, 180. For the text of the Belgic Confession, see J. N. Bakhuizen van den Brink, *De Nederlandse belijdenisgeschriften*, 2d ed. (Amsterdam: Ton Bolland, 1976), 129 (note).

18. The reticence in the Reformed churches probably relates to the ruling elder being chosen and ordained for a certain term only, whereas an ordination for life is the norm in Presbyterian churches. See on this issue Samuel Miller, *The Ruling Elder* (Dallas: Presbyterian Heritage, 1987 [1832]), 278–93.

empowers the elders, as "the power of God for the salvation of everyone who believes" (Rom. 1:16). "The word of God is living and active. Sharper than any double-edged sword, it penetrates even to dividing soul and spirit, joints and marrow; it judges the thoughts and attitudes of the heart" (Heb. 4:12). Those who believe this Word and accept the gospel by a true faith triumph over the evil one (1 John 5:4–5).

The Word, however, was given not only to the elders. In so far as the congregation has received the gospel, the Word of God, it too, therefore, has responsibilities with respect to the keys. Christ's instructions originally given to the apostles (Matt. 18:15–20) now impact, not only the elders, but also in a general way the congregation. After all, the gospel is what opens the door to the forgiveness of sins and life eternal. As that gospel is ministered by members of the congregation in admonishing, exhorting, and encouraging one another in mutual oversight and Christian discipline (Col. 3:16), the keys of the kingdom are being used. It is clear from the manner in which the keys are thus used that the authority and power exercised are of a serving and not autocratic nature. This feature is consistent with the one who gives this authority, the Lord Jesus Christ, who came in love to serve (Matt. 20:26–28). When the keys of the kingdom are used, Christ himself works powerfully and authoritatively by his Spirit through the Word, which is the Word of God and not man (1 Thess. 1:5; 2:13; 1 Peter 1:23; John 6:63).

As we shall see in chapter 9, the elders have special leadership responsibilities in the use of the keys of the kingdom of heaven, but the congregation is also fully engaged. The congregation is able to be involved, for the living Christ dwells in his church by his Spirit[19] and mobilizes his entire people in the struggle against the gates of hell.

---

19. Note how Christ speaks of his presence with his congregation (Matt. 18:20) when he gives the keys of the kingdom to his church (Matt. 18:15–19).

Part 4

Elders as Preservers and Nurturers of Life in the Covenant Community

Ruling and Having Authority

WE WILL NOW CONSIDER the task of the New Testament elders within the context of the perspectives that the Old Testament and the Christian church's inheriting the office have opened up. Such an investigation will deepen our appreciation of what the head of the church expects from his elder office bearers today.

We saw that the key responsibilities of the Old Testament elders revolved around providing the necessary leadership for the Lord's nation (chapter 4) and judging the people in a God-pleasing way (chapter 5). In the next two chapters, these tasks will be considered within the context of the New Testament church. When the duties of giving leadership and judging or disciplining are properly executed, elders are a powerful force for the preservation and nurture of life with God within his covenant community.

It is good to remind ourselves at the outset that just as in the Old Testament, so also in the New Testament, the work of the elders took place within the context of the family. Whereas in ancient Israel the family was constituted of actual blood lineage, after the outpouring of the Holy Spirit on the day of Pentecost, it is the community of believers that forms the household of God (Eph. 2:19; 1 Tim. 3:15; 1 Peter 4:17). This means that the church is the family of the heavenly Father whose members are brothers and sisters of each other (2 Cor. 6:18; Gal. 3:26; 1 John 3:1–2). Present-day elders function within this familial context, just as

their ancient counterparts did. As we shall see, one obvious implication is that elders are to execute their duties in a loving and
serving way, as can be expected of those having jurisdiction in
a familial setting (1 Tim. 3:2–7). Furthermore, authority in the
family is not unlimited, but is clearly circumscribed since the
head of the church is Christ (Eph. 4:15; 5:23; Col. 2:19) to whom
the elders are responsible for the execution of their multifaceted
task (1 Peter 5:2, 4; Titus 1:7).

In regard to the elders' task of ruling and giving leadership,
we will consider:

- Loving leadership
- Stewards of God's house
- Entrusted with the gospel
- Summary: leading, gathering, and nurturing the flock

Loving Leadership

In order to be an elder or overseer one must be able to
manage (NIV) or rule (KJV) his own family (1 Tim. 3:4). The
verb that is translated as "manage" or "rule" (*proistēmi*) has the
ideas of both leading and caring. The context of the usage of
this verb in 1 Timothy 3 bears this out. The apostle writes that
a bishop (or elder) "must be one who manages [*proistēmi*] his
own household well, keeping his children under control with all
dignity (but if a man does not know how to manage [*proistēmi*]
his own household, how will he take care of the church of God?)"
(1 Tim. 3:4–5 NASB).

A basic requirement for taking care of the household of God,
the congregation, is the ability to manage or rule one's own household and children. This truth underlines that office bearers are
essentially dealing with family members, as fathers deal with their
children. This duty should be done in a caring manner.

The connection between ruling and caring is also illustrated
when the apostle Paul writes the Thessalonians and speaks of

"those who are over you [*proistēmi*] in the Lord and who admonish you" (1 Thess. 5:12). The reference is probably to elders, and again the emphasis is not on their superior rank or authority as such, but on their concern for the congregation as evidenced in the admonishing they do. The elders' authority is not to exercise power for its own sake, but to enable the office bearers to act on behalf of Christ for the well-being of the congregation. The same basic meaning of caring leadership and authority on the part of the elders is found in 1 Timothy 5:17: "Let the elders who rule [*proistēmi*] well be considered worthy of double honor" (ESV).

We now return to 1 Timothy 3:4 where we see that the loving leadership expected of an overseer or elder entails his "keeping his children under control with all dignity" (NASB). This leadership requirement has two basic parts. First, his children are to be obedient and submissive, and second, he should elicit such obedience in a dignified manner.

Since the second point can be dealt with more briefly, we will consider it first. The elder's task of "keeping his children under control with all dignity" (NASB) can also be rendered "see that his children obey him with all dignity" (1 Tim. 3:4).[1] The phrase "with all dignity" can technically refer either to the way the father induces the obedience of his children, or to the way the children obey. If a choice has to be made, the phrase is probably best taken to refer to the leadership qualities of the father that are necessary for the eldership. This requirement of his leadership then complements other prerequisites mentioned immediately prior to the passage in question, such as being temperate, self-controlled, respectable, not given to drunkenness, not violent but gentle, and not quarrelsome (1 Tim. 3:2–3). However, perhaps the ambiguity of reference in the passage is intentional. After all, a dignified and serious submission of the children to the father reflects on the father's capable handling of his solemn responsibilities to his children.

This observation brings us to the first requirement of loving leadership noted above, namely that an elder's children are

1. Cf. the NIV's rendering that the elder "see that his children obey him with proper respect."

141

to be obedient and submissive. Literally it says: "having children in submission" (or "obedience"). What does this submission entail? Besides what is generally expected of children, it may have included accepting the leadership of the father also with respect to his faith in Christ. This point is explicitly made when Paul instructs Titus that an elder must be someone "whose children believe and are not open to the charge of being wild and disobedient" (Titus 1:6). In the context of the early Christian church, it would have been a tremendous testimony to the father's wise and loving leadership if not only he, but also the children who were still under his authority in the home, left paganism to believe in Christ as their Savior. This would have been evidence of his being able to lead the church (1 Tim. 3:5).[2]

In applying this guideline to the choosing of elders today, one needs to realize that the children referred to are living at home under the authority of their father. The apostle suggests that a father who qualifies for being an elder should be able to instruct such a child in the Christian faith and motivate him or her to live accordingly and not in wild and worldly ways. Such unruly behavior cannot be tolerated. Does all this mean that one cannot be an elder if one of his children has strayed away from the Lord? It depends. Various factors need to be weighed, such as: Has the father been diligent in instructing the child in the ways of the Lord? Furthermore, at a certain point a child becomes an adult and is solely accountable for his or her actions. Then such a person is no longer a minor for whom the father takes responsibility. Churches stemming from the sixteenth-century Reformation, therefore, have a long tradition of not disqualifying someone from the office of elder if the disobedience of his children is not his fault.[3]

2. Another possible translation of Titus 1:6 is that the elder must be one "having faithful children not accused of dissipation or insubordination" (NKJV). However, with this rendering it is also clear that being accused of wild living and unruly behavior identifies one as being not only disobedient but also of having an unbelieving attitude and conduct.
3. The Regional Synod of Amsterdam in 1601 (*Acta*, Art. 28) decided that when children are disobedient and the parents are not at fault, then the father is not disqualified for the office of elder. See J. Reitsma and S. D. van Veen, eds., *Acta der provinciale en particuliere synoden gehouden in de noordelijke Nederlanden gedurende de jaren 1572–1620*,

Stewards of God's House

Another expression that highlights an important aspect of the ruling function of elders is their being called "God's stewards." That is how the apostle Paul refers to the elder or overseer when he writes Titus (Titus 1:7 ESV). A steward (*oikonomos*) was one who managed a household (*oikos*) in antiquity. Such a steward could be chosen from among the slaves, and the care of the fellow slaves would be his responsibility. If he showed himself to be faithful, he could be entrusted with the entire estate of the master (Matt. 24:45–47; Luke 12:42–44).

When the apostle uses the metaphor of steward for elders, the first and obvious meaning is that elders are to be managers of the house or family of God, the congregation (1 Tim. 3:4, 5, 15). The immediate context of the apostle's speaking of "God's steward" in Titus 1:7 also brings this out. The qualifications for the elder mentioned both in Titus 1 and in 1 Timothy 3 circle around the family. "An elder must be blameless, the husband of but one wife, a man whose children believe and are not open to the charge of being wild and disobedient" (Titus 1:6). The apostle elaborates by explaining: "For an overseer, as God's steward, must be above reproach. He must not be arrogant or quick-tempered or a drunkard or violent or greedy for gain, but hospitable, a lover of good, self-controlled, upright, holy, and disciplined" (vv. 7–8 ESV).

One could paraphrase these apostolic guidelines to Titus by saying that an elder must be a trustworthy family man who knows how to manage and provide for those in his care and over whom he has responsibility. He must be faithful to his wife and not cheat on her by having extramarital relationships ("the husband of but one wife").[4] His family must be Christian and well-behaved. His ability to

---

8 vols. (Groningen: Wolters, 1892–99), 1:304. Prof. F. L. Rutgers in his famous ecclesiastical advices gave counsel along this line by saying that the father whose child "had to get married" could remain an elder on the assumption that he was not co-responsible for this situation; F. L. Rutgers, *Kerkelijke adviezen*, 2 vols. (Kampen: Kok, 1921–22), 1:202. More recently and in the same vein, see Lawrence R. Eyres, *The Elders of the Church* (Phillipsburg, NJ: Presbyterian and Reformed, 1975), 35–36.

4. Similarly 1 Tim. 3:2. The qualification "husband of but one wife" does not mean that he may not have had a previous marriage (1 Tim. 4:3–4; 5:14). See further George W. Knight,

discipline his family is a reflection of how well he can take responsibility in the family of the church (1 Tim. 3:4–5). In this way he shows himself to be above reproach as God's steward, not arrogant, one who has a grip on his temper, disciplined, not out for the last dollar, and hospitable (see also 1 Tim. 3:3, 8). With these qualifications, a good family man could serve in the office of overseer to manage and direct the affairs of the family of God so that everything be done in an appropriate and orderly way (1 Cor. 14:40).

However, as the instructions to Titus make clear, there is a second, larger aspect of what it means to be a steward. The apostle continues by saying, "He must hold firmly to the trustworthy message as it has been taught, so that he can encourage others by sound doctrine and refute those who oppose it" (Titus 1:9). It is clear that God's steward also has responsibilities with respect to the gospel.

Entrusted with the Gospel

In antiquity, besides being in charge of his master's house, a faithful steward could, as noted above, even end up taking care of the entire estate of his master. All the wealth of his lord would be in his safekeeping. In the case of elders, the Lord Jesus has also entrusted to them as his stewards riches of great value. This most precious treasure is the gospel, which is apparent from the metaphorical use of the term "steward" elsewhere. Paul speaks of himself and Apollos as "servants of Christ and stewards of the mysteries of God" (1 Cor. 4:1 ESV). The mysteries of God are those things that are not found by human wisdom and understanding, but are revealed by God. Such is the gospel. No mind could have conceived it, but God revealed it and entrusted it to his earthly stewards (Matt. 13:11–12, 52; Eph. 3:4–6).

The fact that the ruling elders are entrusted with the gospel as stewards of God is in keeping with the Old Testament position

---

The Pastoral Epistles, New International Greek Testament Commentary (Grand Rapids: Eerdmans, 1992), 157–59.

of elders. However, this responsibility of the ruling elders is not always clearly understood.

Elders and the Preaching of the Gospel

As we saw in chapter 4, the Old Testament elders had distinct responsibilities with respect to bringing the Word of God to Israel. For example, every seven years at the Feast of Tabernacles both the priests and the elders had to read the law to the assembled people (Deut. 31:9–12). Not surprisingly, officials, probably chosen from elders, were included in the delegation sent by King Jehoshaphat to teach the people the law of God (2 Chron. 17:7–9).

Also in the Christian church, the ruling elders have been entrusted with the gospel and, as we will see a little later, have the duty to pass on these riches. The ruling elders' having responsibility for the Word of God has considerable implications for their office, and for their relationship with the teaching elder or pastor. While pastors are expected to proclaim the gospel from the pulpit each Sunday anew, the elders as good stewards of the same gospel have duties in regard to this proclamation as well.

First, they have the responsibility to safeguard the purity of the preaching and oppose false teachings. Titus is told that the elder or overseer

> must hold firmly to the trustworthy message as it has been taught, so that he can encourage others by sound doctrine and refute those who oppose it. For there are many rebellious people, mere talkers and deceivers, especially those of the circumcision group. They must be silenced, because they are ruining whole households by teaching things they ought not to teach—and that for the sake of dishonest gain. (Titus 1:9–11)

The elders have to be on the lookout for those who would distort the truth, even within the congregation. As the apostle Paul warned the Ephesian elders: "savage wolves will come in among you and will not spare the flock. Even from your own number men will arise and distort the truth in order to draw away disciples after them. So be on your guard!" (Acts 20:29–31).

In light of these passages we see that elders, who are to hold firmly to the message they have been taught, need to have a competent grasp of the gospel so that they can actually answer those who oppose it without being quarrelsome (1 Tim. 3:3) or entering into senseless controversies (1 Tim. 1:3–4; 6:4–5). A good knowledge of the Word is absolutely essential (1 Cor. 4:2); elders need to know and understand truths of the gospel. One can think in this context of the important role the elders played in the meeting held in Jerusalem to decide whether circumcision was necessary in order for people to be saved (Acts 15:1–2, 6). Far-reaching decisions were made that profoundly affected the future of the church (Acts 15:22–30).

Today also, those who are ruling elders must be equipped to be good stewards of the gospel treasure entrusted to them and be able, if necessary, to correct and admonish a minister of the gospel should he err in a point of doctrine. One must never forget that ruling elders and teaching elders or ministers have an elder office and therefore hold much in common.[5] They are colleagues together for the cause of the message of salvation. The whole idea of biblical experts who lord over the ruling elders is unbiblical and ignores the responsibility of the ruling elders.[6] Of course, being stewards of the gospel does imply that elders must love and study the Word and become familiar with its riches. Only then can they be good stewards and help the teaching elders with their counsel and ensure that the Word rather than human opinion is proclaimed from the pulpit. A superficial acquaintance with Scripture is not enough.

Second, besides safeguarding the purity of the preaching, the ruling elders have the duty to ensure that the preaching is indeed the passing on of the Word. This responsibility entails two parts. The Word must be preached in its fullness. Christ must

---

5. On this see chapter 6, under "The Underlying Unity in the Elder Offices."

6. On the danger of a church being run only by a minister and the necessity of ruling elders, see Samuel Miller, *The Ruling Elder* (Dallas: Presbyterian Heritage, 1987 [1832]), 175–91.

always be the focal point, and the whole counsel of God must be proclaimed. Preaching is the glad news of Jesus Christ. It is the administration of reconciliation (2 Cor. 5:18–21) and the power of God for salvation (Rom. 1:16). All this is at the heart of biblical preaching and must form the kernel of every sermon. Then the earnest proclamation of warning and repentance will also not be missing (Heb. 12:28–29). Furthermore, the Word must be communicated effectively so that it is indeed the Word of God that reaches the congregation and hits home (Heb. 4:12). Often elders are better judges than ministers in determining whether the Word gets through and impacts the lives of God's people. They can assist the minister by informing him how the message comes across and suggest modifications, be it in his use of language or other communication skills, or in the choice of texts. The selection of a text is important and needs to edify the congregation. The elders who know the congregation well can help the minister answer the question as to what text would be especially useful for the congregation to hear a sermon on at a particular time.[7]

The elders' relationship with the minister, however, goes beyond having supervision over the preaching of the gospel. As the counsel of the elders was often of critical importance in the Old Testament and could prevent calamity (Ezek. 7:26), so also today the wise counsel and advice of elders can be a tremendous help to the pastor as he shepherds the flock. With their considered and well-thought-out recommendations, the elders can assist the pastor in his work. The reverse is also true. The office of the teaching elder must likewise be ready to serve the ruling elder with good counsel and advice. Both offices are to work together for building up the congregation (1 Cor. 3:9). They share each other's joys and sorrows as they minister to the flock. But they also share the promises. Work done for the Lord is not in vain (1 Cor. 15:58).

7. See, e.g., A. N. Hendriks, "The Elder and the Preaching," *Diakonia* 4 (1991): 91–97; William Shishko, "How to Assess a Sermon: A Checklist for Ruling Elders," *Ordained Servant* 12 (2003): 43–44; and Gerard Berghoef and Lester De Koster, *The Elders Handbook: A Practical Guide for Church Leaders* (Grand Rapids: Christian's Library Press, 1979), 153–64.

Elders Administering the Word

Being a steward of the riches of the gospel, however, includes more than having oversight of the preaching and assisting the pastor. Ruling elders must also administer the Word within the framework of their office as elder.[8] This duty implies that they will be able to comfort and exhort from the Word as they administer the gospel to the flock entrusted to their oversight. It is noteworthy how the apostle Paul tells Titus that the elder "must hold firmly to the trustworthy message as it has been taught, *so that* he can encourage others by sound doctrine" (Titus 1:9). This doctrine impacts positively on life. "For everything that was written in the past was written to teach us, so that through endurance and the encouragement of the Scriptures we might have hope" (Rom. 15:4). It is the responsibility of elders to pass on the consolation that is found in the gospel. It is also a great privilege. In this way elders pass on the treasures of the gospel to those who suffer from sickness, are lonely, are in mourning, or experience whatever ills befall them in this fallen world. But only knowledgeable stewards will know how to apply the riches of the gospel so that the desired effect is achieved, namely, that there be hope (Col. 2:2).

Now it is noteworthy that the Greek term used of the duty of elders to encourage (*parakaleō*; Titus 1:9) with the riches of the gospel also suggests the task of teaching. As a matter of fact the ESV renders the passage in question (Titus 1:9): the overseer or elder "must hold firm to the trustworthy word as taught, so that he may be able to give instruction (*parakaleō*) in sound doctrine." The Greek word suggests "instruction with a practical bent, something more than simply detailing facts and doctrines, and it carries an element of persuasion and even command."[9] This task of the elder presupposes that he

8. We saw in chapter 6, under "Different Offices," that there are two separate offices: the ruling elder and the teaching elder. The former does not have the task of publicly proclaiming the gospel, a task that the teaching elder does have.

9. I. Howard Marshall, *A Critical and Exegetical Commentary on the Pastoral Epistles*, in collaboration with Philip H. Towner, International Critical Commentary (Edinburgh: T&T Clark, 1999), 167.

knows the sound doctrine so well that he can readily apply it to the lives of those whom he counsels and helps. Teaching the doctrine and message of salvation does not imply abstract theorizing, but passing on the riches of salvation in Christ— riches that impact the lives of believers who are challenged by the fallenness of this world and who struggle with the real consequences of its brokenness. Thus for an elder to be "able to teach" (1 Tim. 3:2) implies not only having knowledge of the Word of God, but also being able to facilitate the impact of the gospel on the lives of those who are in his care. In this way elders in the church, just like their Old Testament counter-parts, have the responsibility to imprint, as it were, the gospel and its demands on the hearts and lives of God's people and to teach them in the deepest sense of the word. They may do so as authority figures, yes, but as loving fathers deal with their own children, encouraging, comforting, and urging them to live lives worthy of God (1 Thess. 2:11–12).

Now in a way all the members of the church of course have the responsibility of so teaching the gospel and its implications to each other. Indeed, the author of Hebrews, frustrated by the lack of understanding he met, scolded his hearers that they were slow to learn: "by this time you ought to be teachers" (Heb. 5:12). This admonition indicates that ideally everyone in the congregation should be able to teach and pass on the Word to others. Peter also urged the believer to "use whatever gift he has received to serve others, faithfully administering God's grace in its various forms. If anyone speaks, he should do it as one speaking the very words of God" (1 Peter 4:10–11). In a similar vein the apostle Paul exhorted: "Let the word of Christ dwell in you richly as you teach and admonish one another with all wisdom" (Col. 3:16). More specifically, older women were told to teach what is good to the younger ones so they would live according to the Word of God (Titus 2:3–5). However, while it is true that all believers have the responsi-bility to teach the Word and to encourage each other in the faith, elders have a special responsibility in this regard and must set the example for others. They are to be the leaders in this respect.

The responsibility of being entrusted with the gospel and the task of passing it on in a meaningful way is immense for it has tremendous consequences. Did the Lord not warn his people of old that "My people are destroyed from lack of knowledge" (Hos. 4:6)? Although the context of this particular warning is the failure of the priests to do their sacred calling of teaching, the fact remains that knowing the Lord is central to the well-being of God's people, whether then or now. We must realize that this knowledge of God is not just knowing some facts about God. Rather, it means being in a right covenantal relationship with the living God who has entered one's life with his glorious promises. Knowing God means that one experiences the Lord's faithfulness and love and that one responds to him with loving obedience in holy awe of his greatness and majesty (see Jer. 31:34).

A most powerful way of teaching the gospel message and its implications for knowing God in a life of communion with him is by example. Such is the duty of every office of leadership in the church that is entrusted with the gospel. As the apostle exhorted Timothy, "set an example for the believers in speech, in life, in love, in faith and in purity" (1 Tim. 4:12). The elders are to be a living embodiment of the gospel. For that reason qualifications for the office include such traits as being "above reproach, the husband of but one wife, temperate, self-controlled, respectable, hospitable . . . not given to drunkenness, not violent but gentle, not quarrelsome, not a lover of money" (1 Tim. 3:2–3).

When an office bearer exemplifies and teaches the gospel message and how it impacts life, he works for the salvation of those who listen to him. "Watch your life and doctrine closely. Persevere in them, because if you do, you will save both yourself and your hearers" (1 Tim. 4:16). Elders who lead with the example of a godly life and display the fruits of the Spirit command the respect of others; they are elders and leaders in the Old Testament sense of the word. Then they stand out as those to whom the congregation owes respect and honor.

Summary: Leading, Gathering, and Nurturing the Flock

In chapter 2 we saw that the work of the elder could be described under the image of the shepherd and the flock. When elders are considered as shepherds, several functions come into sharper focus, namely, their task of leading, gathering, and nurturing the flock. We will briefly look at each of these in turn and thereby also summarize some important points made in this chapter. But before we do so, we need to remind ourselves of the relationship of the elders as undershepherds to the Great Shepherd, Jesus Christ (Heb. 13:20).

It is clear that since the Lord Jesus is *the* Shepherd of the flock (John 10:11, 14; 1 Peter 2:25), the elders as servant-shepherds are responsible to him. This is a tremendous and weighty obligation (Ezek. 34:1–10; Heb. 13:17). The direction in which Christ leads determines the course for the elders guiding those in their charge. The manner in which Christ gathers and nurtures the flock must set the tone for the work of the servant-shepherds. Elders must look to Christ in doing their work, for the will of the Good Shepherd must be done. In the face of such a momentous responsibility, elders can, however, take comfort in the fact that their Master will provide for them in the difficult task they face. When Paul and Barnabas appointed elders with prayer and fasting, they entrusted these elders to the Lord and his provision (Acts 14:23). There is a close bond between those charged with the office of elder and their heavenly superior. He not only charges them with their considerable duties, but he also sustains those who labor for him. He provides all that is necessary. Surely, this remains a most encouraging reality for the elder shepherds.

Leading the Flock

Elders are to give strong, positive leadership. That is inherent in their task as ruling elders. To rule is to give leadership, which is what was meant when the apostle Paul wrote Timothy: "Let the elders who rule well be considered worthy of double honor"

151

(1 Tim. 5:17 ESV). At the beginning of this chapter we noted that the verb "rule" (*proistēmi*) in this passage has the idea of a caring leadership. By giving such leadership, elders act as servants of Christ and direct the flock on the way ahead. This is not just the task of the teaching elder or minister of the gospel; it is also the task of the ruling elder. Did the apostle not write: "Let the elders who rule well be considered worthy of double honor, especially those who labor in preaching and teaching" (1 Tim. 5:17 ESV)? Both types of elders are in view. Ruling elders, as well as those who labor in preaching and teaching, are to lead and so in a caring way direct the flock. How they execute their task may differ. Teaching elders have responsibilities in the pulpit that ruling elders do not have. But both are to have the same burden for the congregation, and both are to rule and lead in a caring way according to the dictates of their office.

To give biblical leadership as an elder is to let the sheep hear the voice of the Good Shepherd. The elder's own opinion about the issue at hand is unimportant. What is crucial is that as office bearers, elders speak according to the mind of Christ. After all, elders, whether ruling or teaching, are to be spokesmen for the Great Shepherd of the flock. The sheep recognize the voice of the Good Shepherd and will follow it (John 10:4). Elders must therefore bring the Word of the Great Shepherd to bear on the lives of the congregation so that they can lead them in the rich pastures of God's instruction and comfort. Then the elders' speaking has authority, and they are able to give the flock the direction it needs in all the circumstances of life. Indeed, then the Word of God is a lamp before the feet of the sheep and a light on their path (Ps. 119:105).

It cannot be overestimated, therefore, how important it is for elders, as servants of Jesus Christ, to know the Scriptures. Christ does not demand higher education from his elders, but he does require that they are familiar with his Word so that through their ministry the sheep recognize the voice of their Great Shepherd and benefit from the leadership he gives. There is nothing more devastating for the flock than elders leaving the clear demands of the Word and confusing the flock by imposing on them a direction in which they do not recognize the voice of the Good Shepherd. And so knowledge of Scripture is basic for the task of the servant-shepherd.

Elders must also have a good knowledge of their flock. In order to lead, elders must know their sheep—their capabilities, their weaknesses, and strengths. Elders who are conscious of their task as shepherds will take the time and effort necessary to become acquainted with the circumstances, joys and sorrows, and trials and challenges of each one of those entrusted to them. Then they will be there when needed, and they will be able to give the necessary direction and leadership through the Word. As appropriate, they will be able to encourage, instruct, correct, and exhort. As shepherds have the well-being of all their sheep constantly in their heart and mind, so elders have a burden for the flock. Also in their lifestyle and example of godliness, elders will reinforce the message of the Word as they direct the sheep in their charge according to the wishes of the Good Shepherd.

Gathering the Sheep

The Good Shepherd gathers his sheep together. He calls them by name and leads them. They listen to his voice and follow him (John 10:3–4). Shepherds pay extra attention to the sheep that have trouble keeping up, or are not well, or are in danger of straying. They coax them on or carry them as necessary. The flock must stay together. Shepherds gather and keep the sheep together. Elders must do likewise.

How are elders to do that? What is the bottom line? What binds the flock together? In simplest terms, it is the communal heeding of the voice of the Good Shepherd that keeps the flock together. More specifically, the elder shepherds must always be conscious of the fact that they are to be instruments of the Chief Shepherd in gathering the flock through his Word. Then the Spirit working through the Word binds the people of God together in the unity of the true faith.

153

Like the apostle Paul, elders, therefore, have the mandate to present the Word of God, the voice of the Good Shepherd, in its fullness (Col. 1:25). Each will do that according to the expectations of his office, whether the teaching or ruling elder. But the essential thing remains that elders are to minister the Word and be faithful to the Word in leading the flock. Only the Spirit working through the Word can gather and bind a congregation together. It is the Spirit who works regeneration and new life by the word of Christ (Rom. 10:17), the gospel, which is "the power of God for salvation" (Rom. 1:16 ESV), the sword that penetrates "even to dividing soul and spirit, joints and marrow; it judges the thoughts and attitudes of the heart" (Heb. 4:12). It is this Word that needs to be administered to the confused, the straying, and the rebellious so that they connect with or rejoin the flock and are gathered together with the others.

The central significance of the Word in binding a congregation together is obvious from the exhortation of the apostle Paul to the Colossians: "Let the word of Christ dwell in you richly as you teach and admonish one another with all wisdom, and as you sing psalms, hymns and spiritual songs with gratitude in your hearts to God" (Col. 3:16). This exhortation is given in the context of bearing with each other, forgiving each other, and being at peace together (Col. 3:12–15). Especially elders as servant-shepherds must be very conscious of the fact that it is in the communal submission to the Word of the Great Shepherd that the unity of the faith is found.

The elders' task of gathering and binding the flock together in the unity of the faith with the Word of God takes much wisdom, patience, and love. The wayward are to be called back with firmness and love (2 Cor. 2:5–8; Matt. 18:12). Heresy is not to be tolerated (1 Tim. 3:15; Rev. 2:14–16), but at the same time patience must be shown in disputable matters (Rom. 14:1–7). Furthermore, elders are not to be contentious and waste their energy on nonissues that divert them from the goal of the unity of the flock (1 Tim. 1:3–5; 2 Tim. 2:23–26). Elders are not to confuse and scatter, but to speak the Word clearly and gather together. The apostolic exhortation also applies to the work of the elders: "Make every effort to keep the unity of the Spirit through the bond of peace. There is one body and one Spirit—just as you were called to one hope when you were called—one Lord, one faith, one baptism; one God and Father of all, who is over all and through all and in all" (Eph. 4:3–6). The goal is "that the body of Christ may be built up until we all reach unity in the faith and in the knowledge of the Son of God and become mature, attaining to the whole measure of the fullness of Christ" (Eph. 4:12–13).

Blessed is the congregation that has wise elders. By the example of their lives and by their exhortation and encouragment in conformity with the Word of the Good Shepherd, they bind a congregation together, thus making more clear the unity that Christ has given the flock by the Spirit who dwells in them. Such a congregation fellowships in the Spirit and experiences the bond that binds them together in Christ. Such a congregation is nurtured and sustained by the Word.

Nurturing the People of God

Christ commanded Peter: "Feed my lambs. . . . Take care of my sheep. . . . Feed my sheep" (John 21:15–17). In this way Christ restored Peter as his disciple after Peter's triple denial of his Savior (John 18:17, 25, 27). At the same time, this threefold injunction underlined how important it is that Christ's flock be nurtured by all those entrusted with its care. Twice the Savior specifically demanded that the flock be fed and once that the sheep be cared for. The Great Shepherd wants his servant-shepherds to give the nurturing task a top priority. They are, after all, *his* sheep (note "my sheep"). Ultimately, it is not only to Peter that this exhortation is directed, but to all those who are to shepherd the flock. For that reason, Peter essentially passed on the exhortation he received to others when he later urged the elders: "Be shepherds of God's flock that is under your care" (1 Peter 5:2). Peter used the more general term that Christ used in his case. And clearly, a central task of shepherding is feeding the flock.

155

But what does this nurturing task entail and what is its purpose? What does one feed the flock of Christ? To begin with the last question, the daily food and drink of the flock is to be the Word of God. That is what makes the lambs, who are so vulnerable, stronger in the faith so that they grow and become more mature. Now teaching elders have a special task in this regard, especially in the weekly proclamation of the Word on the Lord's Day. But ruling elders are also shepherds who need to feed the flock with the Word of God.

The Word is to be *the* food and drink of the flock. "Man does not live on bread alone but on every word that comes from the mouth of the LORD" (Deut. 8:3; Matt. 4:4). God graphically illustrated this truth when he let his people Israel hunger in the wilderness after being led out of Egypt. In this way, he clearly exposed their inability to sustain themselves. Once that was clear, the Lord fed his people for forty years in the desert with manna that daily came down from heaven (Deut. 8:2–3). In this wilderness lesson, the Lord God also wanted to make clear that human beings have been created in such a way that it is impossible for them to truly live a full life as God intended on the basis of material bread alone. Humans are more than body and flesh. They need the Word of life from the mouth of God. After all, was man not created to live in communion with God and to find therein his highest joy? Only that which brings one closer to God is really nurture and food in the biblical sense of the word. And therefore, ultimately, the Savior is the bread of life who gives the life that never ends. Whoever comes to him will never go hungry, and whoever believes in him will never be thirsty (John 6:26–35).

The task of elders in nurturing the flock is, therefore, to point to Christ. Their office includes directing the hungry and the thirsty souls to the living God from whom their strength and sustenance are to come. As God said through Isaiah: "Listen, listen to me, and eat what is good, and your soul will delight in the richest of fare. Give ear and come to me; hear me, that your soul may live" (Isa. 55:2–3). Again, it is the Savior who quenches all thirst and who through the Spirit gives the life that never ends (John

4:14; 7:37–39; 1 Cor. 10:3–4). Through the mouth of faith, God's people are to partake of Christ and so receive the life everlasting (John 6:47–58).

In nurturing the flock, shepherds must also know the condition of their sheep. Not all will be at the same stage of development. There are the newborn lambs that are just starting to learn to eat, and there are the older sheep. Some are more mature than others. Elders as good shepherds must know what food to give those in their care so that true nourishment will be given and there will be growth in Christ. The apostle Paul addressed the "mere infants in Christ" with these words: "I gave you milk, not solid food, for you were not yet ready for it" (1 Cor. 3:1–2). Milk is the basic elementary doctrine of salvation. But as one matures in the faith, more is needed (Heb. 5:12–14), and elders must stimulate an appetite for this. A taste for the Word of God and its delights needs to be nurtured. As Peter exhorted: "Like newborn babies, crave pure spiritual milk, so that by it you may grow up in your salvation, now that you have tasted that the Lord is good" (1 Peter 2:2–3).

As shepherds, elders have a nurturing responsibility. When appetite for the Word of God lags and when knowledge of the living God dims, then God's people are destroyed. Death and not life is the result. As God warned through the prophet Hosea: "My people are destroyed from lack of knowledge" (Hos. 4:6). It is therefore necessary that elders not only know the Bible and be able to guide the sheep in reading it meaningfully, but they should also be aware of helps and aids that can promote a true knowledge of God. In every possible way they should encourage the sheep entrusted to them to have a growing appetite for the Word of life, so that the eagerness with which Jeremiah awaited the Word of God may be theirs as well. "When your words came, I ate them; they were my joy and my heart's delight, for I bear your name, O LORD God Almighty" (Jer. 15:16).

As hunger for the Word is stimulated, the sheep will not eat the junk food of the world with which the spirits of the day seek to satisfy the human appetite. Rather, they will go to the true food to be found in Christ and receive nurture from "the hidden manna" (Rev. 2:17). It is hidden, for the world has not received it. The stronger the longing for the good food of the Chief Shepherd, the greater will be the aversion to the abundant "food" that leads to spiritual death. Indeed, the sheep of the Good Shepherd will then rejoice with the psalmist: "How sweet are your words to my taste, sweeter than honey to my mouth!" (Ps. 119:103).

This rejoicing in the delightful and rich nurture of the Word of God provides a foretaste of the perfect joy to come when "the Lamb at the center of the throne will be their shepherd; he will lead them to springs of living water. And God will wipe away every tear from their eyes" (Rev. 7:17). Life with Christ in perfection! This is also expressed in the image of being given "the right to eat from the tree of life, which is in the paradise of God" (Rev. 2:7). Elders have the privilege of feeding the flock with the Word of Christ so that the yearning grows for fullness of life with him.

The Word of God is central in the task of the elder shepherds in leading, gathering, and nurturing the flock. The Word of the Good Shepherd makes their task possible. That Word must therefore fill the hearts and minds of the servant-shepherds. They must know it intimately and thoroughly. There is no substitute for the voice of the Chief Shepherd of the flock.

Disciplining for Life

THE NEW TESTAMENT ELDERS' involvement in church discipline brings to mind the responsibility of judging that the elders had in ancient Israel. Church discipline is often misunderstood and put in a negative light. Yet it is precisely this task which highlights the tremendous blessing of the eldership for the well-being of the congregation and the promotion and nurturing of life in the Spirit of Christ. We will cover the following topics.

- The elders' self-watch
- The elders' watching the flock
- The process of church discipline
- The exercise of church discipline
- Summary: shepherding the flock

As we deal with disciplining for life, we will build on and, as necessary, elaborate on the Old Testament principles of judging as related in chapter 5.

The Elders' Self-Watch

It is noteworthy that when the apostle exhorted the Ephesian elders to keep watch over the flock entrusted to them, he first urged: "Keep watch over yourselves" (Acts 20:28).[1] The very first object of their judging and disciplining is to be their own lives. Unless elders can apply the Word of correction and admonition to themselves, how will they ever be able to do so to others? Indeed, elders cannot watch over others if they cannot first watch over their own lives. The ethical qualifications for this office are therefore high. Elders must be above reproach, holy, blameless, temperate, self-controlled, respectable, hospitable, not given to drunkenness, not violent but gentle, not quarrelsome, and not lovers of money. They must also have a good reputation with outsiders (1 Tim. 3:1–7; Titus 1:6–9). These requirements for the office necessitate the apostle's admonition: "Keep watch over yourselves" (Acts 20:28).

The verb used in the apostle's exhortation to self-watch underscores that one must be in a constant state of alert.[2] This indicates the vigilance with which elders should live their lives. A spiritual warfare is being waged (Eph. 6:12) and elders need to be consciously aware of this. Their lives and lifestyles must be absolutely exemplary so that there is no reason for the eldership to be discredited (2 Cor. 6:3). Even more than those who do not hold a special office in the church, they must be careful not to give any cause for stumbling by members of the congregation (Rom. 14:13; 1 Cor. 8:9). After all, if Satan is able to attack the credibility of office bearers, then their biblical admonitions will fall on deaf ears, and the congregation will suffer as a result.

The admonition to "keep watch over yourselves" (Acts 20:28) indicates something else as well. It underlines that elders are just as prone to the sins of the world as anyone else and need to be on the alert (Rom. 3:23; 1 John 1:8). They have not yet reached the state of perfection (Phil. 3:12). A basic recognition of this fact will do at least two things.

1. A similar admonition was directed to Timothy: "Watch your life and doctrine closely. Persevere in them, because if you do, you will save both yourself and your hearers" (1 Tim. 4:16).
2. The verb, *prosechō*, is in the present imperative, here indicating ongoing action.

First, elders will do everything within their power to make sure that their lives are focused on Christ (Heb. 12:2). Peter's exhortation to believers surely counts all the more for office bearers: "Be on your guard so that you may not be carried away by the error of lawless men and fall from your secure position. But grow in the grace and knowledge of our Lord and Savior Jesus Christ" (2 Peter 3:17–18). Elders who are aware of their own sinfulness will take all necessary measures to live close to the Lord in a prayerful life of obedience and seek to grow in the Lord by the diligent study of Scripture. Then they will experience the working of the Spirit in their lives and be strong in the Lord (Rom. 1:16; 1 Cor. 1:18).

Second, the realization of their own limitations will make elders sensitive to the struggles of those in their charge. When dealing with the sins of others, they will not look down on them, but empathize with their struggles and stand beside them to assist and encourage them in the ways of the Lord (Titus 1:9; also Gal. 6:1–2; Col. 2:2–3; 1 Thess. 5:11; Heb. 3:13).

The Elders' Watching the Flock

After insisting that the Ephesian elders be on guard for their own souls, the apostle Paul continued by exhorting that elders "keep watch over . . . all the flock of which the Holy Spirit has made you overseers" (Acts 20:28). Keeping watch over *all* the congregation is an awesome task. This responsibility is accentuated by the fact that none other than the Holy Spirit has charged them with this duty. The charge that elders have is of divine origin and therefore is a divine obligation.[3] Elsewhere we read of elders as those who are set over the congregation in the Lord and who admonish, that is, urge the congregation to obey God's ordinances (1 Thess. 5:12). This too is part of their duty of watching out for the well-being of the church.

3. On the divine authorization of the office, see also, e.g., chapter 1, under "A Task Given by God"; chapter 2, under "Shepherds of the Good Shepherd"; chapter 6, under "The Congregation of Christ"; and chapter 7, under "The Elders, the Keys, and the Congregation."

How are elders to handle this responsibility? We need to remember that elders in ancient Israel functioned within the smaller and larger family unit and that the New Testament people of God is the family of God. As noted earlier, elders must exercise loving leadership befitting this family context and act as responsible stewards of God's household.[4] But how specifically are these general guidelines to be implemented? Both the charge to keep watch, and the family context, suggest that elders must be familiar with the lives of those entrusted to their care. So familiar must these be to them that they can admonish and correct in a timely fashion when danger threatens the life of a member of God's household. All this presupposes that elders regularly visit and otherwise keep in touch with those in their care and that a relationship of trust and confidence is maintained. An important instrument for being able to keep watch is the regular visitation of two ruling elders, or a ruling and teaching elder, to the families in their charge.

Family Visitation

The principle of visiting families in their homes to instruct and guide them in the Christian way of life is evident from the example of the apostle Paul who preached and taught not only publicly, but also privately in the homes of congregation members in Ephesus (Acts 20:20). If an apostle considered such private sessions important enough to do while being in Ephesus for about two years, how much more should those entrusted with the oversight of a specific congregation be diligent to visit the homes as necessary?[5] If an apostle could say: "For you know that we

4. See chapter 8, under "Loving Leadership."

5. Calvin understood the apostle's teaching in the homes as indicating the need for shepherds of the flock to visit the homes and care for the individual sheep. See John Calvin, *The Acts of the Apostles*, 2 vols., ed. David W. Torrance and Thomas F. Torrance (Grand Rapids: Eerdmans, 1965–66), 2:175. Similarly, e.g., the American Puritan Cotton Mather (1663–1728) in his *The Rules of a Visit* (1705) as discussed in George W. Harper, "*Manductio ad ministerium:* Cotton Mather as Pastoral Innovator," *Westminster Theological Journal* 54 (1992): 79–97, esp. 85, and more recently, John R. Sittema, *With a Shepherd's Heart: Reclaiming the Pastoral Office of Elder* (Grandville, MI: Reformed Fellowship, 1995), 175. The prevailing current view that Acts 20:20 refers to house congregations meeting

dealt with each of you as a father deals with his own children, encouraging, comforting and urging you to live lives worthy of God" (1 Thess. 2:11–12), then how much more should this be said of elders to whom are given the care and responsibility of specific souls in the congregation? Indeed, the whole task of shepherding entrusted to elders presupposes that they seek out the sheep and tend to their needs (Acts 20:28; Matt. 10:12; Luke 15:4).

The early Christian church initially followed the apostolic example of seeing members in their homes, and this formed a basic element in the normal discipline of the church.[6] Eventually, however, the growing importance of what became the sacrament of penance displaced family visitation as part of the normal means of ministering to the individual members of the congregation. Several factors lie behind this development. The eldership was usurped by a priesthood,[7] and the medieval church basically kept watch over the souls entrusted to them by obligating them to visit a priest and do confession. The sense of security and peace that came from the absolution granted by the priest after the proper confession had been made undoubtedly encouraged the shift to the sacrament of penance.

It was not until the Reformation during the sixteenth century that the important place of the elder was recognized again and the practice of family visitation was revived. While Luther wanted to retain a purified form of penance (and ended up not giving the office of elder its full due), Calvin broke radically with the practice of penance and restored the eldership to its rightful place in the shepherding of the congregation. For how can the

---

together (cf. Acts 2:46; Rom. 16:5) does not exclude the obvious literal meaning of "homes" (as, e.g., in Acts 8:3) and visiting those who reside in them.

6. This can be deduced, e.g., from Cyprian, *Letters* 68.5, where he speaks of flocks having shepherds, and the *Apostolic Constitutions* (c. A.D. 390) 2.18–19 which strongly exhorts bishops to shepherd the people entrusted to their care so that they do not fall into sin. The bishops are urged to exercise preemptive pastoral care as a shepherd seeks the well-being of his sheep in line with God's expectations in Ezek. 34. For an English translation, see Alexander Roberts and James Donaldson, eds., *The Ante-Nicene Fathers: Translations of the Writings down to A.D. 325*, 10 vols., rev. A. Cleveland Coxe (Grand Rapids: Eerdmans, 1969–73), 5:373–74 and 7:403–4. See on this also P. Biesterveld, *Het Huisbezoek* (Kampen: Bos, 1908), 22–24.

7. See chapter 6, under "Some Consequences of the Distinctions."

elder oversee the flock and apply the key of church discipline, if not through the administration of the Word of the Good Shepherd? This is the gospel of Jesus Christ who forgives the sins of believers who confess them on the basis of his single sacrifice (Rom. 3:25; Heb. 10:14; 1 Peter 2:24; 1 John 1:7; 2:1). This word of forgiveness and reconciliation, this absolution from sin, can be administered in the public worship service, and when visiting the family as well. When elders administer the Word of God in the homes of church members, they can not only administer the forgiveness of sins where such are confessed, but can also exhort the flock according to God's Word. The true believers are then encouraged and comforted for they hear the voice of the Good Shepherd (John 10:3–5) through the undershepherds, the office bearers, who faithfully bring the Word of God to bear on their situation.[8]

In both the Presbyterian and Reformed traditions, the office of elder has the responsibility of visiting the homes of those in their charge. This is a wonderful opportunity for the office bearers to ascertain the spiritual well-being of a particular family in its life-setting and to administer the Word of God. Within the confidential confines of the family circle, the Word can be explained and applied. Burdened consciences can be relieved and find rest in the Lord. In the exercise of Christian discipline elders can testify to the penitent that their sins are truly forgiven and, as necessary, they can admonish from the Word of God to prevent corruption of doctrine or morals. The sick and the sorrowing can be comforted and the ignorant instructed. Issues that have cast a shadow over one's life can be dealt with, and difficulties that

8. For the Word being connected to the key of church discipline, see John Calvin, *Institutes of the Christian Religion* 4.1.22 and 4.2.10, ed. John T. McNeill (Philadelphia: Westminster, 1960), 1035–36, 1051. "For these things—forgiveness of sins, the promise of eternal life, the good news of salvation—cannot be in man's power. Therefore, Christ has testified that in the preaching of the gospel the apostles have no part save that of ministry; that it was he himself who would speak and promise all things through their lips as his instruments. . . . We conclude that the power of the keys is simply the preaching of the gospel, and that with regard to men it is not so much power as ministry. For Christ has not given this power actually to men, but to his Word, of which he has made men ministers"—*Institutes* 4.11.1, p. 1213. On the necessity of family visitation, see *Institutes* 4.12.2, pp. 1230–31.

seem too heavy to carry can be brought to the throne of grace. Through such family visitations, elders can have good oversight of those in their care, work for their progress in love for Christ, and systematically build up the congregation in true faith.

It is clear that the task of watching over the people must be considered holistically. As an elder in ancient Israel would have been very much involved in the fabric of the familial society of which he was an integral part, so the New Testament elder is to be as a father to the flock, approaching his task with a broadly based concern for those in his charge. The members of the congregation should, therefore, gladly welcome elders into their homes. After all, the elders are watching over souls as those who must give account. And therefore, "Let them do this with joy and not with groaning, for that would be of no advantage to you" (Heb. 13:17 ESV).

The practice of regular family visitation puts the initiative for the care of the flock with the office bearers; that is, they seek out those over whom they must watch. They go to their homes where their life is concretely lived, where the family comes together, shares events, and speaks about future plans. In coming to the homes and visiting the families, the elders get to know the people they watch over; and the members of the congregation, young and old, become more familiar with the office bearers. As a result, relationships are built up that will be of great value when joy or sorrow can be shared and difficulties needing pastoral direction arise.

Besides the regular visits to the families, the elders will, of course, also need to pay special visits when they know of problems and challenges that need to be addressed. However, the regular family visitation cannot be missed as this will often be the first opportunity of becoming aware of difficulties that need special attention.

When dealing with the oversight of God's people, it is necessary to remind ourselves that keeping watch is never just the duty of those who have a special office in the church. Seeing to the spiritual well-being of brothers and sisters in the Lord is the responsibility of all members of the church. This point brings us to consider the place of the congregation and the elders in the process of church discipline.

The Process of Church Discipline

The Central Place of the Congregation

The responsibility of watching out for the spiritual well-being of others begins in the families of the church. It starts with training children in the way of the Lord. Such an early education in what the Lord requires of a godly life is absolutely crucial for the health and holiness of the congregation. Both by precept and example, parents must diligently teach their offspring and instruct them in the discipline and nurture of God (Prov. 22:6; Eph. 6:4). By becoming familiar with the Lord's demands as given in his Word, children will be equipped to grow in godly love and commitment. But this training will also make the entire family sensitive to God's requirements for all of life so that they can help and encourage members of the larger family of God to walk in the ways of the Lord.

Church discipline is first of all about applying the Word to the concrete here and now so that members of the congregation can encourage, instruct, and warn each other on the basis of Scripture. If there is a falling into sin, such a sin will be recognized by those who have learned to be sensitive to God's holy will for their lives, and they will be able to admonish lovingly to draw the erring back to the Lord (Eph. 4:29–32; Col. 3:12–14). This grassroots activity is very important. Except for public sins known to the entire congregation,[9] the process of warning and keeping the people of God holy should begin with members of the flock seeking to help each other walk in the ways of the Lord. Everyone in the congregation needs this mutual discipline. It is the congregation that is addressed by exhortations such as: "Encourage one

9. For the distinction between public and private sins, see Calvin, *Institutes* 4.12.3, 6, pp. 1231, 1234.

another and build each other up, just as in fact you are doing. . . . warn those who are idle, encourage the timid, help the weak, be patient with everyone" (1 Thess. 5:11, 14), or "See to it that no one misses the grace of God and that no bitter root grows up to cause trouble and defile many" (Heb. 12:15), and "Brothers, if someone is caught in a sin, you who are spiritual should restore him gently. But watch yourself, or you also may be tempted. Carry each other's burdens, and in this way you will fulfill the law of Christ" (Gal. 6:1–2). The related demand to be holy and separate from the world of sin also impacts the congregation's ministry to each other (2 Cor. 6:14–17; 2 Tim. 3:1–5).

This first responsibility of the congregation for each other in combating sin and later, if necessary, involving the elders of the church is in accordance with the principles the Lord Jesus laid down in Matthew 18. There we read:

> If your brother sins against you, go and show him his fault, just between the two of you. If he listens to you, you have won your brother over. But if he will not listen, take one or two others along, so that "every matter may be established by the testimony of two or three witnesses." If he refuses to listen to them, tell it to the church; and if he refuses to listen even to the church, treat him as you would a pagan or a tax collector. I tell you the truth, whatever you bind on earth will be bound in heaven, and whatever you loose on earth will be loosed in heaven. (Matt. 18:15–18)

With these words, the Lord Jesus indicated the steps to be followed for dealing with sin in the congregation.

With respect to these guidelines, we should note that the context is Christ's insistence that love be shown to the little ones, the children, so that they do not stumble. Woe to those who cause them to sin (Matt. 18:1–9). This point is further illustrated by the parable of the good shepherd who seeks out the one lost sheep because he does not want any of his flock to perish (Matt. 18:10–14). Within this context of mutual love, the Lord now gives direction for how this love for each other can be realized. "If your brother sins against you, go and show him his fault, just between the two of you. If he listens to you, you have won your brother over" (Matt. 18:15).

This instruction of the Lord Jesus places the primary responsibility for what we call church discipline with the members of the congregation. It shows something of the radicalness of the love with which church members should love each other. Even if one is not the cause of the offense or sin but rather has been sinned against, even then he or she is to seek out the sinner and serve him for his salvation. This must be done privately. Human nature being what it is, it is easier to show remorse for sin in a confidential setting than in a public one. In other words, the one giving offense must be confronted with his sin in such a way that his repentance and salvation are sought. This is the way of love. Such a manner of dealing presupposes that the one who has been offended is also aware of his own shortcomings (Matt. 18:8–9; 7:1–5) and therefore seeks to remove the offense without unnecessarily drawing the attention of others to it. As with elders (Acts 20:28), self-examination and self-watch must precede the mutual discipline, yes, and even accompany it. As the apostle Paul put it: "Brothers, if someone is caught in a sin, you who are spiritual should restore him gently. But watch yourself, or you also may be tempted" (Gal. 6:1; 1 Cor. 10:12). A happy outcome is that "If he listens to you, you have won your brother over" (Matt. 18:15). Then the mutual discipline has achieved its purpose, and there is no need to involve the elders. Members of the congregation have resolved the matter.

This important place of the congregation in the Christian discipline of the church is consistent with God's instruction to his people in Old Testament times. Had Israel not promised in the presence of God at Sinai to do God's covenant will and to be a kingdom of priests and a holy nation (Ex. 19:5–8; 24:3–8)? The command of love is stated negatively in Leviticus 19:17: "Do not hate your brother in your heart. Rebuke your neighbor frankly so you will not share in his guilt." More positively we read: "The fruit of the righteous is a tree of life, and he who wins souls is wise" (Prov. 11:30).[10] How much more can be expected of the New Testament congregation, which is also "a royal priesthood, a holy nation, a people belonging to God" (1 Peter 2:9), in whom the word of Christ is to dwell richly as members teach and admonish each other with all wisdom in Christ (Col. 3:16; cf. Rom. 15:14)! Church discipline can function properly only within a caring and faithful congregation.

The Lord Jesus continued in Matthew 18 by saying that if the one giving offense "will not listen, take one or two others along, so that 'every matter may be established by the testimony of two or three witnesses.' If he refuses to listen to them, tell it to the church" (Matt. 18:16–17). The one or two who accompany the original brother will first need to ascertain or become convinced that the alleged sin actually happened and that repentance is necessary. Only then will it be possible for them to join in trying to convince the one causing offense of his sin and of the need for repentance. Through this process, those drawn into this case by the offended one become witnesses of whether the offender is willing to be reconciled or not.

Although two or three are now involved, yet at this point, a resolution to the problem is still being worked on privately. This issue is still in the hands of the individual who first confronted the guilty one with his sin. Before the matter goes to the church, one or two must join in trying to convince the brother of his wrong and to win him over. This procedure testifies of the mercy of God. If there is repentance at this stage, the matter is still resolved in a very small circle. The sinner is saved from death, the sin covered (James 5:20), and there is great joy in heaven (Luke 15:7). Clearly this disciplinary procedure is full of love for the wayward one (1 Cor. 13:7).

If the private admonitions do not yield the desired results, then those who admonished are to act as witnesses. They are to be witnesses both of the sin and of the failed admonitions. The word of the single individual who first started the process is not

10. For the responsibility of the congregation in Israel, see chapter 5, under "The Involvement and Responsibility of the People."

enough to testify before the church against the one giving offense. When the Lord Jesus mentioned this provision of witnesses (Matt. 18:16), he quoted from Deuteronomy 19:15. There we read: "One witness is not enough to convict a man accused of any crime or offense he may have committed. A matter must be established by the testimony of two or three witnesses." This important Old Testament principle was especially used to protect innocent people from the death penalty (Num. 35:30; Deut. 17:6), but in Deuteronomy 19:15, the Lord God broadened this principle for all offenses with which one could be charged. The Lord knows the corruptness of the heart (Lev. 19:18), and in his righteousness he protects the blameless. Christ had the same motives and made this principle a rule for his congregation (also see 2 Cor. 13:1; 1 Tim. 5:19). After all, much is at stake, for if the unrepentant persists in his sin, the result is exclusion from the fellowship of life with God and even, possibly, eternal death (James 5:20).

If after the repeated admonitions of the two or three, the one giving offense still refuses to listen, Christ says, "Tell it to the church" (Matt. 18:17). This brings us to the work of the elders in the process of church discipline. However, as will become clear, the congregation retains an important role.

The Role of the Elders

When Christ says, "Tell it to the church," he means that the admonition can now leave the private sphere and be brought to the attention of the church, that is, the local fellowship of believers who come together in Christ's name (Matt. 18:20). When Christ first gave this instruction, the gathering of the disciples of the Lord Jesus was but a rudimentary reflection of the later church. The language that the Lord Jesus uses in Matthew 18 reflects an undifferentiated view of what would later become an organized congregation with a council of elders (as in 1 Tim. 4:14). When Christ says, "Tell it to the church" (Matt. 18:17), he indicates that in one way or another the congregation as a whole is to be mobilized for the spiritual health of the sinner. When the efforts

170

of the individuals involved in the initial private admonitions fail, all the members of the church must become involved. Everything possible must be done for the sake of the straying sheep, and it must be done in an attitude of humility and service (Matt. 18:1–14). It is obvious that without a living congregation, church discipline becomes impossible. The participation of the people of God is vital and indispensable, both in the beginning of the admonitions, and also in seeing the discipline process through to a final resolution.

However, all this is not to say that the leadership in the church does not have its own duties and responsibilities. They do. If the admonitions of the church are not heeded (Matt. 18:17), the leaders, and not the congregation, make the decision to expel. The leaders whom Christ addresses in the first instance (Matt. 18:1) are the Twelve. They would become the apostles of the New Testament church. To these future leaders, Christ says: "I tell you the truth, whatever you bind on earth will be bound in heaven, and whatever you loose on earth will be loosed in heaven" (Matt. 18:18). This reminds us of what Christ says later to his disciples and apostles: "If you forgive anyone his sins, they are forgiven; if you do not forgive them, they are not forgiven" (John 20:23). The special responsibilities of the leadership of the church are also evident from the exhortations that the elders receive to keep watch over the flock (Acts 20:28). The apostle Peter even appeals to the elders as a fellow elder to shepherd those under their care (1 Peter 5:1–2).

What are the leaders of the church expected to do should members of the congregation bring a case of an unrepentant member to their attention? They need to carefully investigate the matter themselves to make sure that the accusations are bona fide and that no false witnesses are involved (Deut. 19:18–19). The leadership of the church has its own responsibility to ensure that the requirement of the testimony of two or three witnesses is being met (Matt. 18:16; 2 Cor. 13:1).[11]

11. For the need of an independent inquiry, see the principle enunciated in Deut. 17:4. The law of Moses recognized the possibility of false witnesses who were to be

This obligation of the leadership or the council of elders in the process of discipline and their eventual judgment is of no small consequence. Like the Old Testament judges, they too need to show no partiality in the realization that "judgment belongs to God" (Deut. 1:17). It is not for man to decide what is right; this is God's prerogative. In other words, the elders serve not themselves or the congregation in the first place, but God. When they make a decision regarding a discipline matter, it must be perceived and received as a decision of the Lord himself.[12]

When the sin and unwillingness to repent are established by the elders, the office bearers now share in the responsibility for the well-being of the individual involved. They will therefore visit and admonish in love. Should these admonitions be blessed, the sinner can be forgiven and the circle of those who are involved is kept relatively small. However, if there is no repentance, then such a person begins to lose privileges of membership and is barred from the celebration of the Lord's Supper. Eventually the entire congregation must become involved. Since both the Presbyterian and Reformed traditions have been profoundly influenced by Calvin, there is a similar series of steps in each tradition that can lead to excommunication from the church if there is no true sorrow for sin.

The first official step in which the congregation is involved is a public announcement by the session or consistory that a member of the church is guilty of a serious sin and that in spite of many earnest admonitions there is no evidence of true repentance. As a result, the session or consistory is obliged to exercise further discipline. The offense is not specified except to indicate which of the Ten Commandments has been transgressed. In this first announcement no name is mentioned and the congregation is asked to pray for repentance.

---

punished in accordance with the punishment they sought for the one wrongly accused (Deut. 19:16–20).

12. When a matter was brought to the judges in ancient Israel, it was brought "to God." Note the phrase "before God" in Ex. 22:8–9, which is often translated "before the judges" (e.g., KJV, NASB, and NIV; but cf. RSV).

If necessary, due to a lack of genuine remorse, a second announcement is eventually made giving the name and address of the one concerned so that the congregation can seek to win over the errant member. One must however be careful not to become involved in the sin of the one to be admonished and so share in his guilt, but to warn him as a brother (2 Thess. 3:6, 14–15; Rom. 16:17).[13] If the admonitions prove fruitless, a date for the excommunication is eventually set. When the individual is excommunicated, it is solemnly declared that he or she is excluded from the fellowship of Christ and from his kingdom. But readmittance can take place, if there is true repentance.

In this process, which is patterned after Matthew 18:15–17, the congregation is very much involved, just as the people were involved in discipline cases in ancient Israel. Once the matter goes to "the church" and becomes also the responsibility of the leadership of the church, their work is a most solemn one. Only the teaching and ruling elders are able to bring the process of church discipline to the final step of excommunication. Also, they are the ones who will open the door to the church again if there is true repentance. This responsibility of the elders is so weighty that we need to consider it more closely.

Excommunication and Readmission

The importance of the collective action of the office bearers in expelling someone from the church, as well as in possibly readmitting, is difficult to overestimate. Remember that the authority of the elders has been entrusted to them by the risen Christ who gave the power of the keys of the kingdom to his church and whose Spirit set the elders in positions of leadership (Acts 20:28).[14] This means that when the elders act, they

13. Second Thess. 3:6, 14–15 does not speak of the attitude of the congregation toward one who has been excommunicated. Rather it describes how one must deal with someone who is being censured but is still within the congregation. See William Hendriksen, *Exposition of I and II Thessalonians*, New Testament Commentary (Grand Rapids: Baker, 1955), 204–6.

14. See chapter 2, under "Shepherds of the Good Shepherd"; chapter 6, under "The Congregation of Christ"; and chapter 7, under "The Elders, the Keys, and the Congregation."

must act in accordance with Christ's wishes. Only then will their judgment be credible. It needs to be in line with the wishes of the great key bearer of the kingdom, Jesus Christ. He "holds the key of David" (Rev. 3:7) according to the prophetic Word (Isa. 22:22), and he acts in accordance with the wishes of God the Father, so that all who believe in the Son will have eternal life (John 3:16; 6:38–40). The elders of the church must likewise act according to the wishes of God (Deut. 1:17). That means their judgment must be "based on truth" (Rom. 2:2), that is, according to the facts of the particular case, "for God does not show favoritism" (Rom. 2:11). There are special privileges for none (1 Tim. 5:21). For elders who are also by nature sinful, much faithfulness and godly wisdom are required to judge rightly. But God will give such faithfulness and wisdom in answer to prayer (Prov. 2:1–11).

The absolute necessity of faithfulness in reflecting God's own judgment in excommunicating someone is obvious when one considers the magnitude of what is happening. Such an excommunication means that the person involved has been excluded from the church, and thus no longer has any part in the blessings that Christ gives his church, blessings such as the forgiveness of sins and life with Christ now and in eternal blessedness. Such a person is to be treated as a pagan (Matt. 18:17) and delivered up to Satan (1 Cor. 5:1–5; 1 Tim. 1:20). Excommunication means that the doors to the kingdom of Christ with all the glorious treasures of his redemption have been shut. It is noteworthy that the solemn act of excommunication was to be done when the congregation was assembled (1 Cor. 5:4).[15]

The horror of excommunication is evident when one considers that the Old Testament equivalent was physical death. Sin for which there was no repentance in the old covenant led to

---

15. The involvement of the congregation is also evident from the use of the imperative plural when the apostle exhorts, "Expel the wicked man from among you" (1 Cor. 5:13). Probably, he also alludes here to a phrase repeated in disciplinary settings of capital punishment in Deuteronomy: "You must purge the evil from among you" (Deut. 17:7; 19:19; 21:21; 22:21, 24; 24:7).

the capital punishment of the perpetrator,[16] most commonly by stoning. Underlining the gravity of it all was the rule that the witnesses would have to cast the first stones (Deut. 17:7). The Old Testament form of excommunication by physically killing the unrepentant gave a terrifying tangibleness of what it meant to be excluded from God's people. Yet the seriousness of punishing sin by excommunication is no less in the New Testament church. As already noted, by being excommunicated, one is being handed over to Satan. Unless there is repentance, one is essentially consigned to eternal death, away from the presence of the God of life and light. This is far worse than any physical death.

How did the death penalty get replaced by excommunication as the ultimate disciplinary step? After the return from the Babylonian exile, Israel was no longer an independent nation. This may be the underlying reason why we read of banishment rather than the death penalty for the unfaithful in the postexilic community at Jerusalem. In response to the challenge of dealing with the sin of those exiles who had taken foreign wives, Ezra called for a renewal of the covenant with God (Ezra 10:3). The people were told to come together. "Anyone who failed to appear within three days would forfeit all his property, in accordance with the decision of the officials and elders, and would himself be expelled from the assembly of the exiles" (Ezra 10:8). Although at that moment Ezra had the authority from the Persian court to impose the death penalty for unfaithfulness, yet he chose the way of banishment for dealing with the unfaithful in Israel (Ezra 7:25–26). By God's providence, Ezra in this way ushered in the use of excommunication for the disciplining of God's holy congregation. A mechanism was now in place that would serve the covenant nation when their foreign overlords would forbid their use of the death penalty for unfaithfulness to God.[17] It was this

16. Death was prescribed for refusal to repent for sin against the first nine commandments, which could be policed by humans. See chapter 5 n. 15.

17. As, e.g., the Romans forbade the Jews the use of the death penalty for sins against their law (John 18:31). When Stephen was stoned, the Jews took the law into their own hands (Acts 7:58). Synagogues apparently still exercised the right to flog an offender (Matt. 10:17; Acts 22:19; 2 Cor. 11:24).

ecclesiastical excommunication that was in effect in Jesus' day. Those who believed in him were therefore afraid of being expelled from the synagogue (John 9:22; 12:42; 16:2). Excommunication became the norm for Christ's church as well.

Punishment by exclusion also meant that readmission was possible should there be repentance. Indeed, a key objective of excommunication was the salvation of the sinner (1 Cor. 5:5). It is therefore to be expected that at any stage in the process of discipline, even after excommunication, the congregation must be prepared to restore the one being censured to his place in the fellowship. "Godly sorrow brings repentance that leads to salvation and leaves no regret, but worldly sorrow brings death" (2 Cor. 7:10). Those who are sorry for their sins, no matter what they entailed, will be forgiven. God graciously forgives (1 John 1:9; Ps. 103:12) and so must the congregation (Matt. 6:14–15; 18:21–35). Both the elders and the congregation must always be ready to embrace the penitent sinner. In a particular case of discipline, the Corinthian church was told that enough was enough, and they now had to forgive and comfort the one punished "so that he will not be overwhelmed by excessive sorrow" (2 Cor. 2:7). It is unclear whether this refers to restoring someone after excommunication or lifting the censure at some previous time. In any event it is clear that godly sorrow for sin must lead to restoration or readmission to full fellowship. An added consideration in this case is that otherwise Satan might get an advantage out of the situation for his schemes (2 Cor. 2:11).

Limitations of the Elders

There are two key limitations of human elders that need to be mentioned at this point. Elders are not all-knowing and, just like those in their charge, they are also by nature inclined to sin. The implications of these constraining realities need to be considered.

Since elders are not omniscient, they may have to end their official dealing with someone because there is not enough evidence to warrant church discipline. It may be simply impossible for them to render a well-considered judgment. They may have their suspicions, but they cannot proceed with admonition. This can happen if there is a denial of the sin and there are no witnesses or only one witness. In such a case, judgment must be left to God. Unlike with Israel, there is no provision for an oath to be accepted as evidence in church discipline (Matt. 5:33–37).[18] So it should be recognized that some cases may need to be left to God because it is impossible for office bearers to adjudicate properly.

Now to be sure, at certain critical junctures in the history of God's people, the Lord himself did reveal and punish sin that was hidden to the congregation. This happened after the fall of Jericho and before the conquest of the land when God exposed Achan's sin of taking for himself what had been devoted to God. As a result he was disciplined by stoning (Josh. 7). At a similarly critical time, shortly after the outpouring of the Holy Spirit at Pentecost, the hidden sin of Ananias and Sapphira's lying about the money they had received from the sale of property was exposed as an offense against the Holy Spirit. They were punished with immediate death (Acts 5:1–11). In the case of the church at Thyatira, there was toleration for one who called herself a prophetess. Perhaps her deception and sin were not clear to the congregation. But she led people into sin. The Lord warned that unless there was repentance, he would cause her and her followers to suffer and die. "Then all the churches will know that I am he who searches hearts and minds, and I will repay each of you according to your deeds" (Rev. 2:23). In all these cases, hidden sin was either punished or exposed.

However, living in the postapostolic age, we today cannot count on God's direct intervention as seen in the above-mentioned cases. The Lord has equipped his church with his fully revealed will in Scripture as well as with the gift of his Holy Spirit. These gifts are sufficient for the church to fulfill her responsibilities.[19]

18. On the use of oaths in Old Testament legal settings, see chapter 5, under "Special Circumstances."

19. On the nature of the postapostolic period and the gifts God gives his church, see, e.g., Richard B. Gaffin, *Perspectives on Pentecost: New Testament Teaching on the Gifts of the Holy Spirit* (Phillipsburg, NJ: Presbyterian and Reformed, 1979).

Yet all this does not mean that the Lord cannot intervene today in ways that are visible to the eye of faith. For example, when the church at Corinth desecrated the Lord's Supper, God caused sickness and even death in the congregation. The apostle Paul told the church that the misery they experienced was the result of their partaking of the Lord's Supper in an unworthy manner (1 Cor. 11:27–30). Then he added: "When we are judged by the Lord, we are being disciplined so that we will not be condemned with the world" (1 Cor. 11:32). Today also the Lord can discipline his children in special ways, for those whom he loves he disciplines (Heb. 12:6). Although afflictions that come one's way are not always punishment for specific sins, as the life of Job shows, yet it is possible that such is the case. When special trials occur, there is always reason to ask whether the Lord could be punishing because of sin that has not been properly cleared up (1 Cor. 11:31–32). We must not make light of the Lord's discipline (Heb. 12:5). Elders also need to keep this in mind and be sensitive to the possibility that sin could be involved in a chastisement (James 5:14–16). If elders strongly suspect sin but cannot prove it, they must express their concerns to the party involved and warn of the wrath of God if there is no repentance.

A second limitation on the work of elders is the reality that elders also are by nature inclined to sin. Every precaution must be taken that the office not be compromised by any wrongdoing. Since it is in their office that the authority of elders resides, their office is protected by the fact that they are subject to church discipline as well. Indeed, no one is exempt from it. The person of the elder, however, needs to be protected. As public servants of Christ they can easily attract criticism and hostility for faithful work they do. For that reason, the apostle Paul reminds Timothy: "Do not entertain an accusation against an elder unless it is brought by two or three witnesses" (1 Tim. 5:19). The old rule of the necessity of two or three witnesses (Deut. 17:6; Matt. 18:16; 2 Cor. 13:1) is brought to the fore. Although it applied to everyone in the church, and therefore to elders also, this reminder appears to have been necessary since this rule was not known in the Greek-Hellenistic law of that time.[20] Furthermore, perhaps the apostle wanted to stress that elders especially needed this protection (1 Tim. 5:17).

On the other hand, elders are not to be sheltered from just accusations. On the contrary: "as for those who persist in sin, rebuke them in the presence of all, so that the rest may stand in fear" (1 Tim. 5:20 ESV). Here we have an application of the rule that those with more responsibilities will be judged more strictly (James 3:1). The rebuke in the presence of all has been interpreted either as a rebuke in the council of all the elders or in front of the entire congregation. The latter is more likely since the context of two or three witnesses reminds one of the rule of Matthew 18:15–18 where in the case of those who persist in sin, the rule applies: "Tell it to the church" (Matt. 18:17). Such a public rebuke is necessary "so that the rest may stand in fear" (1 Tim. 5:20 ESV). Here too, probably the entire church is in view rather than just the elders (cf. Deut. 13:11). However, one can be sure that the elders especially would be reminded of the earnestness of their calling and that as leaders in the church they do not stand above the law, but like everyone else are rightly subject to the discipline of the church.

In conclusion, the high view that the apostle Paul holds of the eldership is obvious from the way he protects elders from ungrounded accusations, but also from the rigorous way in which sin in the eldership has to be confronted. All of this underlines the elders' limitations and vulnerability to sin.

The Exercise of Church Discipline

Keeping the Purpose in Mind

Before discussing some key principles for church discipline, it will be helpful to review its overall goal. Calvin articulated three

---

20. See H. van Vliet, *No Single Testimony: A Study of the Adoption of the Law of Deut. 19:15 par. into the New Testament* (Utrecht: Kemink en Zoon, 1958), 19–25.

specific purposes of discipline.[21] First, discipline must serve God's glory. Harboring sin is a dishonor to God for the holy church (Eph. 5:25–26), which is the body of Christ (Col. 1:24). Second, discipline benefits the congregation, for the removal of evil means the removal of a corrupting influence (1 Cor. 5:6–7; Eccl. 9:18). Similarly, the author of Hebrews admonished: "See to it that no one misses the grace of God and that no bitter root grows up to cause trouble and defile many" (Heb. 12:15; cf. Deut. 29:18). As the context makes clear, the root of bitterness is not a bad attitude but an embittered or rebellious person who can have a disastrous effect on the congregation. Third, church discipline has in view the salvation of the sinner (2 Thess. 3:14; 1 Cor. 5:5).

These three goals of church discipline should be seen against the wider background of God's insistence in the Old Testament that justice be administered among his people so that righteousness be upheld in the covenant community. It bears repeating[22] that the Lord God is the one who established the relationship of peace and righteousness between himself and his people. This relationship the elders had to safeguard and promote. It is no different in the New Testament church where God has reconciled his people to himself through the Passover lamb, Jesus Christ (1 Cor. 5:7). As in the Old Testament, also today, the first priority of elders is not to judge and impose a sentence, such as barring people from the Lord's Supper, or if necessary, ultimately expelling them from the church. No, the first priority and purpose of their disciplinary labor is to help resolve the problem at hand so that God will be glorified and the congregation will be blessed. Reconciliation and the salvation of the sinner must be the goals. In this way the peace of God in the fullest sense of the word is restored, for relationships are healed between the sinner and God, as well as between the fellow members of the family of God, the church.

All of this means that elders must recognize that acting righteously is not simply acting according to the letter of the

---

21. For what follows, see Calvin, *Institutes* 4.12.5, pp. 1232–34.
22. For what follows in the next two paragraphs, see chapter 5, under "Judging and Righteousness."

law in a legalistic manner. Rather, the administration of God's judgment must always be accompanied by a demonstration of God's mercy and love. God's justice and righteousness also reflect his care and covenant faithfulness, and it must be no less with the elders' labors in church discipline. The punishment must match the offense. In this elders need to demonstrate prudence and understanding.

When the above goals in church discipline are kept in view, life in covenant with God is nurtured and encouraged. There is also room for the members of the family of God to grow in a non-threatening and supportive atmosphere of biblical faithfulness, love, and righteousness. All of this will become more clear as we now consider factors influencing the execution of discipline, in particular what warrants excommunication and what kind of toleration is biblically justified.

Cause for Excommunication?

A sin that has been witnessed or that can be established is subject to church discipline. As we saw earlier, church discipline is a family affair in which the family of God, the local congregation, watches over each other in love and compassion. When a sin is noticed, an admonition or an encouragement to reconsider and do things in a God-pleasing way is appropriate. Such is the life of a healthy congregation living in communion with the Spirit of Jesus Christ. Such are the basics of church discipline.

The question that needs to be addressed now is, when is excommunication justified? When must a sin move the council of elders to expel someone from the body of Christ? To be sure, no list of sins worthy of excommunication can or should be drawn up. Discipline can never be restricted to a certain group of sins. Any sin is repulsive to the Lord, and any sin that members of the church are aware of can eventually lead to expulsion from the church. It all depends. There are several factors to consider: sin should be recognized for what it is; the nature of the sin should be discerned; no favoritism should be shown; and the promotion of heresy is not to be tolerated. We will consider each of these elements in turn.

First, elders should be diligent to recognize sin for what it is and act on it. Now this point may seem obvious enough but it needs to be stated. Due to cultural or other circumstances a sin can easily gain a status of being tolerated. However, when a wrongdoing that is condemned in Scripture is condoned in a congregation, that church may find itself in great danger. Tolerated sin spreads and one's sensitivity to God's holy demands is diminished. Almost imperceptibly, there is in effect a hardening in the sin by the entire congregation, simply by its not being challenged and dealt with in a biblical manner.

An example of sinful toleration is found in the Corinthian church. When this congregation condoned sexual sins, the apostle instructed that the guilty brother be handed over to Satan, that is, be expelled (1 Cor. 5:5, 13), so that this evil and destructive influence could be removed from the church (1 Cor. 5:6–7). The apostle's instruction also included: "You must not associate with anyone who calls himself a brother but is sexually immoral or greedy, an idolater or a slanderer, a drunkard or a swindler. With such a man do not even eat" (1 Cor. 5:11). Not only the well-being of the congregation, but also that of the sinner being disciplined is in view. This is clear from the apostle's instruction: "You are to deliver this man to Satan for the destruction of the flesh, so that his spirit may be saved in the day of the Lord" (1 Cor. 5:5 ESV). "The destruction of the flesh" can best be seen as God permitting Satan to gradually weaken the physical frame of the one excommunicated. Sin is sometimes punished by God with sickness, physical failings, and even death, as happened when the Corinthian church desecrated the Lord's Supper table (1 Cor. 11:30).[23]

Second, elders must distinguish the nature of the sin and understand the direction of the person's life. A sin should lead to excommunication only when there is a hardening of the heart and no evidence of repentance. In this connection it can be recalled

---

23. See, e.g., the discussion in Simon J. Kistemaker, *Exposition of the First Epistle to the Corinthians*, New Testament Commentary (Grand Rapids: Baker, 1993), 160–61.

that Scripture distinguishes between a sin done intentionally, with an upraised hand, and one done in weakness.[24] The person who hardens in sin becomes the object of special discipline by the elders. If there is no repentance, such a person ultimately must be cut off (Num. 15:22–31). When dealing with a wayward soul, elders need to consider carefully which type of sin they are dealing with. What was the motivation for the sin? How does the guilty one regard the matter? How is the situation developing? What is the direction of that person's life? Is it toward God or away from him? A sin done in weakness can become a sin of defiance against God and warrant excommunication. The person so disciplined may then hopefully realize how serious his sin is, repent, and be readmitted.

If someone who has been excommunicated continues to harden in his sin and rejects God against better knowledge, he may end up grieving the Spirit (Eph. 4:30), resisting the Spirit (Acts 7:51), and eventually quenching the Spirit completely from his life (1 Thess. 5:19). This last stage is sinning against the Holy Spirit, for which there is no forgiveness. Such a person has completely fallen away (Heb. 10:26–31; Matt. 12:31–32).[25] Many questions can come up in this respect.[26] For their pastoral work, elders need to keep one thing especially in mind. If an elder is admonishing someone who is living in fear of having committed the sin against the Holy Spirit and thus of no longer having a good relationship with the Lord and the church community, the elder can console such a troubled soul with the comfort of the gospel. The very fact that such an individual worries about being cast away from the gracious presence of God is an indication of the continuing work of the Holy Spirit in that person's life. Such a fear speaks

24. See further on this issue, chapter 5, under "Distinctions in Sin and Consequences."

25. See, e.g., William Hendriksen, *Exposition of the Gospel according to Matthew*, New Testament Commentary (Grand Rapids: Baker, 1973), 527–29.

26. Heb. 6:4–6 is often mentioned in this context, raising the question whether it makes sense to pray for someone who is hardening in sin and has been excommunicated. However, Heb. 6:4–6 is not a general rule that conversion is impossible after apostasy, but it is part of a warning in a specific situation of the real danger of falling away, using the historical example of Israel's apostasy. See Philip Edgcumbe Hughes, *A Commentary on the Epistle to the Hebrews* (Grand Rapids: Eerdmans, 1977), 206–22.

of a desire for communion with God, and such a desire can be produced only by the Holy Spirit. So the elder can encourage such a person to repent and turn back to God, for God has not stopped working in his or her life. As the prophet Isaiah put it:

> Seek the LORD while he may be found;
>   call on him while he is near.
> Let the wicked forsake his way
>   and the evil man his thoughts.
> Let him turn to the LORD, and he will have mercy on him,
>   and to our God, for he will freely pardon. (Isa. 55:6–7)

God can and will forgive any sin, no matter how grievous and shameful, if there is true repentance (Ps. 103:11–14; 1 John 1:9).

Third, the elders must show no favoritism in the work of discipline (Lev. 19:15; Deut. 16:19; 1 Tim. 5:21). There is to be no special consideration due to someone's station in life or in the church. Discipline is to be applied to all offenders alike. The fear of the Lord must govern all church discipline, for with God there is no favoritism (Deut. 10:17; 2 Chron. 19:7; Rom. 2:11). When a popular leader is involved in church discipline, emotions that seek to minimize the wrong can easily overrule better judgment if one is not careful. The situation must always be seen from the perspective of God's Word and not human sensitivities. Elders too are subject to ecclesiastical discipline. As a matter of fact, those in leadership positions should be judged and disciplined more strictly (James 3:1).

Fourth, the promotion of heresy is not to be tolerated in the church, which is "the pillar and foundation of the truth" (1 Tim. 3:15). Doctrinal error can be a factor especially in the discipline of church leaders. Elders have the duty to preserve the true doctrine, if necessary, by way of excommunication. Heresy is a grave danger to the congregation, and those who promote it must be disciplined accordingly (Rev. 2:14–16). The apostle Paul, therefore, wrote the Galatian churches that "even if we or an angel from heaven should preach a gospel other than the one we preached to you, let him be eternally condemned! As we have already said, so now I say again: If anybody is preaching to you a gospel other than what you accepted, let him be eternally condemned!" (Gal. 1:8–9). There is to be no respecting of persons when it comes to church discipline and safeguarding the gospel.

Titus was also counseled: "Warn a divisive person once, and then warn him a second time. After that, have nothing to do with him. You may be sure that such a man is warped and sinful; he is self-condemned" (Titus 3:10–11; see also Rom. 16:17). The Greek term used for "a divisive person" can indicate a heretic who created divisions in the church by embracing teachings that the apostles opposed (Titus 3:9). Notice that although such a heretic presented the church with a dangerous situation, patience and love must be shown. Every effort must be made to try to convince the erring one to reconsider. This approach reminds us how the apostle Paul wrote Timothy that those who oppose the Lord's servant "he must gently instruct, in the hope that God will grant them repentance leading them to a knowledge of the truth, and that they will come to their senses and escape from the trap of the devil, who has taken them captive to do his will" (2 Tim. 2:25–26). Furthermore, the apostle Paul's writing to Titus of the first and second warnings (Titus 3:10) reminds one of the steps of Matthew 18 where private admonitions are followed by semiprivate ones and eventually the church excludes the unrepentant. The injunction: "Have nothing to do with him" (Titus 3:10) has the sense of dismiss or reject, that is, remove from the fellowship of the church. Clearly the type of person Paul had in view did not keep his opinions to himself but propagated them with the resulting damage to the church. Such a person, if unrepentant, needed to be excommunicated. He "is warped and sinful; he is self-condemned" (Titus 3:11).

Elsewhere the apostle Paul noted that some had shipwrecked their faith. "Among them are Hymenaeus and Alexander, whom I have handed over to Satan to be taught not to blaspheme" (1 Tim. 1:20). These men were heretics (1 Tim. 1:19), and it appears that the handing over to Satan was the last stage in church discipline (cf. 1 Cor. 5:5). But even then, the intent was not their eternal doom but their well-being. They were put outside the church, in Satan's territory so to speak, in order that they might "be taught not to blaspheme" (1 Tim. 1:20).

False teachers were very dangerous for the young churches, and therefore preemptive action was also counseled. The apostle John exhorted that those who did not continue in the teaching of Jesus should not be taken into one's home and welcomed (2 John 10). The reference here is to traveling teachers who would instruct the congregations meeting in homes. If such a teacher did not acknowledge Christ as having come in the flesh, he was a deceiver and the antichrist (2 John 7) and should not be admitted into the home. After all, admitting someone like that would be sharing in his wicked work (2 John 11).

In summarizing and concluding this section we note that any sin can eventually become cause for excommunication. To judge fairly, the elders need to distinguish the nature of the sin they are dealing with, recognize sin for what it is, show no favoritism, and show no toleration to the promotion of heresy. This brings us to the issue of toleration.

Toleration?

A vexing question elders are often faced with is, how much can be tolerated before we commence formal ecclesiastical discipline? Obviously, a clear boundary between church and world must be maintained. But where does one draw the line between recognizing human fallibility and falling into sin and living in sin in defiance of God's will? Or, as we framed the question earlier, how does one factor in divine flexibility and human inability so that judgment rendered on earth is a true reflection of that in heaven? How can the Old Testament principles of flexibility and compassion, as well as of justice and holiness, which we considered earlier, function for the elder today?[27] Let us consider these questions in the light of Scripture and illustrate the issues where

27. See chapter 5, under "Divine Flexibility."

possible by examples from church history and so seek to benefit from the godly struggles of those who have gone before us.

In order to place the issues under discussion in the right context, we need to remember that as believing Israelites were expected to heed the Ten Commandments in response to the salvation of God detailed in the prologue (Ex. 20:2; Deut. 5:6), so Christians today should seek to do God's will out of love and gratitude for what God has done for them in Christ (Rom. 6:13; 12:1–2). The law is the rule of thankfulness.[28] For believers, the law is not a yoke and a burden as it would be for slaves who fearfully obey an oppressive master. Christians have been set free from that fear, for they have received the Spirit of adoption by which they cry "Abba, Father" (Rom. 8:15; also, Gal. 3:25–26). Children of God respond to God's call to live a pure and holy life (1 Thess. 4:7) by endeavoring to love him with their entire being (Deut. 6:5). However, in spite of their best efforts, they know they fall short. But such failing does not arouse fear of condemnation because Christ has removed the curse of the law for those who love him (Gal. 3:10–13). In Calvin's words, as children of God we offer our best to God without fear of condemnation, "firmly trusting that our services will be approved by our most merciful Father, however small, rude, and imperfect these may be. Thus also he assures us through the prophet: 'I will spare them as a man spares his son who serves him' (Mal. 3:17)." Calvin goes on to note that the word "spare" is used in the sense of "to be indulgent or compassionately to overlook faults."[29]

Elders must seek to imitate God in evaluating and weighing the obedience of those in their care. In their service as nurturers of the covenant life with God, elders are to encourage those who struggle with sin and weaknesses with the comfort that Christ has fulfilled the law. Elders are also to be long-suffering with respect to the shortcomings of those in their care as the heavenly Father is. Then their judgment will be a reflection of God's judgment.

28. Significantly, the Heidelberg Catechism places its discussion of the law under its section "Thankfulness."
29. Calvin, *Institutes* 3.19.5, p. 837.

All this brings to mind the family context of the office of elder in both the Old and New Testaments. Elders function in a sense as fathers who need to foster and stimulate the life with God in the family of God and not seek an unrealistic perfection which in this life is impossible. Christians do not live under law in that sense, but under grace. Not enforced legalism but encouraging gratitude and love for God and seeking the salvation of the sinner should be the elders' goal. All this has nothing to do with tolerating sin in a God-displeasing way, but it has everything to do with setting life's challenges to be holy in the liberating context of the salvation that Christ has achieved for us.[30]

With these general principles in mind, elders still need much wisdom in evaluating ethical and doctrinal issues so that they are worthy representatives of God's will for his people. Let us consider some of the factors involving ethical concerns. After that we will turn to matters of doctrinal purity and toleration.

In the enforcement of ethical matters, it is very easy for us to give human rules and ordinances a status equal to God's Word. This must never be allowed. The Lord God summarized his entire will for his people in the Ten Words of the Covenant. Much detail was given in the Mosaic legislation, but a good part of this deals with ritual law with which God carefully hedged in Israel's life in the time of the old covenant. God was not interested in listing every possible scenario for sin, with specific punishments for each disobedience. Much of the ethical law found in Scripture illustrates the application of the Ten Words of the Covenant. God was not after obedience to the letter of the law as such. He wanted Israel's heart, soul, and strength in loving commitment to him (Deut. 6:5).[31] The temptation to multiply rules and regulations for God's people to follow must be resisted. History, however, teaches that believers have often succumbed to this temptation.

The Pharisees zealously increased the requirements of the law and laid a heavy burden on God's people (Matt. 23:4). But the

30. It is significant that Calvin in his *Institutes* addresses matters of toleration in the section on Christian freedom, 3.19.1–16, pp. 833–49.
31. See chapter 5, under "The Unique Character of God's Law."

Lord Jesus called to himself those weighed down by such extra legal requirements. The Savior said: "Come to me, all you who are weary and burdened, and I will give you rest. Take my yoke upon you and learn from me, for I am gentle and humble in heart, and you will find rest for your souls. For my yoke is easy and my burden is light" (Matt. 11:28–30). Christ opposed the legalism of the scribes and Pharisees. For example, when the Pharisees asked him whether it was lawful to heal on the Sabbath, the Lord Jesus was confronted with one of their legalistic distinctions. According to the Pharisees, it was lawful to heal on the Sabbath only when a life was in danger. The Lord Jesus responded that if it was permissible to do good to a sheep on the Sabbath, "how much more valuable is a man than a sheep! Therefore it is lawful to do good on the Sabbath" (Matt. 12:12). Christ exposed the untenability of their legalism and healed the man of his shriveled hand (Matt. 12:13).

Although Christ repeatedly exposed unbiblical legalism on the part of the Pharisees, especially by healing on the Sabbath (also, e.g., Luke 13:10–17; John 5:1–15), the danger of human rules and ordinances being imposed on the church and even being used unjustly to rid the church of believers has remained with God's people in various forms. In the days of Augustine, there was the overscrupulousness of the Donatists; and in the time of the Reformation, it was Anabaptists who insisted on a church that was perfect in every respect.[32] Indeed, there are examples of Dutch Anabaptists refusing church membership to someone in 1700 because he wore a wig and excommunicating a brother in 1715 for traveling to the Cape of Good Hope.[33] History suggests that the danger of making human regulations the litmus test for church membership is one to be aware of today also.

Calvin wisely observed that once we start on the path of making binding human rules for which there is no biblical basis, we enter a maze that is difficult to escape. Consciences will become

32. For Calvin on these two examples see his *Institutes* 4.12.11–12, pp. 1238–40.
33. For these and other examples, see H. Bouwman, *De Kerkelijke tucht naar het Gereformeerde kerkrecht* (Kampen: Kok, 1912), 199.

189

progressively bound so that in the end the Christian "will come to the point of considering it wrong to step upon a straw across his path, as the saying goes." Despair at the untenability of what is imposed or despising God because of the unjust demands is often the result.[34]

The intent behind many human rules and regulations may be a sincere desire for the holiness of the church. However, elders must not pretend to be wiser than God and go further than he does in his Word. The Lord leaves room for the application of the law and has not regulated our life in all its minute details. There is a certain Christian liberty regarding ethical matters. When those in the Corinthian church disputed whether it was permissible to eat meat offered to idols, the apostle allowed for both eating and not eating this meat. If one's conscience could handle eating the meat, that was fine; if not, he should not eat it. Both positions were to be tolerated. However, one must not cause a brother who is weak in the faith to sin (1 Cor. 8). "'Everything is permissible'— but not everything is beneficial. 'Everything is permissible'—but not everything is constructive. Nobody should seek his own good, but the good of others" (1 Cor. 10:23–24).

The apostle Paul counseled the church at Rome in a similar manner on a variety of issues. Again, he stressed that judging each other should be avoided and that the well-being of fellow believers should be sought (Rom. 14:13–23). He also admonished: "We who are strong ought to bear with the failings of the weak and not to please ourselves. Each of us should please his neighbor for his good, to build him up" (Rom. 15:1–2). There is Christian freedom, but as the apostle admonished: "Do not use your freedom to indulge the sinful nature; rather, serve one another in love. The entire law is summed up in a single command: 'Love your neighbor as yourself'" (Gal. 5:13–14).

Examples from church history illustrate the great care that is needed to determine what merits excommunication. For example, in answer to the question whether or not it would be useful to

34. See Calvin, *Institutes* 3.19.7, p. 839.

have a list of sins worthy of excommunication, the Dutch national synod of 's-Gravenhage (1586) decided that this was unnecessary since the most important transgressions are mentioned in the form for the celebration of the Lord's Supper.[35] When the synod of Middelburg (1591) did come up with a list of censurable sins, it was very short and referred to the first and second parts of the Ten Commandments.[36] Another example is the Church Order of Drenthe (The Netherlands), which was adopted in 1638. This document specified that sin should be judged to be a sin only on the basis of God's Word so that the consciences of those involved not be tormented and troubled with faulty opinions and wrongheaded prejudices. Furthermore, this same Church Order directed that a sinner be admonished in such a way that those admonishing not too readily comment on and censure every little shortcoming. Where would be the end of reprimanding? Scripture therefore frequently urges forbearance. After all, the elder also is inclined to sin and has his limitations (Matt. 7:1–5). On the other hand, this Church Order also affirmed the duty to be on the alert if the one who fell into sin was coming into ever greater danger and harm, or if offense was taken, or if God was blasphemed by this sin.[37] Being forbearing is not the same as being lax in disciplining the body of Christ. Where there is a clear hardening in sin, there should be no hesitation to proceed, even with eventual expulsion in accordance with Scripture (1 Cor. 5:13).

Concerning doctrinal purity in the church and the possibility of tolerating that which is not in strict accord with sound doctrine, the following needs to be noted. First of all, as we saw earlier in this chapter, God's Word clearly stresses the need for maintaining sound doctrine. Nothing that will be said about tolerating doctrinal views should be understood to compromise this clear demand of Scripture. The church is to be a confessional church (1 Tim. 3:15). With the office bearers

35. See for the decision referred to F. L. Bos, *De Orde der kerk* ('s-Gravenhage: Guido de Bres, 1959), 284–85. For a complete text of the questions directed to this synod, P. Biesterveld and H. H. Kuyper, *Kerkelijk handboekje* (Kampen: Bos, 1905), 215–24.

36. For the text see Bos, *De Orde der kerk*, 285.

37. For the relevant text of the Church Order of Drenthe (1638) see ibid.

and leaders in the church no heresy can be condoned. As we saw earlier in this chapter under the heading "Cause for Excommunication?" there is zero tolerance for church leaders who propagate false teaching. The normal route of admonishing and trying to convince the person of his error is to be followed. In the end, if there is no repentance from propagating heresy, deposition from office and possibly even excommunication must follow.[38]

The question now is whether *any* deviation from true doctrine can be tolerated in a confessional church. Historically, there has been some toleration in doctrinal matters among church members. This has been the case if certain members came to erroneous views through lack of insight and ignorance, did not propagate them, and agreed to listen to the sound teaching and preaching of the true faith. In this way, room was made in the Reformed churches in the Netherlands for those who were still sympathetic to Arminian ideas after the adoption of the Canons of Dort. As much as possible, those straying from the Reformed teaching were treated with compassion and patience to preserve the unity of the church. However, if such members were unwilling to learn the true faith and threatened the unity of the congregation, they could eventually be excommunicated.[39] A more recent example is the general toleration of different millennial views within Presbyterian and Reformed churches today, with less freedom being given to office bearers.[40]

38. Typically a distinction was made between pastors and elders and deacons. In sixteenth- and seventeenth-century Netherlands, a pastor who persisted in his error and in teaching it was to be excommunicated. Those who publicly recanted and showed themselves willing to learn the true doctrine could be called back to the ministry after two years. Elders and deacons holding heretical views were to be deposed from their office, but a waiting period of a year was necessary before any thought was given to excommunication in order to see how they conducted themselves. If they wanted to be reconciled to the church, an acknowledgment of guilt was sufficient. See for examples in the history of the Reformed churches in the Netherlands, Bouwman, *Kerkelijke tucht*, 192–93.

39. After the adoption of the Canons of Dort, the Regional Synod of Leiden decided in 1619 (and reinforced by the Regional Synod of Gouda in 1620) to admit to the church those with Arminian sympathies. See Joh. Jansen, *De leertucht over de leden der kerk* (Kampen: Kok, 1936), 28–32; Bouwman, *Kerkelijke tucht*, 193–95.

40. Typical is the position of the Orthodox Presbyterian Church, which has historically accepted into membership those holding divergent views on eschatol-

Doctrinal integrity based on Scripture, and as summarized in confessional statements, needs to be maintained if a church is to remain a confessional body. Where justifiable, however, differences should be tolerated. If one believes that "souls upon leaving bodies fly to heaven; while another, not daring to define the place, is convinced nevertheless that they live to the Lord," who would create a schism over that? This example is from Calvin, who further notes: "First and foremost we should agree on all points. But since all men are somewhat beclouded with ignorance, either we must leave no church remaining, or we must condone delusion in those matters which can go unknown without harm to the sum of religion and without loss of salvation."[41]

To summarize, elders are charged with seeking the holiness and well-being of the church. At the same time, situations can arise in which forbearance and patience is the biblical route. However, tolerance may never be exercised at the cost of true unity in holiness of life and the doctrinal integrity of the congregation. If toleration in ethical and doctrinal matters results in a congregation moving in different directions, this toleration cannot continue. That is why the apostle Paul emphasized the duty of both the strong and the weak to live to the Lord. He is to be the focal point and direction of a Christian's life (Rom. 14:6–12; 15:5–7; 1 Cor. 10:31). Also, the strong have the obligation to help the weak (Rom. 14:1–15:2; 1 Cor. 8:9–13). Furthermore, toleration, both in ethical and doctrinal matters, may never come at the cost of the blurring of the boundary between the church and the world. This boundary must be clearly maintained, as we have seen earlier in this chapter. After all, discipline is a great gift of God; it must be used so that through it the riches of the gospel can be enjoyed by the people of God.

ogy. See, e.g., "Millennial Views" in the Question and Answer section of the official Web site of this church, accessed on July 11, 2008, from http://www.opc.org/qa.html?question_id=300.

41. Calvin, *Institutes* 4.1.12, p. 1026.

Summary: Shepherding the Flock

In a sense, the process of discipline and some of its important general principles can be summarized by the image of the shepherd and the sheep and the associations this calls to mind. Elders are in the service of the Good Shepherd, Jesus Christ (John 10:11, 14), and they need to mirror the Savior's love, dedication, and concern for the flock. In chapter 8 we saw how the shepherd image informs us of the elders' task in leading, gathering, and nurturing the flock. We will now briefly consider how this image helps us understand the elders' judging and disciplinary responsibilities. Again, the central position of the Word of God will be evident.

The Word of the Good Shepherd

Clearly, the elder's task of disciplining the Lord's flock is a most daunting one. In order for the elder to be credible, he needs to be faithful to the Word of the Good Shepherd. After all, the sheep must not hear the voice of the elder in the first place, but they must recognize the demands of the Good Shepherd himself through the labors of the elder. The authority of the elder comes from Christ, and so it is the Savior's voice that needs to come through loud and clear. Christ's sheep will recognize the voice of the Good Shepherd and heed it (John 10:4, 27). Obviously, the elder will need to know the Scriptures for him to function in his judging and disciplining capacity. Knowing the Scriptures also entails having the wisdom to apply the Word to the concrete situation.

Such wisdom is essential when one considers that whatever the elder does must serve the honor and glory of the Chief Shepherd, the building up of the congregation, and the salvation of the sinner. Furthermore, the expectations of the Word often seem to be in tension with each other. The Word urges the flock to aim for perfection (2 Cor. 13:9, 11), yet allowances are to be made for the sinful nature of the sheep and their living in an unholy world

194

(Rom. 7:17–20). It requires that the elder be firm in opposing sin (1 Cor. 5:5) but also gentle if the circumstances warrant it (Gal. 6:1). An identical sin, but set in different contexts, can therefore require different approaches. Much prudence is needed to work properly with the Word of the Good Shepherd.

Wisdom from Above

This wisdom necessary for disciplining the Lord's flock can only come from above. But the elder can take courage that this wisdom is accessible to him. God will give it for all circumstances of life to those who ask him for it (Prov. 2:1–11; James 1:5). It is worthwhile for our topic of shepherding, disciplining, and guiding the sheep to consider what this wisdom entails. James informs us that "the wisdom that comes from heaven is first of all pure; then peace-loving, considerate, submissive, full of mercy and good fruit, impartial and sincere" (James 3:17). Surely, all this is precisely what the elder-shepherd needs.

Let us briefly consider these features of wisdom. That wisdom is "pure" is especially stressed. Such wisdom is holy and undefiled. It shows moral and spiritual integrity, taking its cue from Christ (1 John 3:3). This purity shows itself in being "peace-loving," that is, both seeking and making peace. True wisdom is conciliatory. It is also "considerate," that is, fair and reasonable, not rigid and exacting in relations with others.[42] Furthermore, true wisdom is "submissive," that is, "easily persuaded, with the implication of being open to reason or willing to listen."[43] "Full of mercy and good fruit" are other features of wisdom. Wisdom that is full of mercy reminds one of James's earlier exhortation to "act as those who are going to be judged by the law that gives freedom, because judgment without mercy will be shown to anyone who

42. See James Adamson, *The Epistle of James*, New International Commentary on the New Testament (Grand Rapids: Eerdmans, 1976), 155, where he also notes that Aristotle contrasted this word with "strict justice."

43. Johannes P. Louw and Eugene A. Nida, eds., *Greek-English Lexicon of the New Testament Based on Semantic Domains*, 2d ed., 2 vols. (New York: United Bible Societies, 1989), 1:423.

has not been merciful. Mercy triumphs over judgment!" (James 2:12–13; Matt. 5:7). By speaking of the law that gives freedom, James implies that the law should not be understood legalistically, simply as a list of rules. Rather the law is the way to show our love to God and our neighbor. Then one has freedom and is not a slave to sin. Wisdom that is full of mercy will show mercy to those who do not deserve it—otherwise it would not be mercy. In this we follow the example of God himself (Mic. 6:8). Finally, James mentions that wisdom is "impartial and sincere," that is, all the evidence is heard before coming to a conclusion. In this way an impartial judgment is given and the elder's sincerity is evident.

Wisdom such as the above presupposes and requires a deep love for the one being disciplined. Indeed, love is an absolutely essential ingredient for shepherding and disciplining the flock. When we speak of love, we mean in the first place the love of Christ, a love that elders must also possess (Phil. 2:2). That must motivate and determine everything.

Shepherding in Love

The Good Shepherd laid down his life for his sheep (John 10:11). The Old Testament elders knew of the paschal lamb without defect that set Israel free from Egyptian bondage (Ex. 12:1–11). How much greater is the privilege of elders today to know *the* Lamb of God (John 1:29) who was *the* Passover lamb (1 Cor. 5:7). With his blood he set his people free from the righteous judgment of God (Rom. 3:25) and purchased the flock with the awesome price of his blood (1 Peter 1:18–19). No elder can ever forget this. The sheep in his care belong to the Great Shepherd of the sheep (Heb. 13:20; 1 Peter 2:25). The love he showed the sheep must be reflected in the elders' shepherding the flock.

Now of course, as we have seen, church discipline is in the first place the task of the congregation, although the elders have a very important role to play. It is noteworthy in the context of our topic that the apostle Paul wrote to the Philippian church and office bearers: "Do nothing out of selfish ambition or vain conceit, but in humility consider others better than yourselves. Each of you should look not only to your own interests, but also to the interests of others. Your attitude should be the same as that of Christ Jesus" (Phil. 2:3–5). The unselfish, humble serving of each other in love is what must characterize a congregation as well as the shepherds of the flock. This love shows itself in different ways.

Elders who are motivated by love will care for every sheep entrusted to them without prejudice. As a matter of fact, those that wander away may at a certain point take all their available time and energy. But those going astray are important as the parable of the shepherd leaving ninety-nine sheep to look for that missing one shows (Matt. 18:12–14). They must be pursued with love for they belong to the flock Christ purchased with his blood.

Wandering away from the flock can begin with doubts. Jude exhorted: "Be merciful to those who doubt" (Jude 22). Elders need to be compassionate to those who question the faith and wonder why. They need loving support and understanding to keep them in the flock. Jude continued: "snatch others from the fire and save them" (Jude 23). These are those who have become affected by the fire of sin and destruction (cf. Zech. 3:2). They need to be rescued, and elders can be instruments for that by warning of their imminent ruin. This is the way of love. Regarding those who persist in sin, Jude warned: "to others show mercy, mixed with fear—hating even the clothing stained by corrupted flesh" (Jude 23). Even though these people have gone a long way off, yet, "show mercy." How far love goes! But care is needed. "Show mercy, mixed with fear—hating even the clothing stained by corrupted flesh." The image is of stained undergarments, representing the contaminating influence of sin (Isa. 64:6; Rev. 3:4). Even as elders seek the salvation of the lost, they need to recognize the corrosive influence of sin and maintain a healthy respect for it. But if elders can be God's instrument for snatching such persons from the clutches of the evil one, then such rescued sheep will eventually wear the pure robes of salvation (Rev. 7:9, 13–14) and the angels in heaven will rejoice (Luke 15:7, 10)!

Those who wander off and go their own way are not always the most lovable, from a human point of view. Yet the love of Christ must be shown to them. After all, all members of the church received the covenant promises of salvation when they were baptized (Acts 2:39). That love also shows itself in the way the admonishing is done. "Do not rebuke an older man harshly, but exhort him as if he were your father. Treat younger men as brothers, older women as mothers, and younger women as sisters, with absolute purity" (1 Tim. 5:1–2). Like the Good Shepherd, elders too must be compassionate to those entangled in Satan's snares. "Brothers, if someone is caught in a sin, you who are spiritual should restore him gently" (Gal. 6:1). The sheep that is beginning to stray must sense in the kind and caring attitude of the elders that it is genuine heartfelt concern for his eternal well-being that fuels the admonitions and rebukes.

That same concern and love can eventually lead to the expulsion of the erring member from the fellowship of believers. It would be most cruel if such a lost sheep was allowed to stay within the fold and be under the impression that all was basically well. This would only give a false security. Love warns and admonishes. Love does not downplay the seriousness of sin, but shows precisely where the sin lies (1 Cor. 13:6–7). Excommunication shows the situation as it is, namely, that a sheep of the flock has wandered away from the fold and needs to be called back.

Even after excommunication, love shows itself in the prayers that continue to ascend to heaven for the lost sheep and the warnings that continue to be given.[44] Excommunication does not in itself condemn someone to hell. Rather it warns the person that if there is no repentance, he will be eternally condemned.[45] However, if there is a turning back, then, in the words of the apostle Paul, "You ought to forgive and comfort him, so that he will not be overwhelmed by excessive sorrow. I urge you, therefore, to

44. Indeed, the classic form for excommunication of the Reformed churches in the Netherlands urges the congregation not to consider the one who has been excommunicated as an enemy, but to warn him or her as a brother or sister in hopes there will be repentance.

45. See Calvin, *Institutes* 4.12.10, p. 1238.

reaffirm your love for him" (2 Cor. 2:7–8). Reconciliation and restoration await the repentant soul. The whole process of discipline must therefore be saturated with love so that, should there be excommunication, the way back is facilitated as much as possible. Needless to say, all of this presupposes the work of the Holy Spirit in the labors of the elders (Gal. 5:22–23).

Serving the Great Shepherd

We conclude this chapter by considering two apostolic charges given to the elders, one by Paul (Acts 20:28), the other by Peter (1 Peter 5:2–4). As apostles they spoke on behalf of the Great Shepherd of the sheep, Jesus Christ (Heb. 13:20). These apostolic charges will help us to pull together important aspects of the disciplinary and judging tasks of the elders.

In his farewell address to the Ephesian elders, the apostle Paul urged the elders: "Keep watch over yourselves and all the flock of which the Holy Spirit has made you overseers, to shepherd the church of God, which he bought with his own blood" (Acts 20:28, my translation). Several things stand out in this charge. First, as we noted earlier, the one charged to watch over the lives of others must watch over his own soul. He must constantly be on the alert so that he can be an example of godliness to the flock. Where the shepherd leads, also in conduct of life, the sheep follow.

Second, notice that the entire congregation is to have the attention of the elders. There are to be no exceptions. All are their responsibility—the prominent and the lowly, the rich and the poor, the young and the elderly, the lovable ones and the difficult sheep. All form part of the flock. The image of the shepherd underscores the dependency of the sheep on the protective guidance of the elders. Elders are, therefore, not those who live in ivory towers. They must know life and be familiar with the challenges and temptations that their sheep face in the world and warn the sheep of the flock accordingly.

Third, the Holy Spirit has made elders overseers, and so their office is from God. This divine origin of the eldership adds tremendous weight and dignity to their calling. Set over the congregation by God himself, they have an awesome responsibility to live up to God's expectations. Through the labors of the elders, the Spirit himself ministers to the congregation, using the elders as his instruments. The faithful elder can, therefore, count on the gifts he needs by using the means of the Spirit, training himself in godliness, and searching the Scriptures so that he may be equipped for every good work (2 Tim 3:14–17).

Fourth, these responsibilities are summed up with the words: "The Holy Spirit has made you overseers, to shepherd the church of God, which he bought with his own blood" (Acts 20:28). The purpose of being overseers or elders is "to shepherd the church of God." Being an overseer and being a shepherd are therefore closely related. Remarkably, both terms, "shepherd" and "overseer," are used of Christ. He is called the "Shepherd and Overseer of your souls" (1 Peter 2:25). Christ sets the tone for the work of the elders. His work as Shepherd and Overseer of the souls of his people means that he purchased them with his own blood, a fact Paul mentions in his charge to the elders (Acts 20:28; cf. 1 Peter 1:18–19).

Fifth, the love, care, and concern Christ showed for his people by buying his flock with his own life are unfathomable, and elders must never forget them. That central fact must color the attitude and actions of elders. They deal not just with certain church members. No, they are dealing with the priceless possession of their Savior. He is jealous for his people, and he will ask his elders to give an accounting (Jer. 23:2; Ezek. 34:1–16; Zech. 10:3). Elders are therefore duty-bound to give their all in watching over the well-being of the flock by encouraging, warning, seeking, guarding, and guiding the sheep in the ways of the Good Shepherd. Moved with the love of Christ they will do everything possible to search out the straying, gather the sheep together, safeguard, and shepherd the priceless flock in their care.

Coming now to Peter's charge to the elders, we notice that he also stressed that the sheep belong to God. Peter wrote:

Be shepherds of God's flock that is under your care, serving as overseers—not because you must, but because you are willing, as God wants you to be; not greedy for money, but eager to serve; not lording it over those entrusted to you, but being examples to the flock. And when the Chief Shepherd appears, you will receive the crown of glory that will never fade away. (1 Peter 5:2–4)

In addition to what has already been said about Paul's charge, the following additional points merit mention. First, in light of his past, Peter was surely not just using imagery when he exhorted the elders to be shepherds of the flock. When Christ was on trial, Peter denied the Lord three times. When he was restored, the Savior asked Peter three times whether he loved him. Three times Peter answered in the affirmative, and in response the Lord gave him a triple charge: "Feed my lambs. . . . Take care of my sheep. . . . Feed my sheep" (John 21:15–17). Peter was charged to be a shepherd of the flock of Christ, and now as a fellow elder (1 Peter 5:1) he also charged his colleagues with the same task. As Peter was to carry out this charge in the context of his love for his Master, so the other elders were to do likewise. They were to serve as elders, not because they had to, but because they were willing, as God wanted them to be (1 Peter 5:2). After all, to shepherd a flock that belongs to God is a privilege that must never be done grudgingly and reluctantly, but with love, gratitude, and devotion to the Chief Shepherd.

Second, elders were not to be "greedy for money, but eager to serve" (1 Peter 5:2). Since workers deserve their wages (Luke 10:7), some elders were remunerated for their services. The office of what we today call the teaching elder or minister falls under the rule that "those who preach the gospel should receive their living from the gospel" (1 Cor. 9:14). Nevertheless, it happened that some tried to profit unfairly from their office. Such were false teachers, out for themselves and not the flock (2 Peter 2:1–3, 14–15; Jude 12). Being an elder is not about getting something for yourself, but about giving yourself as a shepherd to those assigned to your care.

Third, Peter stressed that elders were not to lord it over those entrusted to them, but to be examples to the flock (1 Peter 5:3). Literally the original reads: "not lording it over the lots," that is, that which is assigned by lot or simply given as a portion or share. In the context of this charge to the elders it means: "the various parts of the people of God which have been assigned as 'portions' to individual elders or shepherds."[46] Each elder had a specific part of the congregation allotted to him for which he was especially responsible. This underlines the close bond that should exist between an elder and those whom he is shepherding. An elder is not to abuse this relationship by asserting an unbiblical domination over those entrusted to him. That can easily happen, for example, when a sheep has stumbled and fallen into sin. The elder should not then use the occasion to imply that he is superior to his brother. Rather, the elder should be at his side in his troubles, knowing that as an office bearer he too is by nature inclined to sin. "God opposes the proud but gives grace to the humble" (1 Peter 5:5). The whole attitude of the elder should be one of humble service as befitting one who is answerable to the Chief Shepherd. Elders are there to nurture, guide, protect, and seek the well-being of the sheep. As the Lord Jesus came to serve and not to be served, so his undershepherds must do as well (Mark 10:43–45; Luke 22:25–27; John 13:12–16).

Peter touches on this principle of service which is for God's glory when he writes:

> Each one should use whatever gift he has received to serve others, faithfully administering God's grace in its various forms. If anyone speaks, he should do it as one speaking the very words of God. If anyone serves, he should do it with the strength God provides, so that in all things God may be praised through Jesus Christ. To him be the glory and the power for ever and ever. Amen. (1 Peter 4:10–11)

46. F. W. Danker, ed., *A Greek-English Lexicon of the New Testament and Other Early Christian Literature*, 3d ed. (Chicago and London: University of Chicago Press, 2000), 548.

These words remind us of the exhortation of the apostle Paul: "Your attitude should be the same as that of Christ Jesus: who, being in very nature God, did not consider equality with God something to be grasped, but made himself nothing, taking the very nature of a servant, being made in human likeness" (Phil. 2:5–7). Elders who reflect this attitude of Christ are faithful servants.

To say that elders should not lord it over the flock is of course not the same as suggesting that they have no authority. As servants of the risen Lord and Chief Shepherd, elders do have authority and are, therefore, worthy of honor (1 Tim. 5:17). But their authority is a serving authority. Elders have a burden for the congregation. This awesome calling necessitates that those in their charge respect them, not because of their persons as such, but because of their office. As the apostle Paul exhorted the Thessalonians: "Now we ask you, brothers, to respect those who work hard among you, who are over you in the Lord and who admonish you. Hold them in the highest regard in love because of their work" (1 Thess. 5:12–13). In a similar vein the recipients of Hebrews were told: "Obey your leaders and submit to their authority. They keep watch over you as men who must give an account. Obey them so that their work will be a joy, not a burden, for that would be of no advantage to you" (Heb. 13:17).

This brings us to the final point respecting Peter's charge to the elders. He told the faithful elders that "when the Chief Shepherd appears, you will receive the crown of glory that will never fade away" (1 Peter 5:4). What a tremendous note of encouragement! The Chief Shepherd does not have merely a part of the flock, but oversees the whole flock of sheep. To him elders are responsible. For him they work as servant-shepherds. Their work of discipling and judging may often seem unappreciated or unnoticed on earth. But one day the Chief Shepherd will return. He will appear in visible form before their very eyes and bring the reward for the faithful office bearers: "the crown of glory that will never fade away"!

While the Good Shepherd wore the crown of thorns (Matt. 27:29), he will give his faithful servants the crown of glory. The word Peter uses for "crown" indicates the wreath that in the Greek-Roman world of that time was given to athletes in recognition of their achievements in competitions. It was also presented to those who made significant contributions to the state. This wreath was possibly made of the amaranth foliage and flower because these were thought not to fade quickly. However, the wreath that Christ will give to his faithful elders is unfading because of the glory associated with it. Indeed, glory defines this crown or wreath. This glory is the glory with which the Chief Shepherd is crowned (Heb. 2:9), and it is this crown of Christ's glory that the servant-shepherds will share in, as for that matter will all the people of God (2 Tim. 4:8)! This crown lasts forever (1 Cor. 9:25) and is the crown of life (James 1:12; Rev. 2:10) and of righteousness (2 Tim. 4:8).

Part 5

Maintaining and Building on the Heritage

10

Two Current Issues: Female Elders and Elders for Life

LET US NOW briefly consider two current questions that are important for maintaining and building on the biblical heritage of God's gift of the eldership. They are

- Female elders?
- Elders for life?

Female Elders?

Our present egalitarian culture has asked why women cannot be elders. Is the apparent biblical exclusion of women from the office of elder not culturally determined so that we today are not bound by this restriction? Does not limiting the eldership to males unjustifiably exclude the use of the gifts that women have to offer to the church? Such questions have become a burning issue.[1]

---

1. The literature on this topic is vast. Two studies arguing for female elders are: Craig S. Keener, *Paul, Women, and Wives: Marriage and Women's Ministry in the Letters of Paul* (Peabody, MA: Hendrickson, 1992), and Richard Clark Kroeger and Catherine Clark Kroeger, *I Suffer Not a Woman: Rethinking 1 Timothy 2:11–15 in Light of Ancient Evidence* (Grand Rapids: Baker, 1992). A representative collection on excluding women from the eldership is: John Piper and Wayne Grudem, eds., *Recovering Biblical Manhood and Womanhood: A Response to Evangelical Feminism* (Wheaton, IL: Crossway, 1991).

The cultural context is an important matter. But the key issue is of course what Scripture itself tells us about changing contexts and the unchanging demands of God. Scripture makes it clear, for example, that the ritual laws connected with the temple are a thing of the past (Col. 2:16–17; Heb. 9:1–10:18). However, the Ten Commandments and the underlying demand of love for God and neighbor are still in force (Matt. 19:17–19; 22:37–40). Also still in force are creation ordinances, such as marriage, which were established at creation and maintained throughout Scripture. Now with respect to the eldership, it is noteworthy that the apostle Paul appeals to creation when he writes about the position of women in the church. However, such passages, which historically have been taken to affirm male eldership, have been reinterpreted. It is therefore necessary for us to consider these portions of Scripture and how egalitarians are interpreting them in our day. We will focus on three New Testament passages that have been considered most important for defending a male eldership, namely, 1 Timothy 2:11–14; 1 Corinthians 11:3–16; and 14:33b–35.

1 Timothy 2:11–14

> A woman should learn in quietness and full submission. I do not permit a woman to teach or to have authority over a man; she must be silent. For Adam was formed first, then Eve. And Adam was not the one deceived; it was the woman who was deceived and became a sinner. (1 Tim. 2:11–14)

Since authoritative teaching and governing of the church are part of the elder's responsibility (1 Tim. 3:2, 5), this prohibition, based on God's work of creation, seems to bar women from the office of elder for all time. The following two counterarguments have however been brought against this conclusion. First, if one properly understands the social background, this general prohibition cannot be maintained. Paul asked women to be silent only because they first needed to learn before asking questions. Such an imposition of silence in order to learn would fit the cultural context of Paul's time. The apostle had no intention to silence women permanently. Indeed Paul wanted them to learn (1 Tim. 2:11) so that they could eventually teach.[2] Second, the very fact that Paul needed to forbid women to teach shows that Timothy was apparently unaware of such a general prohibition. Paul's forbidding "a woman to teach or to have authority over a man" (1 Tim. 2:12) was, therefore, a specific command referring to the specific situation in Ephesus where uneducated women were apparently spreading false teaching in a domineering manner. In conclusion, Paul's prohibition is not to be taken as a general rule.[3]

In response, the following can be noted. To suggest that Timothy was unaware of a general ban on women teaching and having authority over men is a weak argument. After all, the apostle wrote not just to Timothy but also through him to the church, including those whom Paul had in mind with his prohibition. By writing what he did, the apostle strengthened Timothy's position and authority to enforce the apostolic teaching.[4] As for the idea that women had to be silent because of their lack of education, there is no biblical evidence for this. Nowhere in 1 or 2 Timothy does the apostle identify a woman teaching false doctrine. If this had been the reason, why would the apostle not have simply written: "You are not permitted to teach since you are uneducated"? This observation takes us to the central problem with the above interpretations.

The apostle Paul based his prohibition on the fact that Adam was formed first and then Eve and that Adam was not the one deceived, but the woman. This means that the teaching prohibition for women reflects the fact of Adam's prior creation and that the woman fell into sin first. Paul's prohibition is, therefore, a universal rule, for it is based directly on creation and what happened at the very beginning. This is the most obvious way to read the text. Arguments to the contrary are simply not convincing.[5]

2. Keener, *Paul, Women, and Wives*, 107–8, 112.
3. Ibid., 103–13.
4. Benjamin L. Merkle, "Paul's Arguments from Creation in 1 Corinthians 11:8–9 and 1 Timothy 2:13–14: An Apparent Inconsistency Answered," *Journal of the Evangelical Theological Society* 49 (2006): 541 note 47, also 545–47.
5. Cf., e.g., Keener, *Paul, Women, and Wives*, 116–17, with Merkle, "Paul's Arguments from Creation," 542–47.

But what about 1 Corinthians 11:3–16? Does not the apostle there base on creation as well the injunction that women should cover their heads during worship? Yet most conservative scholars take Paul's directive as a cultural matter that does not apply today. Is this not inconsistent? To be consistent should the prohibition of 1 Timothy 2:12 then not be taken as a cultural issue as well, a prohibition that is not binding on us? To answer these concerns, we turn to 1 Corinthians 11.

1 Corinthians 11:3–16

> Now I want you to realize that the head of every man is Christ, and the head of the woman is man, and the head of Christ is God. Every man who prays or prophesies with his head covered dishonors his head. And every woman who prays or prophesies with her head uncovered dishonors her head—it is just as though her head were shaved. If a woman does not cover her head, she should have her hair cut off; and if it is a disgrace for a woman to have her hair cut or shaved off, she should cover her head. A man ought not to cover his head, since he is the image and glory of God; but the woman is the glory of man. For man did not come from woman, but woman from man; neither was man created for woman, but woman for man. For this reason, and because of the angels, the woman ought to have a sign of authority on her head.
>
> In the Lord, however, woman is not independent of man, nor is man independent of woman. For as woman came from man, so also man is born of woman. But everything comes from God. Judge for yourselves: Is it proper for a woman to pray to God with her head uncovered? Does not the very nature of things teach you that if a man has long hair, it is a disgrace to him, but that if a woman has long hair, it is her glory? For long hair is given to her as a covering. If anyone wants to be contentious about this, we have no other practice—nor do the churches of God. (1 Cor. 11:3–16)

The apostle is discussing matters proper for worship. It is clear that he is using arguments from creation. But how? What is the real issue at stake? Is it head coverings as such or something more than that? Surely it is something more, for, as a careful reading of the passage shows, the apostle is concerned with keeping the distinctions between male and female in worship. The use or nonuse of head coverings was not the point as such but was simply a cultural outworking of the truth that needed to be maintained, namely, that God created males and females differently. It is important to notice that Paul does not here use the creation account to make the case for head coverings for women, but to affirm that man "is the image and glory of God; but the woman is the glory of man" (1 Cor. 11:7). That fact and the related fact that "the head of the woman is man" (1 Cor. 11:3) are the truths that the apostle was affirming when bringing creation into the argument. Creation thus shows that the woman's demeanor should be humble and submissive to male leadership. How this truth is exhibited varies from culture to culture and is ultimately a secondary point.[6]

Also, Paul's argument from nature suggests that God's creational gender and role distinctions are the primary issues in view. The apostle writes: "Does not the very nature of things teach you that if a man has long hair, it is a disgrace to him, but that if a woman has long hair, it is her glory? For long hair is given to her as a covering" (1 Cor. 11:14–15). "Nature" does not refer to culture or social conventions but to God's design in creation. These differences must therefore also be exhibited in accordance with the cultural conventions of the time in which one is living. In Corinth that meant that women should cover their heads. Indeed, the fact that this was a universal rule is indicated by the apostle's adding, "If anyone wants to be contentious about this, we have no other practice—nor do the churches of God" (1 Cor. 11:16). Such a universally accepted custom reflects an underlying principle.

In summary, then, the apostle does not bring in creation in order to make the case that head coverings must be worn.

6. See for what follows Merkle, "Paul's Arguments from Creation," 534–38. See also Thomas R. Schreiner, "Head Coverings, Prophecies and the Trinity," in Piper and Grudem, eds., *Recovering Biblical Manhood and Womanhood*, 124–39.

Rather, he brings creation into his argument to show the universal and continuing truth that gender and role distinctions were determined by God at creation. That truth should also be reflected in one's culture. In the culture of Paul's day this meant that women should wear head coverings in worship. Thus, while the universal truth of gender and role distinctions needs to be maintained, the manner in which a particular culture exhibits that truth can change.[7]

One other passage is often used to argue that women should not be ordained as elders, namely 1 Corinthians 14:33b–35.

1 Corinthians 14:33b–35

> As in all the congregations of the saints, women should remain silent in the churches. They are not allowed to speak, but must be in submission, as the Law says. If they want to inquire about something, they should ask their own husbands at home; for it is disgraceful for a woman to speak in the church. (1 Cor. 14:33b–35)

The apostle wrote these words while addressing matters of worship. An egalitarian interpretation of this passage suggests that Paul was addressing a situation in which relatively uneducated women were disrupting the service with irrelevant questions. The immediate remedy was to stop them asking such questions until they could be educated.[8] In other words, we have a situation similar to what was suggested for 1 Timothy 2:12. However, as in the case of Paul's letter to Timothy, also here there is no biblical evidence that a lack of education on the part of the women motivated the prohibition for them to speak and ask questions.

How should this passage be interpreted? This command to be silent cannot be understood as an absolute demand. Women

---

7. For additional arguments that the apostle's main concern is gender and role distinctions, and not that women's heads should be covered, see Merkle, "Paul's Arguments from Creation," 534–36.

8. Keener, *Paul, Women, and Wives*, 70.

were, after all, permitted to pray and prophesy in the church, as well as to sing hymns (1 Cor. 11:5; 14:26). On the other hand, the injunction to be silent is important. It is made three times (1 Cor. 14:34–35), all within the context that women must be in submission, as the law says (1 Cor. 14:34). So the demand for silence needs to be understood within that framework. The reference to the law probably refers to the Old Testament, with the creation account being specifically in view.[9]

If the command to be silent is to be understood in the context of submission, it seems most reasonable to understand this prohibition in the light of Paul's injunction that prophecies needed to be judged (1 Cor. 14:29). When prophecies were being weighed and evaluated, women were to keep silent. If they wished to criticize or ask about a prophecy, this should be done at home, out of respect for the men. The context and the flow of thought in 1 Corinthians 14:29–40 suggest that this is the best interpretation. The careful weighing of prophecies would fall under the command that a woman was not "to teach or to have authority over a man" (1 Tim. 2:12).[10]

We can conclude that three critical passages, 1 Timothy 2:11–14, 1 Corinthians 11:3–16, and 14:33–35, should continue to be used to support the position that women should not be ordained as elders. The egalitarian reinterpretation does not convince.

The Participation of Women in the Church

Among reasons given for opening the office of elder to women is the fact that women were involved in what appears to be ministry-related roles in the early church.[11] What are we to make of that? Could this indicate that women were in

9. When the apostle used the term "law" in 1 Cor. 14:21, he quoted from Isaiah. Paul also used the term "law" to refer to the five books of Moses (Rom. 3:21; Gal. 4:21). Since Paul had appealed to the creation account earlier with regard to the relationship of men and women (1 Cor. 11:8–9), one can reasonably suppose that this is the case here as well.

10. For an extensive defense of this interpretation, see D. A. Carson, "'Silent in the Churches': On the Role of Women in 1 Corinthians 14:33b–36," in Piper and Grudem, eds., *Recovering Biblical Manhood and Womanhood*, 151–53.

11. E.g., Keener, *Paul, Women, and Wives*, 237–57.

positions of authority over men and so could be considered for the eldership?

Scripture indicates that women and men share in the gifts of the Spirit and have a vital contribution to make for the well-being of the church. The Spirit also gave to women the gift of prophecy (Acts 2:17–18; 21:9; 1 Cor. 11:5), prayer (1 Cor. 11:5), and teaching (Acts 18:26). These gifts of women must be utilized for the benefit of God's people. "Each one should use whatever gift he has received to serve others, faithfully administering God's grace in its various forms" (1 Peter 4:10; 1 Cor. 12:5). Now one should realize that having and using these gifts as such says little about the legitimacy of ordaining women to the office of elder. One does not need to be an elder in order to have and use these gifts. A review of the evidence confirms this fact.

We saw that 1 Corinthians 11 teaches that a woman's prophesying and prayer should be done in such a way that the distinctions between male and female are maintained. This entails that the woman should show herself submissive to male leadership. Priscilla and Aquila taught Apollos (Acts 18:26). But not too much can be made of this since we do not know how the two shared the teaching or what the teaching entailed. We do know that it took place in the privacy of their home and thus was not public, authoritative teaching from one who held an office in the church. To argue from this instance that Priscilla would have qualified for the eldership is reading far more into the text than it allows.

In another context, the apostle Paul urged the older women to "train the younger women to love their husbands and children, to be self-controlled and pure, to be busy at home, to be kind, and to be subject to their husbands, so that no one will malign the word of God" (Titus 2:4–5). This passage also does not support official authoritative teaching of men by women. A basic rule of interpreting Scripture is that the less clear passages should be explained by those that are more clear. As we have seen, Paul's injunction to Timothy, based on creation, is very explicit and precise: "I do not permit a woman to teach or to have authority over a man" (1 Tim. 2:12). A brief passage about Priscilla's teaching Apollos that leaves unanswered questions for some issues raised in our culture cannot be a justification for affirming an authoritative teaching office in the church for women when Scripture explicitly forbids this on the basis of God's creation order. Furthermore, as noted earlier, the gifts of women are never specifically mentioned as functioning in the special office of elder or overseer. This observation suggests that the women's ministry or service in the church complemented and was supportive of the work of the elders and overseers.[12]

Another issue is that Priscilla, as well as the women Euodia and Syntyche, are called fellow workers in the gospel (Rom. 16:3; Phil. 4:2–3). In 1 Corinthians 16:16, Paul exhorts the Corinthian Christians to submit to such fellow workers and laborers. Thus it would seem that these Christians are to be subject to female fellow workers as well, indicating that they held a position of authority, even over men, in the church. Furthermore, the terms "laborers" and "labor" are used of office bearers (e.g., 1 Thess. 5:12; 1 Tim. 5:17) as well as of work that women do for the church (Rom. 16:12).[13] However, to conclude from this usage of the terms "fellow workers," "labor," and "laborers" that women functioned in the office of elder is unwarranted. These terms are far too vague and general to prove the existence of women elders. There are many ways in which women could be coworkers and laborers for the gospel without being in an ordained office. Here again we must be guided by the more clear passages to understand the less clear.

Justification for women elders has also been sought in Romans 16:7, which is understood to indicate that a woman served as an apostle. If a woman could be an apostle, why could she not serve as an elder? This passage reads, "Greet Andronicus and Junias, my relatives who have been in prison with me. They are outstanding among the apostles, and they were in Christ before

12. See, e.g., Thomas R. Schreiner, "The Valuable Ministries of Women in the Context of Male Leadership: A Survey of Old and New Testament Examples and Teaching," in Piper and Grudem, eds., *Recovering Biblical Manhood and Womanhood*, 209–24.

13. The Greek terms are *synergos* "fellow worker" and *kopiaō* "to labor" (*kopiōn* "laborer").

I was" (Rom. 16:7). A key issue is whether Junias was male or female. Considerable research has been done on this question. When all has been said and done, there is no definitive proof that this was a woman's name.[14] There are also other elements in the passage that caution us against using it as a proof text for a female apostle. The text could mean that Andronicus and Junias were outstanding in the eyes of the apostles, although this view is not widely held. More importantly, the term "apostle" can mean different things. It need not refer to the stature that one like Paul had (1 Cor. 15:5, 7). Elsewhere, Paul used the term in a nontechnical sense as a messenger or representative (2 Cor. 8:23; Phil. 2:25), and that could very well be the case here.[15]

Other Factors

Something Paul wrote to the Galatians is frequently raised in defense of women elders: "There is neither Jew nor Greek, slave nor free, male nor female, for you are all one in Christ Jesus" (Gal. 3:28). These words, however, cannot be used to justify female elders. They underline the unity of believers in Christ. But this unity does not mean that all have the same function and place in the congregation. The apostle's concern in Galatians 3 is neither the position of man and woman as such nor the elimination of their distinctives, but the issue is their sharing fully the salvation in Christ.[16]

Additionally, Christ honored the creation ordinance of male headship when he called twelve male disciples (Matt. 10:2–4), which led directly to a male apostolic office upon which the church was founded (Eph. 2:20; Rev. 21:14). An analogous male eldership can therefore be expected.

14. Al Wolters has argued persuasively that Junias is probably a Hellenistic form of a masculine Hebrew name. See his "*Iounian* (Rom. 16:7) and the Hebrew Name *Yehunni*," *Journal of Biblical Literature* 127 (2008): 397–408.

15. See on Junias, e.g., Douglas Moo, *The Epistle to the Romans*, New International Commentary on the New Testament (Grand Rapids: Eerdmans, 1996), 921–24, and John Piper and Wayne Grudem, "An Overview of Central Concerns," in Piper and Grudem, eds., *Recovering Biblical Manhood and Womanhood*, 79–81.

16. See, e.g., S. Lewis Johnson, Jr., "Role Distinctions in Church: Galatians 3:28," in Piper and Grudem, eds., *Recovering Biblical Manhood and Womanhood*, 154–64.

Furthermore, as noted earlier, the church developed within the context of the family and is to be understood in terms of the family. Male headship in the church is consistent with male leadership in the family and with the fact that a Christian marriage is to reflect the relationship that the church has with Christ (Eph. 5:22–25). The loving submission to the husband, the caring head, based initially on creation, gets new impetus and justification in the re-creation work of Christ. This work includes his church where male headship is an important principle. The Christian father who manages his own household well has an important qualification to lead the church as an elder (1 Tim. 3:4–5).[17]

In Conclusion

Scripture teaches and requires a male eldership. Not surprisingly, some have concluded that the pressure to authorize women elders "owes more to secular, pragmatic and social factors than to any regard for biblical authority."[18] Indeed, a dissertation investigating why three major Dutch churches opened the office to women concluded that biblical data about the relevant issues played only a marginal role in the decision-making process.[19] If Scripture is the final authority, there is no justification for the ordaining of women elders.

The exclusion of women from the office of elder does not mean, of course, that women have no place or task in building up the body of Christ. We have already noted that the Holy Spirit gives women gifts for the edification of the church. But these gifts can be used without being ordained into the office of elder.

17. See further, e.g., Vern Sheridan Poythress, "The Church as Family: Why Male Leadership in the Family Requires Male Leadership in the Church," in Piper and Grudem, eds., *Recovering Biblical Manhood and Womanhood*, 233–47. Keener's point that Paul demanded submission of the wife to the husband to mollify Roman authorities lest they feel their patriarchal view of marriage being challenged is not credible given the reasons adduced and what the apostle wrote elsewhere, e.g., in 1 Cor. 11:3. See Keener, *Paul, Women, and Wives*, 133–83.

18. J. I. Packer, "Let's Stop Making Women Presbyters," *Christianity Today* 35.2 (February 11, 1991): 19.

19. Koen Kyungkeun Lim, *Het spoor van de vrouw in het ambt* (Theologie en Geschiedenis; Kampen: Kok, 2001), 288.

In God's sovereign wisdom he has given both male and female specific roles in his church. These roles complement each other; they are not competitive.[20]

Elders for Life? Definite or Indefinite Tenure

Presbyterian churches normally ordain elders for life, or to phrase it more accurately, for an indefinite tenure since there can be reasons for one's eldership to be terminated.[21] Reformed churches, on the other hand, tend to ordain elders for a set number of years. When their term is up, they cease to be elders. If elected to office again, they need to be ordained again. What is one to think of these dissimilar traditions? Before attempting to form a judgment on the issue, we will need to consider the historical roots of the different practices as well as any biblical evidence upon which these practices may be based.

Some History

Calvin was apparently in favor of elders serving for one year, but he did not exclude the possibility of a longer time period.[22] In Scotland, *The First Book of Discipline* (1560) reflects Calvin's view. Under the eighth head, "Touching the Election of Elders and Deacons," we read: "The election of Elders and Deacons ought to be used every year once . . . lest of long continuance of such officers men presume upon the liberty of the kirk. It hurteth not that one be received in office moe years then one, so that he be

20. See further on the important role of women in the life of the church, Schreiner, "The Valuable Ministries of Women in the Context of Male Leadership," 209–24.

21. As noted by G. I. Williamson at the 1989 International Conference for Reformed Churches held in Langley, British Columbia. See *Proceedings of the International Conference of Reformed Churches, June 19–28, 1989* (Winnipeg: Premier, [1989]), 57. For reasons for removal from office, see John Murray, "Arguments Against Term Eldership," in his *Collected Writings of John Murray*, 4 vols. (Edinburgh: Banner of Truth Trust, 1976–82), 2:351–52.

22. The "Ecclesiastical Ordinances" (1541) in Philip E. Hughes, ed. and trans., *The Register of the Company of Pastors of Geneva in the Time of Calvin* (Grand Rapids: Eerdmans, 1966), 42.

appointed yearly by common and free election."[23] Here we see one of the primary motives for a yearly election, namely the fear that some by virtue of their office might usurp the liberty of the church. This was not an idle threat. In Geneva elders were chosen from civil councils and in Scotland elders were initially taken from the Lords of the Congregation and the Burgh Councillors.[24]

When *The Second Book of Discipline* was adopted in 1578, the office of elder was recognized as a perpetual one although not all those ordained needed to serve simultaneously or continuously. This recognition need not be regarded as principally different from *The First Book of Discipline* since it allowed that elders remain in office for more than one year.[25] In any case, rather than being appointed annually, they now entered the office for life. This was reaffirmed by the Act of the General Assembly of 1582.[26] However, "it took some time for the impact of these acts of the Assembly to take effect, as there is evidence of annual elections of elders continuing to take place, while in 1656 it was still believed that 'the order and practice' of the Church was regular elections."[27] As late as 1705 an overture was presented to the General Assembly asking that new elections for elders be for a four-year term.[28] Indefinite tenure has, however, become the accepted norm in Presbyterian churches.

In the history of the Reformed churches, eldership for life was known; but eventually all had a limited term of office. Elders were chosen for life in the Reformed congregations in sixteenth-century London and Cologne.[29] Questions were raised about the practice among the Dutch refugee congregations in England, and

23. James K. Cameron, ed., *The First Book of Discipline with an Introduction and Commentary* (Edinburgh: Saint Andrew, 1972), 175, see also 36.

24. See, respectively, "Ecclesiastical Ordinances" (1541) as given in Hughes, ed. and trans., *The Register of the Company of Pastors*, 41, and T. F. Torrance, "The Eldership in the Reformed Church," *Scottish Journal of Theology* 37 (1984): 505.

25. James Kirk, ed., *The Second Book of Discipline with an Introduction and Commentary* (Edinburgh: Saint Andrew, 1980), 89–94, 192.

26. G. D. Henderson, *The Scottish Ruling Elder* (London: James Clarke, 1935), 204.

27. Torrance, "The Eldership in the Reformed Church," 506.

28. Henderson, *The Scottish Ruling Elder*, 203–4.

29. See A. van Ginkel, *De Ouderling: oorsprong en ontwikkeling van het ambt van ouderling en de functie daarvan in de Gereformeerde Kerk der Nederlanden in de 16e en 17e eeuw* (Amsterdam: Ton Bolland, 1975), 241.

a conference held in 1560 dealt with this point. The conference decided to maintain life eldership for the following reasons. First, there is an essential unity of the office of minister of the Word and elder. The ministers are called elders and the elders are called bishops or shepherds (1 Peter 5:1–2; Acts 20:28). Second, those who served faithfully as elders or deacons were not removed from their office but were "moved up" to the ministry of the Word as Stephen and Philip were (Acts 6:8–14; 21:8). Third, the office is not temporary, for Paul exhorts the elders of Ephesus to take heed to themselves and to the flock without indicating how long they should serve. They are told to persevere. Fourth, on a more practical level, the fact that some elders had to leave the office in order to be able to provide for their families does not mean that it is profitable to have term eldership. As apprentices in normal life are trained for a long period of work in which experience becomes an important asset, so also the congregation is not served by constantly having new office bearers.[30] Last, but not least, it needs to be remembered that besides the reasons given by the conference, the Dutch refugee congregations in London were under the supervision of the Church of England, which was hierarchical. The English church opposed meaningful congregational input in the governing of the congregation, as would happen with regular elections of office bearers.[31]

In the Netherlands, the practice of indefinite tenure for the elder was also not unknown. In North Holland, it was implemented until 1587, possibly due to a lack of candidates. Interestingly, the Provincial Synod of Utrecht declared in 1612 that it was desirable for elders to be chosen for life although the synod recognized that this was no longer possible and thus accepted the established practice of eldership for a definite term. However, in the province of Groningen elders were chosen for life until the end of the eighteenth century.[32]

30. H. Bouwman, *Gereformeerde kerkrecht*, 2 vols. (Kampen: Kok, 1928, 1934), 1:603–4.
31. Ibid., 1:605.
32. Van Ginkel, *De Ouderling*, 214–43; Bouwman, *Gereformeerd kerkrecht*, 1:605. Bouwman notes that life eldership in the city of Groningen was due to political circumstances.

Nevertheless, already very early in the history of the Reformed churches in the Netherlands, the Colloquy of Wesel in 1568 and three years later at the Synod of Emden decided that elders be ordained for a definite term. This was mainly for practical reasons. Such definite tenure eventually became the accepted norm within the Reformed churches, although exceptions were allowed.

The concern cited by the Wesel meeting in deciding to restrict the term of an elder was that those faithfully executing their office as elder could do so only at considerable personal monetary cost. In other words, the financial burden became too heavy because the elders served at the expense of their normal employment or business.[33] This reason must be seen in the context of the struggle of establishing Reformed church life and the persecution of those days. Faithful office bearers often risked their lives, and the necessity to protect themselves often meant loss or reduction of their income. The Synod of Dort of 1578 gave a two-year term as a norm, but also gave the freedom to the secret or persecuted congregations to shorten or lengthen this term of office according to their circumstances.[34]

However, practical considerations such as these were not the only reason for restricting the term of office. In advice which the 1581 Synod of Middelburg had requested on the issue, Professor L. Danaeus of Leiden gave as reasons for limited term eldership the following: First, Scripture does not demand a life eldership; second, lifetime eldership can lead to ecclesiastical tyranny; third, with term eldership more people can have an opportunity to get involved in the government of the church; and fourth, term eldership is now a general practice, although, if desired, one can deviate from that.[35] The synod never had the time to formally deal with this advice, but it was clear that it agreed. The Church Order

---

Four elders were chosen from the "Burgemeesters" and "Raadsheeren," four from the academic circle, and four from the citizenry.

33. The Articles of Wesel, V.17; for the original Latin text, see F. L. Rutgers, ed., *Acta van de Nederlandsche synoden der zestiende eeuw* (Dordrecht: Van den Tol, 1980), 27. For the decision of Emden in 1571 (Art. 15 of the Acts) in the original Latin text see ibid., 62–63.

34. For the original Dutch text of the Acts of Dort 1578 (1.13) see ibid., 239.

35. See the text in ibid., 459–62; see also 364.

adopted by the Synod of Middelburg included the provision of definite tenure. However, if the situation or the best interests of the congregation demanded it, exceptions could be made.[36] This provision for exceptions was incorporated in Article 27 of the Church Order of Dort (1618–1619).[37]

Term Eldership or Not?

When surveying the question whether an elder should be elected to a definite or indefinite term, it is striking that practical considerations seem to have been the main impetus behind ordaining elders for a specific length of time. Biblical considerations played a secondary role, in part because there is no clear prescription in Scripture regarding this issue.

For Calvin and churches influenced by him, both Presbyterian and Reformed, there was initially a real concern that elders who served for too long a period of time could become domineering, particularly since elders were chosen from civil councils. Especially in the Netherlands, this danger continued to be worrisome. Another practical factor that played a role in the Low Countries was the financial burden that would accrue for an elder entrusted with lifelong responsibilities for caring for the church. The times were uncertain, the state of the church relatively fragile, and much time and energy would have to go into the proper discharge of the office, often at the cost of neglecting one's private affairs or business.

Other practical considerations included the argument that should an ordained elder not appear to have the gifts necessary for the office, it would be relatively simple with definite tenure not to put up such an individual for election in the future. Without giving offense, someone could be eased out of the office. Furthermore, with elders regularly retiring from service, other gifts in

36. Ibid., 383.
37. For the Dutch text, see P. Biesterveld and H. H. Kuyper, *Kerkelijk handboekje* (Kampen: Bos, 1905), 233; for an English translation, David W. Hall and Joseph H. Hall, eds., *Paradigms in Polity: Classic Readings in Reformed and Presbyterian Church Government* (Grand Rapids: Eerdmans, 1994), 179.

the congregation could be employed in the office of elder, and possible tendencies toward hierarchy could be opposed. It was noted as well that lifelong service was not explicitly demanded by Scripture.

The force of circumstances could also favor indefinite tenure, as was evident in the case of the Dutch refugee congregation living under the auspices of the hierarchical Church of England. A lack of suitable candidates for definite terms possibly made indefinite tenure attractive in North Holland.

The difficulty with practical considerations is that over time they can lose their initial rationale. It is, therefore, not surprising that practical considerations have also been raised against eldership for a definite term. Such a restricted time of service in the office can create the inappropriate notion of a trial period in the mind of the congregation that elects the elders. Term eldership can also tend to create this impression in the mind of the elders and lead to a decreased sense of responsibility and office. Furthermore, it may interfere with the continuity and stability of the office. Finally, term eldership could give the impression that the church is a democracy and that the eldership should be passed around.[38]

Since practical considerations cannot, in the end, be decisive, scriptural arguments for indefinite tenure have been raised, and they therefore should be considered. These arguments have been summarized as follows.[39] First, "there is no *overt* warrant from the New Testament for what we call 'term eldership.'" Indeed, it is argued that inferences drawn from the New Testament militate against the practice. "The permanency of the gifts which qualify for the office, and the judgments of the church that Christ is calling this man to the exercise of the office" are inconsistent with a limited term, all the more when one considers that the gifts increase in fruitfulness and effectiveness with the usage of them over time. Finally, there is "the unity of the office of ruling. In

38. Murray, *Collected Writings*, 2:355–56.
39. Ibid., 2:352–56. The emphasis in the quotations subsequently given is in the original.

respect of ruling in the church of God, the ruling elder and the teaching elder are on complete parity." If there is no term office for the one, why should there be for the other? Could the practice of term eldership for ruling elders be a hangover of an unwholesome clericalism? Over against the argument that the minister of the Word makes this calling his life work, whereas the ruling elder does not, the following can be noted. In the first place this line of thinking does not invalidate that the ruling elder is called to the permanent discharge of the office of elder; second, with respect to 1 Timothy 5:17–18, the ruling elder can be remunerated part-time as well as full-time; and, third, the ruling elder is also worthy of his hire.

Although these biblical arguments have varying degrees of cogency, it remains a fact that there is no clear biblical instruction that the eldership must have an indefinite term. Furthermore, to affirm that the ruling elder is called to the permanent discharge of his office is an unproven assertion. In fact, does Scripture not seem to indicate that one can change from one office to another? If that is so, then the office is not essentially permanent. Consider that Philip, although first chosen and ordained to wait on tables (Acts 6:1–6), is later described as an evangelist (Acts 8:5, 12; 21:8). This example makes one hesitant to speak of the call to the permanent discharge of the office. It should therefore be possible, for example, for one who served first as an elder to serve later as a deacon. Indeed, it is better not to speak of the permanency of the office. Has the Reformation not rejected the Roman Catholic idea of the indelible character of the office by which the office cannot be separated from the one who discharges it? This is because the office does not have an indelible character; therefore Presbyterian elders who move away from a church where they were ordained should properly resign from their office. For the same reason, someone who previously served as an elder for a specified term in a Reformed church needs to be ordained to office again.

Another justification for indefinite term of office would seem to be that the New Testament office was rooted in the Old Testament eldership. Since that office was apparently for life, one could argue that this would justify making the New Testament office for life as well. This factor, along with some of the arguments mentioned above, could indicate that indefinite term eldership is the closest to the biblical ideal. Yet, in view of the history of the Presbyterian and Reformed churches, one must be careful not to force the issue and insist that an eldership of indefinite tenure is the only right way.

Remarkably, the annual election of elders was initially the norm both in the Scottish Presbyterian churches and in the continental Reformed ones. As we saw above, even after the *Second Book of Discipline* (1578) affirmed that the office of elder was perpetual, it took many years before annual or regular election of elders ceased in Scotland. The issue was not forced. On the other hand, in the Reformed churches eldership for life was known and vigorously defended, but eventually term eldership became the norm. But here too, much leeway was given as the churches slowly adopted a common position of a definite tenure. And so Presbyterian and Reformed churches consciously went their own separate ways. Ultimately, it seems that since specific New Testament direction on the length of the term for the office is lacking, practical considerations played a very important role.

The fact that the history of definite and indefinite tenure shows that it took quite some time for churches of the Reformation eager to do God's will to achieve unanimity on a certain way of doing things leads to another observation. Not only is it difficult to be dogmatic and insist on only one way, but when all has been said and done, issues of tenure will, in the end, not make a lot of real practical difference whether one is elected for life or for a limited term. After all, although the Presbyterian polity ordains elders for an indefinite tenure, periods of relief can be and are given.[40] Practically speaking, this is not so

40. This relief from duty is justified by *The Second Book of Discipline* VI.7 on the basis of the rotation system for priestly tasks detailed in 1 Chron. 24:1–9 (cf. Luke 1:23). See Kirk, ed., *The Second Book of Discipline*, 88–90, 192.

very different from the Reformed system where a faithful elder serves for a specified term, is off for one or two years, and then is re-elected and ordained for a further term. Indeed, Reformed churches know of those who basically serve all their lives as elders, but they do so in specified terms, with periods of rest in between. Furthermore, especially in small churches, it may at times be advisable to have a retiring elder stand for election immediately again or simply to extend his term of office. Such flexibility is possible in Reformed church polity.[41]

---

41. The Church Order of Dort (1618–19), Article 27. For an English translation, see Hall and Hall, eds., *Paradigms in Polity*, 179. Modern revisions of this church order tend to spell out this flexibility more specifically, e.g., the Church Order of the Canadian Reformed Churches, Art. 24, *Book of Praise: Anglo-Genevan Psalter*, rev. ed. (Winnipeg: Premier, 1993), 664.

The Privilege of
the Eldership

THE PRIVILEGE of the eldership is not sufficiently recognized in our egalitarian culture, and this lack of recognition can easily infect the church. Let us then, in closing, consider this privilege.

There is, first, the privilege of being an elder. This high office includes having a special relationship to God who entrusts elders with their weighty responsibilities. Illustrative of the high place that God has assigned this office is that in the history of redemption the Lord has granted to the elders the special prerogative of seeing him and being in his presence. We will explore this theme of Scripture and how it impacts our understanding of the office today, including its place in relation to the members of the church.

Second, there is the privilege that a congregation enjoys in having elders. Elders who labor in the midst of the church are a considerable blessing and are essential to the health of the people of God. This privilege has consequences in terms of needing to honor these servants of the Lord in anticipation of the return of Christ.

In this chapter we will therefore deal with

- The elders' privilege of seeing God
- The congregation's privilege in having elders

The Elders' Privilege of Seeing God

To see God and to be in his presence! Is this not the wish of every child of the heavenly Father who wants to be right with God and yearns for communion with him? David articulated this desire: "As for me, let me see your face in righteousness; let me, when I awake, be satisfied with (seeing) your form" (Ps. 17:15).[1] Believers have the promise that one day they will see God "as he is" (1 John 3:2). What they now know in part, they then will know fully (1 Cor. 13:12).

In the days of Moses those holding the office of elder were privileged to see God already in this life and to experience his presence in a special way. This illustrates something of the high esteem God accorded this office. Their being able to see God also tells us something of the blessing this office was for the people of the Lord, both then and now. We will consider Exodus 24:9–11 and then turn briefly to Isaiah 24:23–25:12, and Revelation 4–5.

Exodus 24

At Mount Sinai the elders of Israel actually saw the God of Israel and had a meal in his presence. "They saw God, and they ate and drank" (Ex. 24:11). What does their seeing God mean? We need first to consider briefly the context of this momentous event.

With a mighty arm, the Lord God had set his people free and carried them on eagles' wings to himself at Mount Sinai (Ex. 19:4). There he identified himself as "the LORD your God, who brought you out of Egypt, out of the land of slavery" (Ex. 20:2) and then gave the Ten Words of the Covenant (Ex. 20:3–17). Through Moses he also revealed more laws and ordinances to which the people enthusiastically responded: "Everything the LORD has said we will do" (Ex. 24:3)!

After this affirmation, Moses proceeded to build altars and offer sacrifices in a ceremony of covenant renewal. The book of

---

1. The translation is from Gert Kwakkel, *"According to My Righteousness": Upright Behaviour as Grounds for Deliverance in Psalms 7, 17, 18, 26 and 44* (Kampen: Van den Berg, 2001), 71, 81; similarly, e.g., New English Bible.

the covenant was read, and the people reaffirmed their commitment to obey the Lord (Ex. 24:7). Moses then took blood from the sacrifices and sprinkled it on the people, saying: "This is the blood of the covenant that the LORD has made with you" (Ex. 24:8).

Now it was only after the blood was sprinkled that Moses and Aaron, Nadab and Abihu, and seventy elders of Israel went up Sinai, as God had commanded, and saw God (Ex. 24:1, 10). They went near to God, but could do so only on the basis of the sacrifices and sprinkled blood, which spoke of forgiveness and a good relationship with God. However, there were distinctions when it came to being in God's presence.

Only a select few actually climbed up Sinai to go to God. The people as a whole were not allowed. They were not even permitted to touch the mountain, lest they die (Ex. 19:10–25). But a privileged few, including seventy elders, were allowed to come closer. There were gradations of holiness at Sinai where God met his people. These different levels of holiness would later be reflected in the tabernacle. The least holy place would be the enclosed courtyard outside the tabernacle where the people could come—that would be the closest the average Israelite got. The next level of holiness would be the holy place to which the priest would come, and finally the holy of holies which only the high priest would be allowed to enter. Such gradations were first seen at Mount Sinai. The people were before the mountain but could not come close and touch it. They were, so to speak, in the outer court. But Moses, Aaron, Nadab, Abihu, and the seventy elders could climb up the mountain. They entered, as it were, the holy place. Yet only Moses could go all the way into the very presence of God, the holy of holies, so to speak (Ex. 24:1–2, 15–18).

The priests and elders did get to see God. It is, however, striking that when a description is given, we simply read that they "saw the God of Israel. Under his feet was something like a pavement made of sapphire, clear as the sky itself" (Ex. 24:10; cf. Ezek. 1:26). One gets the distinct impression that they looked up and saw through a translucent pavement. No actual description of God himself is given. His feet are mentioned, but not even his throne. They saw *something* of God enthroned, but not clearly. This calls to mind how a little later Moses would ask God to show him his glory. But God answered: "You cannot see my face, for no one may see me and live" (Ex. 33:20). The seventy elders saw something of God enthroned. He was close. His feet were visible! But at the same time he was distant, even for the select few who could come up, see God, and have a meal. Yet what an awesome privilege! In his mercy, God allowed them to come close. The God who had been hidden in the thunder and cloud now permitted himself to be seen. And God "did not raise his hand against these leaders of the Israelites; they saw God, and they ate and drank" (Ex. 24:11). Apparently nothing was said. The event transpired in holy silence. Human beings in God's presence—heaven and earth close together.

Why did the elders have the privilege of coming close to God, just prior to the Sinaitic holy of holies, so to speak, to which Moses would be allowed to go? Why is it that they here shared this privilege with the priests, Aaron and his sons Nadab and Abihu? What aspect of their office as elder is revealed here? The answer is that they were there as representatives of Israel. God had renewed his covenant with his people, and now these elders as representatives of the nation ate and drank a meal that belonged to the ceremony of covenant renewal. In this way, the restored fellowship between God and his people was confirmed and celebrated. The fact that there were seventy elders is symbolic of the entire nation and may refer to the seventy descendants of Jacob who had come to Egypt centuries earlier (Gen. 46:27).

There is another aspect of this event that informs our understanding of the eldership. That God chose elders to represent the nation at this covenant renewal indicates their great importance. God singled out the elders to be in his presence, which must have enhanced their authority with the people. If God had such a high esteem of their position in Israel, how much more should the people esteem them for the sake of their office![2]

2. Being allowed into the very presence of God is indicative of the esteem God also expects others to show to such a person. When Moses' authority was challenged by

The elders of the people were allowed to see God and celebrate a meal of covenant fellowship with him, a meal made possible by the atoning blood. What a revelation of the mercy and grace of God! This meal was full of promise since it anticipated the full redemption to come (Heb. 9:18–28). After all, if the *representatives* and leaders of the people could participate now, would this not be an indication that eventually all the people would be able to do so?

That would be some time coming, but this observation does take us to the next occasion where we find the elders in the presence of God, namely in Isaiah 24–25.

Isaiah 24–25

This time the setting is not Mount Sinai, but Mount Zion! God is enthroned in splendor and majesty. The glory of his presence radiates from him (Isa. 24:23; cf. 4:5; 60:1). What is the context? The world has been judged with divine judgment. Devastation is everywhere and the earth languishes and withers for its people have disobeyed the Lord (Isa. 24:1–13, 16b–20). There is no redemption or forgiveness for their sin. Judgment comes in all its terror and the scene is apocalyptic. But there is a righteous remnant, and they shout for joy and sing "Glory to the Righteous One!" (Isa. 24:16a).

In a scene full of terrestrial upheaval with the assurance of punishment for the wicked, there is a sudden shift to the splendid promise that "The LORD almighty will reign on Mount Zion and in Jerusalem." And where God is, there is glory! His glory is so overwhelming that "the moon will be abashed, the sun ashamed." What are these heavenly bodies compared to the light of the splendor of the Lord who reigns in glory? God is on Mount Zion and in Jerusalem in all his majesty. And beholding his glory are elders (Isa. 24:23)!

Miriam and Aaron, the Lord supported Moses by reminding the rebels that Moses came into God's presence and that God spoke with Moses "face to face, clearly and not in riddles; he sees the form of the LORD. Why then were you not afraid to speak against my servant Moses?" (Num. 12:8).

These are the elders of God. The passage says literally "his elders," referring to the Lord of hosts.[3] That means the elders are responsible to the Lord. They are to follow his commands. This the elders often did not do. As a matter of fact, earlier in the book of Isaiah we read that the Lord entered into judgment against the elders and leaders of his people and accused them of ruining the Lord's vineyard and plundering his people (Isa. 3:14). Elsewhere the Lord indicted the elders for misleading the people (Isa. 9:15–16). All this reminds us of the awesome responsibilities that leaders like elders have. The Lord calls office bearers to account for their actions. But the Lord also promises that elders, *his* elders, will be there in the presence of the Almighty when he reigns victoriously on Mount Zion and in Jerusalem. That promise entails that there will be a faithful remnant among the elders, thanks to the grace of God. Over against the abundant sin and destruction, he maintains the work of his hands and triumphs over his enemies.

The promise of the elders being in God's glorious presence on Mount Zion prompts comparison with the elders' experience on Mount Sinai. There are some similarities. On both occasions the event takes place on a mountain, and a key element is proximity to God. However, there are two crucial differences that reflect the progress of God's self-revelation to his people. The first difference is that whereas the elders in Exodus 24 saw only the feet of God, according to Isaiah 24 they will be in the presence of the very glory of God. In Exodus 24, the glory of God was found inside the cloud that covered the summit of Sinai. The people saw something of the glory filtering through the cloud; it looked like a consuming fire (Ex. 24:17). Only Moses had been allowed to enter (Ex. 24:18). However, according to Isaiah 24, the elders will find themselves in the immediate presence of this glory. "His glory will be before his elders" (Isa. 24:23 ESV). They will be in his holy of holies (Isa. 4:5).

---

3. So ESV. The NIV is in error to translate "its elders," referring to Jerusalem. If that was the case, the Hebrew would have read "her elders" since Jerusalem is treated as feminine. See, e.g., Isa. 40:2; 51:17–18; 52:2; 62:6; 66:10.

The second difference concerns the meal and those invited. After Isaiah spoke of the glory that would be before the elders, he interrupted his account with a song of praise (Isa. 25:1–5), and then resumed it with the description of a rich banquet with aged wine and fine meats. This sumptuous festivity on the mountain with God speaks of the future glory. This festivity will, however, be the privilege not only of elders or of Israel, but this meal will be for all nations. God's grace will go out to all peoples. It will be a meal of rejoicing because the Lord God will triumph over death and remove the veil of mourning from the peoples and wipe the tears from their eyes (Isa. 25:6–8; 1 Cor. 15:54; Rev. 21:4). In view of this context, the elders in Isaiah's vision in effect represent the complete New Testament church. This truth is more fully expressed in the vision of Revelation 4 and 5 to which we now turn.

Revelation 4–5

When the apostle John was shown heaven, he saw God's throne and surrounding it were twenty-four other thrones on which were seated twenty-four elders. They were dressed in white, symbolizing their having been cleansed from sin. They had crowns of gold on their heads, symbolizing the authority to rule with Christ (Rev. 4:4). In all likelihood, these twenty-four elders represented the twelve tribes of Israel (Rev. 7:4–8) and the twelve apostles, the New Testament church (Rev. 21:14). In other words, the elders around the throne likely represented the entire holy catholic church of Christ, spanning both Old and New Testament times.[4] They were in the very holy of holies of God's presence, worshiping and praising God, and putting their crowns before his throne. They were there because the Lamb of God had triumphed by being slain and by purchasing with his blood people from every tribe and language and nation (Rev. 5:9). The blood of the covenant sacrificed on the altar of the cross of

4. This traditional interpretation has enjoyed wide support. Simon J. Kistemaker, *Exposition of the Book of Revelation*, New Testament Commentary (Grand Rapids: Baker, 2001), 187.

Golgotha is the basis for the elders and the church being in the glorious presence of God. The presence of the elders speaks of the official presence of the church, a presence later specifically mentioned in Revelation 7. There we read of a great multitude that no one could count, from every nation, tribe, people, and language, standing before the throne and in front of the Lamb. There they worship God and he will wipe away every tear from their eyes (Rev. 7:9–17). That is the future to which the elders' being in God's presence in Exodus 24 already pointed.

Concluding Observations

When we reflect on the elders seeing God, we can make several summary observations. First, when the people were still not allowed to draw near to God on Sinai, that prerogative was given to the elders. God obviously thought highly of this office. The priority that this office had with God is also evident from his maintaining this office through the ages. Although elders often failed in their task and God had to call them to account, yet the Lord kept this office going. In dark days of apostasy, he promised that elders would be part of a faithful remnant. The Lord considered this office of utmost importance. How privileged the church therefore is to still have this office today, both as ruling and teaching elders. In our current egalitarian age where special privilege and responsibility are disdained and church offices are ridiculed, we must not lose sight of the tremendous gift of God in the eldership. The elders, therefore, need to be encouraged and appreciated by the congregation. They need such support, for the eldership is not only a tremendous privilege but also an awesome responsibility. Elders bring God's Word to bear on the life of the congregation and represent God's children before God. This brings us to the next observation.

When the elders saw God, they did so as representatives of the people. Their being representatives of the church before God's throne in Exodus 24 anticipated the day when, according to God's promises (Isa. 25:6–8; Rev. 7; 14:1–3), all God's children will be in his glorious presence and enjoy him forever in holy worship. Because of the sprinkled blood of the new covenant, God's people today are not en route to Sinai with its terrifying fire, darkness, and gloom as when God warned them not to touch or come near. Rather, God's people are en route to the heavenly Mount Zion, the city of the living God (Heb. 12:18–24; Rev. 14:1). Indeed, they can even draw near to the holy of holies through the blood of Jesus in full assurance of faith (Heb. 10:19–23).

The fulfillment of God's promises means that one day not only the elders but the entire people of God, symbolized by the 144,000, will actually be before God's throne (Rev. 14:1–3). They will have a meal with God, the great wedding feast of the Lamb (Rev. 19:7, 9). The entire church will worship, praise, and glorify God in joy unending! The day will come when all God's children will see their God and Savior in a way that surpasses all revelation that we enjoy today. Heaven will come down to earth, and the dwelling of God and his glory will be with his people in perfection (Rev. 21:3, 23). In the meantime, in anticipation of that great day, the church may continue to enjoy the great privilege of having elders who labor in their midst. Their presence in the church is a constant reminder that God once chose this office to come near and see him, a privilege which pointed ahead to the day when all God's people will see him in glory.

The Congregation's Privilege of Having Elders

History teaches that in spite of the great importance and honor that God attached to the office of the ruling elder, this office can sometimes be taken for granted. It even has the tendency to disappear or become an empty formality. Having elders was clearly a priority in the first Christian congregations (Acts 14:23). However, within the grand context of history, it did not take very long for the office to become usurped by a new priesthood in the fourth century. It was only in the sixteenth-century Protestant Reformation that the office was recovered.

235

The Calvinist wing of the Reformation especially restored the eldership to its proper place.[5]

Our appreciation of this office will be helped by reviewing briefly the main duties and expectations of the ruling elder and so recalling some highlights of our earlier discussions. Presbyterian and Reformed readers will notice how their traditions have included these duties in their confessions, church order documents, and forms for ordination.

The Indispensable Tasks of Ruling Elders

In the most basic sense, the identity of ruling elders is shaped by their being shepherds. Along with the teaching elders, they are to lead, nurture, and gather the sheep as servant-shepherds of Jesus Christ. In other words, it is through their ministry that the voice of the Good Shepherd must be heard and impact the lives of those in their charge. This means that the Word of God is central to their office. With the Word, they are to instruct, comfort, and admonish all those in their care. If necessary, they exercise Christian discipline for those who do not believe and refuse to repent, and they ensure that the sacraments are not profaned. In applying the Word for the edification of the church they have a leadership role and are to stimulate the congregation to do its duty.

The second cluster of responsibilities circles around the elders' identity as stewards of the house of God. Along with the teaching elders they must make sure that all things are done decently and in good order and so tend the flock in their charge. It is in the name of Jesus Christ and with his authority that elders rule and manage the church, as well as give access to the kingdom treasures of the forgiveness of sins and life eternal.

In the third place, because of the central importance of the Word of God, elders have the duty to safeguard sound doctrine, remembering that the church is the pillar and foundation of the truth. They must prevent wolves from entering the sheepfold of

---

5. See chapter 6 n. 27 and chapter 9, under "The Elders' Watching the Flock."

the Good Shepherd. It is not the experts who necessarily have the last say, but elders who know the Scriptures and can detect whether the voice of the Good Shepherd is being heard.

All these are awesome duties and expectations. No wonder that the requirements for the office are very high—a godly life, excellent knowledge of Scripture, and a genuine love for the sheep. Elders must constantly seek to cultivate these virtues. Elders who do not grow in the Lord, in knowing Scripture, and in love for the flock are not living up to their responsibility, which includes setting an example for those in their care. Elders who know their dependence on the Lord and seek to grow in him can, however, be confident that the Chief Shepherd will sustain them and provide for them by his Word and Spirit for the task he has entrusted to them. Reflecting on all of this, one can only conclude that it is a tremendous grace of God that he has given faithful elders to his people.

The Blessing of Faithful Elders

If the office of elder functions as it should, then the flock is tended with loving care. Godly living is encouraged. Sin is opposed or nipped in the bud, and holiness is fostered. People are encouraged to take up the challenge of strengthening the bond of faith and participating in godly discipline. With the gentle or not so gentle stimulation of the elders as necessary, sin is kept in check, unbiblical thinking and lifestyles are resisted, and the body of Christ realizes and encourages fellowship in the Spirit. Although all should watch over their neighbors and tend to their spiritual needs, faithful elders, giving godly leadership, go a long way toward ensuring that this actually happens.

The marvel of the eldership is that all this work is done without domineering, but in a serving spirit, as servant-shepherds of the Great Shepherd of the sheep. The elders' authority derives from Jesus Christ who came to serve and whom elders serve. It is especially the Word as it bears on the lives of God's people that gives elders the authority to speak and to act in accordance with the wishes of their sender. When speaking according to the Word, the elders will be careful to discipline in love with a view to the salvation of the sinner. This means not acting legalistically, but according to God's justice and righteousness, which reflect his care for the sheep and his covenant faithfulness towards those who stumble. This takes much godly wisdom, but ministering to the flock with such an attitude of compassion and understanding will nurture the growth of the congregation in holiness. This holiness needs to be maintained without compromise, but in such a way that the elders recognize the nature of the sin they are dealing with and act in a manner consistent with the expectations of the Good Shepherd. God will give the wisdom and love necessary for the elders to do their task.

Blessed is the congregation whose elders labor faithfully. Committing many hours to this labor of love, such elders set an example for others to follow and stimulate the congregation to reach out and care for each other. Such elders are a tremendous blessing from the Lord. They seek the preservation and nurture of the church. They should never be taken for granted, but should be cherished and supported in every way. Without an active ruling eldership a church, humanly speaking, is lost.

The Consequences of These Privileges

Privilege brings responsibilities. The privilege of being an elder brings the enormous obligation of living up to the demands of that sacred office. Elders must carry themselves as those worthy of the office, show exemplary piety, adorn their office with a godly life, and so be an example to others. Elders, however, are not the only ones who have responsibilities flowing from the privilege of their office.

Honor and Obey. A congregation that is blessed with godly and diligent elders has the responsibility to recognize this privilege by honoring the elders. At their ordination, Presbyterian and Reformed churches therefore typically charge the congregation to respect the elders who labor in the church and to esteem them very highly in love because of their work.

Today's secular culture generally has little respect for civil authority and for those who are in the Lord's special service. It therefore needs to be stressed that it is a God-given duty to honor those who labor in the congregation as elders, either as ruling or teaching elders. "Obey your leaders and submit to their authority. They keep watch over you as men who must give an account. Obey them so that their work will be a joy, not a burden, for that would be of no advantage to you" (Heb. 13:17). The apostle Paul admonished: "Now we ask you, brothers, to respect those who work hard among you, who are over you in the Lord and who admonish you. Hold them in the highest regard in love because of their work" (1 Thess. 5:12–13).

Both of these admonitions have several elements in common. First, elders are in the service of God. It was God's idea and not man's to have this office. The almighty Creator and Re-Creator is pleased to use human instruments, which are of themselves weak and fallible, for his great redemptive purpose. Honor must therefore be rendered them as to the Lord, for in their office they represent their Sender.

Second, those who labor faithfully are to be honored. They keep watch and do not withhold warnings and admonitions, but faithfully pass on the Word of God as it impacts the lives of those in their charge.

Third, the honor due to the faithful office bearers includes obedience, submission to their authority, respect, and holding them in the highest regard in love. The reason is that in obeying the elders, one respects and obeys the authority and word of Christ that they represent. Because elders speak and act on behalf of the Good Shepherd and his claims, honoring and obeying is never done in fear but in loving respect as rendering obedience and love to Christ. As those seeking the well-being and protection of the congregation against the attacks of the evil one, elders deserve the loving respect and support of those in their charge.

These three common elements underline the nature of the eldership. Elders are not in it for themselves, but for Christ and his name's sake. "Hold them in the highest regard in love because of their work" (1 Thess. 5:13). One should obey the office bearer so that his work will be a joy and not a burden, "for that would be of no advantage to you" (Heb. 13:17). It is a great privilege to have representatives of Christ labor in the congregation. But this means that God's people are obligated to make their task as pleasant as possible, knowing they work for Christ and not for themselves. Office bearers are also human and need strength and encouragement. They have a right to the love, honor, and obedience of those in their charge. And when that is given, the congregation benefits. There is an advantage involved, for what a privilege it is to be directed, admonished, and comforted by representatives of Jesus Christ himself! If office bearers are encouraged and free to do their work in a congregation that respects their office, how much more eagerly will they represent the interests of Christ to the best of their ability. Everyone profits as a result.

It is therefore very important that respect for the office bearers be engendered and encouraged in the church. Such respect should, of course, be stimulated and earned by the godly example of the elders themselves by their faithful labor. This respect should also be nurtured by the congregation. In homes where parents regularly pray for the office bearers, respect for their task and position will grow. The office bearers need the support of the church community, and parents have the duty to pass the attitude of respect on to their children. Showing and teaching respect for those who labor on behalf of Christ is very important. Not only does this benefit the church because faithful shepherds are encouraged, but such respect for the office of elder can also awaken in young men the desire to serve the Lord by means of this office. And what an office it is. The eldership of today goes back ultimately to the time of Moses! It is an office that God honored by inviting a representative body of elders into his presence. It is an office that today functions in the light of eternity!

In Anticipation of the Day. Remarkably, the admonitions to respect and honor the elder found in Hebrews 13 and 1 Thessalonians 5 are both situated within the larger context of the coming day of the Lord. In Hebrews, the author had mentioned the coming of that great day as a day of reckoning and judgment. He had urged his readers to a life focused on Christ in godliness in light of the fact that the Day is approaching (Heb. 10:19–25). It will be a day of reckoning for those who despised the Son of God (Heb. 10:26–31). Now in his concluding remarks, the author reminds the reader of this great day by saying that the leaders of God's people will need to give an account to the Lord for the work they do (Heb. 13:17; cf. Ezek. 3:17–21). Elders always work in anticipation of that great day when their Lord and Savior returns and asks an accounting.

Similarly the apostle Paul had written of the coming of the day of the Lord and the need to be vigilant and to encourage each other in the faith (1 Thess. 4:13–5:11). In that context he also urged the believers to respect those who labor among them and who are over them in the Lord (1 Thess. 5:12–13).

Elders do their work in the light of eternity. Their shepherding work affects the eternal destiny of those in their charge. This breathtaking fact not only urges them to do their work as well as possible, but it also determines the manner in which the congregation receives their work. The congregation must realize that the elder is not accountable to the church, but the church is accountable to God who set the elders over them.

The fact that elders work within the perspective of the coming of the Lord should also do something else. It should bring great joy both to the elders and the flock in their care. After all, the One who charged the elders with their responsibilities hastens to return. And when he returns he will give the crown of glory to faithful elders (1 Peter 5:4), and those who received their dedicated ministry as from the Lord will be called into the eternal glory (1 Peter 5:10). Then all will see God and worship him before his throne (1 John 3:2; Rev. 7:9–17)! With that perspective, the work of elders is truly something to treasure and appreciate.

Questions for Study and Reflection

These questions are meant to be discussed by everyone—both elders and those who do not have a special office. Six chapters, however, have a final question specifically addressed to the elders for their benefit. All questions refer back to Scripture passages and/or issues mentioned in the chapter under discussion.

Chapter 1: An Overview of the Office

1. Illustrate how egalitarian and worldly standards can affect how we regard the elders and what we expect from them.

2. How does your church select office bearers? If you are involved in the process, how and why are you involved? Is such participation optional? Should the casting of lots have a place in the selection of elders? Are there New Testament examples of such a manner of selection after the outpouring of the Holy Spirit?

3. In what ways do the elements of serving and shepherding come together in the office of the elder?

4. How does the description in Galatians 6:16 that the church is the "Israel of God" highlight the continuity between Old and New Testaments? Can you find other indications in the New Testament that underline this continuity?

5. Does knowing that the eldership goes all the way back to the Old Testament influence how you regard the elders in your church? Elaborate.

QUESTIONS FOR STUDY AND REFLECTION

6. *For elders*. As an elder you have been given authority to serve. What does this imply for the way you do your work as an elder? Has there ever been an instance when your authority was not exercised in a serving manner? How can such situations be avoided?

Chapter 2: The Shepherd and His Flock

1. What tasks did a shepherd need to perform for his sheep? How is your personal life affected by knowing that the Lord is the Good Shepherd?

2. According to Scripture and as discussed in this chapter, what qualifications must an elder have to be an undershepherd of Christ? Are some qualifications more important than others? In addition, how should one weigh factors such as being busy with other activities and/or with a growing family?

3. What practical consequences result from an elder being in the service of the Good Shepherd? How do you see this identity functioning in your own church? Also, to what extent should you involve an elder in your personal faith life?

4. If an elder is an undershepherd in Christ's service, what are the responsibilities of the sheep? How do these obligations influence you, and what difficulties can result from fulfilling these duties?

5. In John 10:14, Jesus says: "I know my sheep and my sheep know me." What comfort is it to you that Jesus knows his sheep? What does it mean for you to know him?

6. *For elders*. Part of the task of shepherds is to protect the flock from danger. What dangers do you see threatening the flock under your care? What are you doing about it?

Chapter 3: A Bearded Head

1. What are your thoughts, in the light of Scripture, on the ideal age of an elder, especially in terms of today's culture and society?

2. If the eldership arose in the Old Testament from within the family unit, may fathers today assume the tasks of elders? How should the church counsel those who play the father's authority against the elders' authority, for example, with respect to catechizing?

3. Does an elder need to be married in order to function as a "family man" in the family of God?

4. Does an elder need to be well educated in order to function in the office? Explain.

5. First Timothy 3:10 speaks about first being tested before being considered for the eldership. What does this mean? Why is this important? How can this be done?

6. *For elders*. In light of the general biblical criteria for being an elder as described in this chapter, how would you evaluate your strengths and weaknesses? How would you be able to further equip yourself for the office?

Chapter 4: Elders as Leaders in the Old Testament

1. No one can do the work of an elder in his own strength as the gift of the Spirit in Numbers 11 shows. How must an elder or one aspiring to the office be receptive to the work of the Spirit?

2. Mention several ways in which elders can lead church members in knowing God's will for Christian living.

3. The history of Israel shows that with the passage of time, the influence and benefit of the eldership can change. What pressures are there on biblical eldership today? How can they be counteracted?

QUESTIONS FOR STUDY AND REFLECTION

4. What can elders and members of the congregation do to acquire and grow in true wisdom? Why is this so important?

5. In ancient Israel, the office of elder was an institution that countered tendencies to hierarchy. In today's church, how can the proper function of the elder's office combat such tendencies? Illustrate how the failure of the elder's office contributes to hierarchy in the church.

6. *For elders.* What do you experience as the most challenging aspect in "carrying the burden of the people" (Num. 11:17) as elders and leaders in the church? Can you think of ways by which you could better equip yourself to handle these difficulties?

Chapter 5: Elders as Judges in the Old Testament

1. In the Old Testament, elders functioned as God's representatives. In what ways do you see elders fulfilling this duty today?

2. Under the heading "The Involvement and Responsibility of the People," this chapter dealt with three ways in which the people participated in executing justice in ancient Israel. How are these three ways still relevant today?

3. Scripture teaches that responsibility for godly discipline and knowledge starts in the homes. Mention several ways that elders today can assist and strengthen families in fulfilling this responsibility.

4. What are the key principles for justice being administered in the city gate in Old Testament times? How are these principles relevant today?

5. What was the goal of the elder judging in the city gate? How does this impact our understanding of resolving disputes today?

6. What is righteousness according to Scripture? How do justice and love come together in countering sin? Is punishment still

in order after sins have been confessed and forgiven? Why or why not?

7. Illustrate how God's law is gracious for his people. Explain how the aspects of divine love and grace in God's law will affect our understanding of the Ten Commandments.

Chapter 6: The Christian Congregation Inherits the Office

1. To whom are elders accountable? From where does their authority come? How does this affect your relationship to the elders in your church?

2. How soon should elders be ordained in a new church plant? Why? Are any special gifts needed for being an elder in a new church plant?

3. What tasks do the teaching and ruling elders have in common? How do they differ?

4. How does the New Testament describe the preaching of the gospel as a priestly task in administering reconciliation between God and his people? What are the implications for the preaching?

5. In view of the context of James 5:13–15, how does this passage apply to the work of elders today?

6. In the history of the church there has often been a tendency to hierarchy and clericalism. Is this biblical? Why or why not?

7. If we expect ministers to be prepared for office by rigorous theological training, should we expect elders also to undergo significant training in preparation for holding office? If so, what should that training include? If not, how then can we protect the parity of office between minister and elder?

Chapter 7: Elders and the Keys of the Kingdom

1. What is the Old Testament background to the concept of the keys of the kingdom?

2. What is *the* key that unlocks and opens the way to the treasures of the kingdom? How is this key administered by elders? What are the treasures this key gives access to?

3. What is the meaning of Matthew 16:18b? What comfort does this give?

4. What responsibilities do members of the congregation have with respect to the key of the gospel? What obstacles could prevent them from following Scripture's teaching?

5. Handling the keys of the kingdom is an awesome responsibility since access to the treasures of God's grace is involved. What is the best preparation for using the keys in a manner pleasing to God?

6. Discuss the significance of the laying-on-of-hands ceremony. For which offices should it be used? Explain.

Chapter 8: Ruling and Having Authority

1. What leadership qualities are necessary for elders? Why?

2. How must elders safeguard the preaching of the gospel? What qualifications for this task are especially important?

3. How are elders to administer the Word as they shepherd the flock?

4. How do you make the admonition of Colossians 3:16a a reality in your life?

5. Is it a biblical concept that elders need to earn respect before the congregation owes respect? Why or why not? Is

there a correlation between earning respect and exercising authority?

6. *For elders*. How do you assist and encourage the minister in his preaching and pastoral tasks? Are there ways to improve the cooperation between the ruling and teaching elders and the effectiveness of the respective offices?

Chapter 9: Disciplining for Life

1. What is the importance of elders visiting families and single members? How and how often do you think these visits should be done? What are some of the challenges, and how can these obstacles be overcome?

2. Where does the watching out for the well-being of the congregation begin? Why is this beginning of critical importance?

3. What is the role of each member of the congregation in church discipline, and how can elders help the congregation in fulfilling this role? Why is it unbiblical to say "Let the elders take care of the discipline in the church"?

4. What is the difference between living in sin and falling into sin? Why is this difference important to note, and is it always obvious? Why or why not? How quickly or slowly should the disciplinary process go? Is there a minimum age to consider before office bearers should proceed to the final step of excommunication?

5. What are some of the factors to reflect on when it comes to tolerating someone's shortcomings? What is the bottom line?

6. *For elders*. How can elders help each other in disciplining themselves?

Chapter 10: Two Current Issues: Female Elders and Elders for Life

1. Should the office of elder be open to women? Give biblical support for your answer.

2. In what ways do you think that women can make the best contribution to the body of Christ?

3. What is *the* distinguishing feature that separates modern secular feminist principles from those of Scripture? In what ways can the current worldly culture of feminism influence the church?

4. For what reasons could a ruling elder's service in a Presbyterian church be terminated?

5. What are the advantages and disadvantages of definite and indefinite tenure as ruling elder? Which would you prefer and why?

6. If the definite tenure system is used, what is the ideal length of time for an elder to serve? Why? How long an interval should there be before a retired ruling elder can be renominated? Why?

Chapter 11: The Privilege of the Eldership

1. Why did God allow the elders at Sinai to see him? To what does their being on Sinai as representatives of God's people point?

2. One day all God's people will be in God's presence and "see him as he is" (1 John 3:2). Now the church is en route to that day (Heb. 12:18–24). How should our being pilgrims affect our attitude toward the elders of the church or the attitude of the elders toward the congregation? Explain.

3. How can you best honor the elders God has set over you? Elaborate.

4. Do you think that the office of elder is appreciated as much as it could be? Why or why not? How can respect for the office be promoted?

5. What steps should you take to be an effective coworker with the elders for the good of the church and the glory of God? Be specific and discuss.

Select Resources on Elders

Allison, Archibald Alexander. "Biblical Qualifications for Elders." *Ordained Servant* 3.4 (1994): 80–96, available online at http://www.opc.org/OS/pdf/OSV3N4.pdf.

Berghoef, Gerard, and Lester De Koster. *The Elders Handbook: A Practical Guide for Church Leaders*. Grand Rapids: Christian's Library Press, 1979.

Brown, Mark R., ed. *Order in the Offices: Essays Defining the Roles of Church Officers*. Duncansville, PA: Classic Presbyterian Government Resources, 1993.

Brown, Michael, ed. *Called to Serve: Essays for Elders and Deacons*. Grandville, MI: Reformed Fellowship, 2006.

Calvin, John. *Institutes of the Christian Religion*. Edited by John T. McNeill. Translated by Ford Lewis Battles. 2 vols. Philadelphia: Westminster, 1960.

Clowney, Edmund P. *The Church*. Contours of Christian Theology. Downers Grove, IL: InterVarsity, 1995.

De Jong, P. Y. *Taking Heed to the Flock: A Study of the Principles and Practice of Family Visitation*. Eugene, OR: Wipf and Stock, 2003.

Dickson, David. *The Elder and His Work*. Edited by George Kennedy McFarland and Philip Graham Ryken. Phillipsburg, NJ: P&R, 2004.

Eyres, Lawrence R. *The Elders of the Church*. Phillipsburg, NJ: Presbyterian and Reformed, 1975.

Feenstra, Peter G. *The Glorious Work of Home Visits*. Winnipeg: Premier, 2000.

Gaffin, Richard B. *Perspectives on Pentecost: New Testament Teaching on the Gifts of the Holy Spirit*. Phillipsburg, NJ: Presbyterian and Reformed, 1979.

Hall, David W., and Joseph H. Hall, ed. *Paradigms in Polity: Classic Readings in Reformed and Presbyterian Church Government*. Grand Rapids: Eerdmans, 1994.

Henderson, G. D. *The Scottish Ruling Elder*. London: James Clarke, 1935.

Keller, Phillip. *A Shepherd Looks at Psalm 23*. Grand Rapids: Zondervan, 1981.

Kloosterman, Nelson D. *Visiting Members*. DVD set. (A two-DVD set containing ten 30-minute elder and deacon training sessions on the principles and practices of visiting church members. Available from http://www.auxesis.net.)

Knight, George W. *The Pastoral Epistles*. New International Greek Testament Commentary. Grand Rapids: Eerdmans, 1992.

Lightfoot, J. B. *The Christian Ministry*. Edited with introduction by Philip Edgcumbe Hughes. Wilton, CT: Morehouse-Barlow, 1983. (This work was originally published as an excursus in Lightfoot's commentary on Philippians in 1868.)

Mappes, David A. "The Discipline of a Sinning Elder." *Bibliotheca Sacra* 154 (1997): 333–43.

Miller, Samuel. *The Ruling Elder*. Dallas: Presbyterian Heritage, 1987 (1832).

Murray, John. "Office in the Church." In *Collected Writings of John Murray*, 2:357–65. 4 vols. Edinburgh: Banner of Truth Trust, 1976–1982.

Piper, John, and Wayne Grudem, eds. *Recovering Biblical Manhood and Womanhood: A Response to Evangelical Feminism*. Wheaton, IL: Crossway, 1991.

Robertson, O. Palmer. *The Israel of God: Yesterday, Today, and Tomorrow*. Phillipsburg, NJ: P&R, 2000.

Shishko, William. "How to Assess a Sermon: A Checklist for Ruling Elders." *Ordained Servant* 12 (2003): 43–44, available online at http://www.opc.org/OS/pdf/OSV12N2.pdf.

Sietsma, K. *The Idea of Office*. Jordan Station, ON: Paideia, 1985.

Sittema, John R. *With a Shepherd's Heart: Reclaiming the Pastoral Office of Elder*. Grandville, MI: Reformed Fellowship, 1995.

Williamson, G. I. "The *Two- and Three-Office Issue* Reconsidered." *Ordained Servant* 12 (2003): 5–6, available online at http://www. opc.org/OS/pdf/OSV12N1.pdf.

Wright, Christopher J. H. *Old Testament Ethics for the People of God*. Downers Grove, IL: InterVarsity, 2004.

A Selection of Additional Specialized Resources

These resources are virtually all in addition to the items mentioned in the footnotes and in the Select Resources on Elders.

Part 1: Introduction: Chapters 1–3

The definition of ecclesiastical office in chapter 1 derives from C. Trimp, *Ministerium* (Groningen: De Vuurbaak, 1982), 6. Trimp's work is also important for part 3.

For a study of shepherd imagery in the Bible, see Timothy S. Laniak, *Shepherds after My Own Heart* (Downers Grove, IL: Apollos/InterVarsity, 2006).

About coming of age, see J. Fleishman, "The Age of Legal Maturity in Biblical Law," *Journal of the Ancient Near Eastern Society of Columbia University* 21 (1992): 35–48.

Part 2: Old Testament Origins: Chapters 4–5

Important studies on elders and their role include: H. Reviv, *The Elders in Ancient Israel* (Jerusalem: Magnes, 1989); John L. McKenzie, "The Elders in the Old Testament," *Biblica* 40 (1959): 522–40; J. R. Bartlett, "The Use of the Word [*ro'sh*] as a Title in the Old Testament," *Vetus Testamentum* 19 (1969): 1–10; and J. P. van der Ploeg, "Les anciens dans l'Ancien Testament," in *Lex tua veritas: Festschrift für H. Junker*, ed. Heinrich Gross and Franz Mussner (Trier: Paulinus, 1961), 175–91.

For elders in the monarchy, see Nili Sacher Fox, *In the Service of the King: Officialdom in Ancient Israel and Judah*, Monographs of the Hebrew Union College 23 (Cincinnati: Hebrew Union College Press, 2000); and H. Tadmor, "Traditional Institutions and the Monarchy: Social and Political Tensions in the Time of David and Solomon," in *Studies in the Period of David and Solomon and Other Essays: Papers Read at the International Symposium for Biblical Studies, Tokyo, 5–7 December 1979,* ed. T. Ishida (Winona Lake, IN: Eisenbrauns, 1982), 239–57.

For the elders in the days of Ezekiel, see Ian M. Duguid, *Ezekiel and the Leaders of Israel,* Supplements to Vetus Testamentum 56 (Leiden: Brill, 1994), 110–32.

On the meaning of justice and righteousness, see Hemchand Gossai, *Justice, Righteousness and the Social Critique of the Eighth-Century Prophets,* American University Studies, Series VII, Theology and Religion 141 (New York: Peter Lang, 1993); and Ze'ev W. Falk, "Law and Ethics in the Hebrew Bible," in *Justice and Righteousness: Biblical Themes and Their Influence,* Journal for the Study of the Old Testament Supplement 137, ed. Henning Graf Reventlow and Yair Hoffman (Sheffield: Sheffield Academic Press 1992), 82–90.

On maintaining justice and the need for all Israel as priestly kingdom to know the law, see Moshe Greenberg, *Studies in the Bible and Jewish Thought* (Philadelphia: Jewish Publication Society, 1995), 11–24; and D. J. Wiseman, "Law and Order in Old Testament Times," *Vox Evangelica* 8 (1973): 5–21. On judicial procedure, see Ludwig Köhler, *Hebrew Man* (London: SCM, 1973), 149–75; and Donald A. McKenzie, "Judicial Procedure at the Town Gate," *Vetus Testamentum* 14 (1964): 100–104.

More specifically, on the distinctions in sin, see C. Van Dam, "The Meaning of [*bisheghaghah*]," in *Unity in Diversity: Studies Presented to Prof. Dr. Jelle Faber,* ed. Riemer Faber (Hamilton: Senate of the Theological College of the Canadian Reformed Churches, 1989), 13–24. On the flexibility of God's law, I have benefited from W. H. Gispen, "De soepelheid der Mozaïsche wet," *Gereformeerd Theologisch Tijdschrift* 57 (1957): 106–11; also see David F. Wright, "Calvin's Pentateuchal Criticism: Equity, Hardness of Heart, and Divine Accommodation in the Mosaic Harmony Commentary," *Calvin Theological Journal* 21 (1986): 33–50.

Part 3: Continuity and Transformation: Chapters 6–7

For the offices in the early Christian church, see Roger Beckwith, *Elders in Every City: The Origin and Role of the Ordained Ministry* (Carlisle, UK: Paternoster, 2003). On the office of priest, see Collin Bulley, *The Priesthood of Some Believers: Developments from the General to the Special Priesthood in the Christian Literature of the First Three Centuries* (Carlisle, UK: Paternoster, 2000).

For the continuity of synagogue institutions and the Christian church, see further James Tunstead Burtchaell, *From Synagogue to Church: Public Services and Offices in the Earliest Christian Communities* (Cambridge: University Press, 1992).

R. Alastair Campbell, *The Elders: Seniority within Earliest Christianity* (London/New York: T&T Clark, 2004), argues for elder as a term of honor and not office. Benjamin L. Merkle, *The Elder and Overseer: One Office in the Early Church*, Studies in Biblical Literature 57 (New York: Peter Lang, 2003), sees elder as an office, but denies any official distinction between ruling and teaching elders. For a classic defense of the twofold elder office, see *Jus Divinum Regiminis Ecclesiastici or The Divine Right of Church Government originally asserted by the Ministers of Sion College, London, December 1646*, rev. and ed. David W. Hall (Dallas: Naphtali, 1995), 123–67. For Calvin's exegesis concerning the office of elder see Elsie Ann McKee, *Elders and the Plural Ministry: The Role of Exegetical History in Illuminating John Calvin's Theology* (Geneva: Droz, 1988).

For a survey article on the laying on of hands, see David F. Wright, "Ordination," *Themelios* 19.3 (1985): 5–10.

Part 4: Elders as Preservers and Nurturers of Life in the Covenant Community: Chapters 8–9

On responsible Christian liberty, see Nelson Deyo Kloosterman, Scandalum Infirmorum et Communio Sanctorum: *The Relation between Christian Liberty and Neighbor Love in the Church* (Neerlandia, AB: Inheritance, 1991).

On excommunication and readmission from the time of Ezra on, see Ze'ev W. Falk, *Introduction to Jewish Law of the Second Commonwealth*, 2 vols. (Leiden: Brill, 1972, 1978), 2:160–63. For Calvin's practice of church discipline in Geneva, see his "Ordonnances ecclésiastiques" (1541), available in *The Register of the Company of Pastors of Geneva in the Time of Calvin*, ed. and trans. P. E. Hughes (Grand Rapids: Eerdmans, 1966), 47–49. On Hebrews 6:6 see J. Geertsema, "Is Conversion after Apostasy Impossible? A Look at Hebrews 6:6," *Clarion: The Canadian Reformed Magazine* 51 (2002): 36–39, 58–61; and Robert A. Peterson, "Apostasy in the Hebrews Warning Passages," *Presbyterion* 34 (2008): 27–44.

Part 5: Maintaining and Building on the Heritage: Chapters 10–11

For a thorough discussion on many aspects of 1 Timothy 2:9–15, see Andreas J. Köstenberger, Thomas R. Schreiner, and H. Scott Baldwin, eds., *Women in the Church: A Fresh Analysis of 1 Timothy 2:9–15* (Grand Rapids: Baker, 1995). For an egalitarian perspective on this chapter, see Richard Clark Kroeger and Catherine Clark Kroeger, *I Suffer Not a Woman: Rethinking 1 Timothy 2:11–15 in Light of Ancient Evidence* (Grand Rapids: Baker, 1992). For critique of this work, see reviews by Al Wolters in *Calvin Theological Journal* 28 (1993): 208–13, Robert Yarbrough in *Presbyterion* 18 (1992): 25–33, Richard Oster in *Biblical Archaeologist* 56 (1993): 225–27, and S. M. Baugh in *Westminster Theological Journal* 56 (1994): 153–71.

Clark Pinnock reviewed two feminist books: E. S. Fiorenza, *In Memory of Her* (New York: Crossroad, 1983), and R. R. Ruether, *Sexism and God-Talk* (Boston: Beacon, 1983), and two nonfeminist books: J. B. Hurley, *Man and Woman in Biblical Perspective* (Leicester: Intervarsity, 1981), and S. B. Clark, *Man and Woman in Christ* (Ann Arbor: Servant, 1980). Pinnock defines feminism in part as "a belief in social role interchangeability, especially in regard to leadership roles in church and society." Pinnock's conclusion is that "Feminism has a problem of biblical authority. . . . If it is the Bible you want, feminism is in trouble; if it is feminism you desire, the Bible stands in the way." See Clark H. Pinnock, "Biblical Authority and the Issues in Question," in *Women, Authority and the Bible*, ed. Alvera Mickelsen (Downers Grove, IL: InterVarsity, 1986), 51, 58.

Romans 16:7 is interpreted in Eldon Jay Epp, *Junia, the First Woman Apostle* (Minneapolis: Fortress, 2005). For a critique see Michael Burer, "Reassessing Junia: A Review of Eldon Epp's *Junia*," *The Journal for Biblical Manhood and Womanhood* 13 (2008): 56–59, available at http://www.cbmw.org.

Index of Scripture

263

264

23:2–3—53
24:20–21—111
28—53
28:12—30
28:12–14—54, 59
28:14—53
30:2–3—86
30:20—86
34:29—54, 65

Ezra
5:3–11—9
5:9—55
6:7–8—55
6:14—55
7:25–26—175
10:3—175
10:7–17—10
10:8—6, 55, 65, 175
10:14—65

Nehemiah
8:1–12—109
8:8—110
9:20—48

Esther
1:19—88
8:8—88

Job
12:12—27
13:18—75
23:4—75
29:7–25—75
32:6–9—28
42:7—28

Psalms
1—83, 90

19:7—92
23—15, 18
26:1—78
28:9—20
33:5—80
35:11—75
51:4—77
69:12—74
72—64, 73
72:2–4—124
72:12–14—124
77:20—20
78:70–72—22
80:1–2—20
95:7—19
103:11–14—184
103:12—176
105:22—33
119:93—92
119:100—58
119:103—158
119:105—92, 152
121:4–5—20
121:7–8—20
148:12—28

Proverbs
1:7—58
1:8—70n6
2:1–11—174, 195
3:1—70n6
4:1–2—70n6
6:34–35—85
9:10—58
11:30—169
15:3—72, 76
15:27—67
16:18—37
18:17—75n9
20:8—64

22:6—166
24:23—67
28:16—67
31:8–9—73

Ecclesiastes
4:13—28
9:18—180

Isaiah
1:11–13—86
1:17—78
1:23—64
3:13—75
3:14—64–65
4:5—231
5:14—123
9:14–15—54
10:1–2—64
11:2—46
22:15–19—123
22:21—124
22:22—124, 174
24–25—228, 231–33
24:23—65
25:6–8—234
30:18—80
40:11—17, 19, 44
44:28—21n
45:8—80
46:13—80
53—9
55:2–3—156
55:6–7—184
60:1—231
63:10–14—46
63:16—56
64:6—197
64:8—56
66:19–21—112

Jeremiah
2:8—22
3:15—23
6:13–14—111
7:12–14—49
7:21–23—86
8:10–11—111
10:21–23
15:16—157
18:18—55, 57, 60
19:1—54
22:17—67
23:1–5—23
23:2—200
23:11—111
26—74n8
26:7–8—111
26:11—75
26:16–19—75
26:17–19—65
29:1—10, 54
31:10—20
31:34—150
33:13—17
50:4–5—23
50:6—23
50:19—20

Lamentations
1:19—59
4:16—54, 57, 59
5:12—54, 57
5:14—65

Ezekiel
1:26—229
3:17–21—24–25, 241
7:26—54–55, 57, 60, 110, 147
8—54, 60
8:1—10, 55

8:9–12—54
9:6—28, 54
14—54, 60
14:1—55
20—54, 60
20:1—55
20:3—55
20:37—17
33:2–9—24–25
34—55, 163n6
34:1–6—23
34:1–10—151
34:1–16—200
34:5–8—17
34:11–16—20–21
34:12—17
34:23—21
37:24—21
44:24—109

Daniel
4:27—80

Hosea
4:6—150, 157
6:6—88

Joel
1:14—60

Amos
2:4—91n
5:12—64
5:15—74n7
5:21–26—86
6:12—64

Micah
2:12—17
3:11—64, 111

5:2–5—21
6:8—196

Habakkuk
2:9—67
3:17—17

Zephaniah
3:5—82

Zechariah
3:2—197
7:3—111
10:3—200
13:7—21

Malachi
2:6–9—59
2:7—108–9
2:16—86
3:17—187

Matthew
2:6—21
4:4—156
5:3—123n4
5:7—196
5:33–37—177
6:14–15—176
7:1–5—168, 191
7:15—107
9:2–7—124
10:1–8—101n
10:2–4—216
10:6—24
10:12—163
10:17—175n17
11:28–30—189
12:7—88
12:12—189

269

274

Index of Subjects and Names